Far Eastern Cookery

OTHER BOOKS IN THE SERIES

GODS, MEN AND WINE: William Younger

THE FRENCH AT TABLE: Raymond Oliver

CHEESE AND CHEESE COOKERY: T. A. Layton

GERMAN COOKERY: Hans Karl Adam

CLASSIC SAUCES AND THEIR PREPARATION: Raymond Oliver

SOUPS: Robin Howe

EGGS: Margaret Sherman

BAKERY, CAKES AND SIMPLE CONFECTIONERY: Maria Floris

MEAT: Ambrose Heath

THE WINES OF BURGUNDY: H. W. Yoxall

Forthcoming titles
SPANISH COOKERY: Mary Hillgarth

HERBS, SPICES AND FLAVOURINGS: Tom Stobart

THE INTERNATIONAL WINE AND FOOD SOCIETY'S GUIDE TO

Far Eastern Cookery

Robin Howe

The International Wine and Food Society   MICHAEL JOSEPH

A Publication of
The International Wine and Food Society Limited
Marble Arch House
44 Edgware Road, London, w.2.

President : André L. Simon

This book was designed and produced by
George Rainbird Limited
Marble Arch House
44 Edgware Road, London, w.2.

Printed by Ebenezer Baylis and Son Limited,
The Trinity Press, Worcester, and London
Bound by Webb Son and Company Limited, London
7181–4027–3

General Editor : Robin Howe

House Editor : Rosemary Joekes

Designer : Judith Allan

Contents

Throughout this book British measurements are given first:
the American equivalent follows in brackets.

COLOUR PLATES

Introduction

One of the most frequent questions asked me is: 'How do you collect all your recipes?' The answer has a Mallory-like simplicity. By going to the countries of origin.

Well, this has been true almost all my life. As the wife of a newspaperman I have travelled far and wide.

Collecting recipes is fruitful, not only for putting them into books or even simply to use them for one's own pleasure, but also because one meets so many people of all ranks. The only place properly to learn about Oriental cooking is in private homes, which makes me think that the moral of this surely is, if one wants to know something about a country and its people, forget politics and concentrate on cooking.

Far Eastern cooking is highly developed, seemingly at first sight intricate but, as will be seen, this is not so. In this book there are no recipes for stewed elephants' ears, devilled tigers' livers or even stuffed peacocks. Obviously mentioned here and there is an ingredient which seems to us in the West exotic. But stop for one moment to consider some of the items in our own larders. Our Western diet is by no means free of 'frogs and snails and puppy dogs tails' and much of what appears normal to us is exotic to the Oriental. Our 'smelly' cheese and blood sausages are a couple of examples which spring to mind.

And the recipes themselves? They are surprisingly simple even those with an apparent endless list of ingredients. Oriental cooking does not usually require exact measurements. On the contrary, family life being what it is in the East no one is sure how many will turn up for a meal so therefore an extra handful of this or that is added. My own efforts to get exact measurements were met with barely suppressed amusement. However, since we in the West prefer to cross our t's and dot our i's I finally sorted it all out, both for the English and American form of measuring.

It is certainly not necessary to attempt a complete Oriental *batterie de cuisine* to use the recipes in this book. In my own home I have tried out these dishes but not using the methods of the East. Instead of a patient cook pounding or grinding, I used my electric mixer. Instead of coal fires, gas.

Instead of Oriental utensils, Western type, easy to clean and light to handle. Kitchen equipment the world over is, I think, interchangeable.

The purpose of this book is to make housewives familiar with the cooking of the Far East. Those recipes which I have chosen are authentic and those which appealed to me and which I can do myself. I like Far Eastern food but do not feel compelled to produce a Far Eastern meal as such, although it is fine from time to time. What I like to do is to intersperse my Oriental dishes among those of the West; a Japanese *chawan-mushi*, for example, makes a good beginning to a Western meal, and curry can be followed by a Western dish.

One last thought. Within the last few years every large city in the West knows all the alchemy of Eastern spices; tropical foods come in their seasons. What cannot be bought fresh is in tins or jars or even frozen. So shopping for the ingredients called for in this book is not going to be all that difficult, on the contrary, entertaining. And for out-of-city shoppers there are many mail order firms only too willing to oblige.

India

The cooking of India is more interesting for its rules, its regulations and its taboos than for its food, both regarding quality and variety.

In most Indian homes the sanctity of the kitchen is still preserved. This sanctity derives from the dietary laws which insist not only that the food eaten by Hindus be pure but that it must be cooked under conditions which are also pure. This has nothing to do with hygiene, but concerns rather the caste of the cook, the type of utensil used and the way the food is cooked. This is difficult for the Westerner to understand. Indians believe that food was created by the Supreme Deity for the benefit of man and, therefore, the art of cooking and eating food must be a sacred rite to be observed with all possible ceremony.

Cooking, it is maintained by the Hindus, is one of God's revelations to man and, as such, a realization of man's intelligence. However, after some study of the methods of Indian cooking I realized that, just as in Indian dancing and music where there is no script and each artiste has his own interpretation of the classic rules of their ancient arts, so the cooks of India also have their own themes and variations.

Not only the ancient rules but also geography and climate affect the dietary laws. Where the soil produces an abundance there is often a relaxation of the rules to permit the Indians to avail themselves of this bounty. Fish is eaten in the coastal areas, even by Brahmins. In Madras, where there is less variety of produce than in the fertile Punjab, the people remain more orthodox, while the sturdy Punjabi, with his fairly regulated winter rains and perhaps too because of Muslim influence, is a fairly free-eating man.

Thus you have Hindus who eat fish, some who eat meat, others who refuse all bulbous foods. Some who eat alone, others who follow the Sanskrit hymn, 'All guilt is he who eats with no partaker'. Some are so caste-ridden that man and wife cannot eat together, if either should be of a lower caste. The man from the north may have no idea how the man from the south eats, or vice versa—and neither cares. If they emigrate within their own country they take their eating and cooking habits with them.

As if the general austerity of diet is not enough, there are days of greater austerity, or days when salt may not be taken or spiced food; times when fasting goes on for one month with only a glass of milk taken in the morning, or wives who fast for their husbands.

Indian cooking is certainly an ancient art and many Indian dishes require skill and patience to prepare. Special dishes require the cook to spend all day cutting up vegetables, simmering milk, pounding rice and spices, or squatting over a charcoal stove for hours on end.

In the actual preparation of everyday food it is basically the same as in the West but in India time does not matter. Once the food is cooked, another hour or so of cooking is of no consequence. It is odd that in a country where cooking is said to be an exact art no one has qualms about cooking vegetables so long that they lose both taste and vitamins. Nor is a meal meant for six or eight people. An Indian meal is like a piece of elastic, made to stretch.

Generally, in the homes of the better-off classes and the Westernized Indian, tables and chairs are the rule for eating, but fingers are preferred to forks. Many Indians of this same class will use Western china, and for meals to which Westerners are asked cutlery is used. In the south many people still eat off a banana leaf which is practical and traditional.

The most general method of serving food is from a *thali* which is a deep round tray which can be made from gold, silver or other metals. This type of *thali* has not changed since Megasthenes visited India in the third century B.C. Sometimes the *thali* is placed on a regular table, sometimes on a low one and one sits cross-legged in front of it with one's feet tucked under it, shoes removed, of course, or on a very low stool with the *thali* on the ground.

Around the edge of the *thali* are small bowls in matching metal. Each bowl contains a different food but all are spiced, potatoes, cauliflower, aubergine (eggplant), beans or cabbage, or even meat and fish dishes. There will be a bowl of curd, another of a thick curry sauce, one of *dahl* (lentils) and often a sweet dish. In the centre is a pile of rice surrounded by small heaps of chutney, some hot dried chillies and often a small whole grilled aubergine. A banana may be added. One eats with the thumb and first two fingers of the right hand. As the little bowls are emptied they are replenished. *Chapaties* are not served when there is rice for both have the same function, to absorb food. At the end of the meal if there is any liquid remaining in the bowls it is usual to pour this over the rice and scoop it up.

Among Westernized Indians eating is simpler and this is the way most Westerners are served curries. Men and women eat together. On the table is a huge pile of rice in a platter and around are the several curries, chutneys, curd and a bowl of *dahl*. First one takes rice and then the curries. The thoughtful hostess provides vegetarian and non-vegetarian food, fish and meat, and all are put on the plate at the same time. Having taken the rice and curry one chooses chutney, *dahl* and curd. Often *puris*, light fluffy wheat balls fried in deep fat, are served, or *pappadams*.

At the end of the Indian meal *pan* is usually served. This consists of a green leaf smeared with a lime paste or sometimes a paste made from rose petals which gives the *pan* a special flavour; this is sprinkled with crushed betel nut and a blend of special spices, cloves, cardamom etc. and the whole made into a small envelope-bundle and fastened with a clove. *Pan* is chewed as an aid to the digestion.

Very few Indians drink alcohol. Some peasants and most industrial workers like to drink toddy, a fermented drink tapped from the toddy palm and, incidentally, a source of vitamins. Westernized Indians drink what the government calls 'foreign liquor'. Goa produces a liqueur made from the cashew fruit which, when allowed to mature, can be very good indeed. The bulk of the population practises voluntary prohibition. Soft drinks are popular, among them buttermilk made from buffalo

Indian and Pakistani cooking utensils: (1) *dekchie*; (2) *krahai*; (3) *tanduri clay oven*; (4) *tawa*

milk, or soured milk mixed with sugar and soda water, which is excellent and cooling. There are numerous fruit drinks and drinks made from fermenting vegetables, such as beetroots or the black carrot (*scorzonera*) etc. A popular drink is pure sugar cane squeezed through a type of mangle; *nimbu pani*, which is simply lime juice and water and one of the best of drinks; *rasam*, from the south, a highly spiced pepper-water which can take the roof off your mouth, some gaudy-looking pink or purple drinks made with milk but often quite pleasant if somewhat sweet.

CURRIES

Everyone in India eats curries, either the rich curry of the princes or the simple curries of the villagers. Curry *is* Indian cooking. The staple food of the Indians consists of a cereal of some kind, rice, wheat or maize. This is either boiled, as in the case of rice, or made into unleavened cakes, such as *chapaties, puris, parathas* etc. Such foods have little flavour of their own, and therefore require a strong sauce. Curry was the answer, a sauce of meat, fish, poultry, game or vegetables, all skilfully blended with a variety of spices.

The origin of the word curry is the Tamil word *kari* meaning a sauce. It also means spiced food and has been eaten in India for 5,000 years, or so it is claimed and I am not prepared to argue the point. The first 'modern' mention of curry is in A.D. 477. Various travellers over the centuries have commented on the Indian habit of eating and serving their rice and curry, including the Greek 'Ambassador' Megatheneses: 'Among the Indians at a banquet a table is set before each individual . . . on the table is placed a golden dish on which they first throw the rice and then add many sorts of meats dressed after the Indian fashion. . . .'

Most of the spices used in Indian cooking were originally chosen as much for their medicinal or antiseptic properties as for their flavour. In the days when there was no refrigeration, antiseptics were of extreme importance. Modern tests have proved the correctness of the Indian's preference for spices. The oil extracted from cloves and cinnamon bark has been found to be as effective in small quantities as carbolic acid and considerably better flavoured.

The basic spices for curries are traditional. They are turmeric, used both as a flavouring and colouring; chillies, very hot to give a pungent flavour as well as colour (Indian curries are often a bright red); ginger to add a subtle flavour and also aid the digestion; garlic and onions (when used) have a heating effect; cloves are crushed to a powder to give an aromatic perfume, or are eaten whole after a meal, or, for that matter, at any time of the day to sweeten the breath; poppy seeds which are rich in oil and used for thickening, and tamarind because it is mildly laxative and has a slightly acid flavour. To these basic flavours are added variously cumin, coriander, cardamom seeds, *neem* leaves from the national tree of India, other flavouring leaves called ambiguously curry leaves, with coconut in the south, grated and squeezed to a coconut milk.

Spices usually are freshly ground each day, although today with fewer servants and a new tendency towards saving time, many cooks pound a week's supply of the dry spices, such as turmeric, chillies, coriander etc. These are kept in tightly sealed jars, next to the large jars of lentils—there are several varieties in daily use in India. Ginger, tamarind and garlic are pounded freshly as required.

Most foreigners consider curries hot. Most Indians protest they are not. It is a matter of taste and region. In the south you will find curries which use as many as fifty hot chillies. In the north, the

Punjab for example, the curries are less hot, considerably so, and only half a dozen chillies will be asked for in a recipe. In Bombay and West Bengal it seems it is simply a matter for family taste.

It is said of India: 'The climate is hot, the dishes are hotter and the condiments the hottest'. And the answer to the question: 'Are Indian curries hot?' is that it depends on the cook and his material.

CURRY POWDER

For a small quantity:

¾ oz. (⅓ cup) dark cardamom seeds
6 large pieces cinnamon bark
¼ oz. (1 tablespoon) whole cloves

¼ oz. (1½ tablespoons) black cumin seeds
a large pinch each of mace and nutmeg

Grind all these ingredients either in the blender or, better still, in a coffee grinder (which is not used for coffee). Pass this mixture through a sieve and store in airtight bottles. It will keep for at least 2 or 3 weeks provided the bottle is airtight.

MIXED SPICES (*Garam Masala*)

This is a condiment made of cardamoms, cumin and cloves, all dry-roasted on a griddle or heavy frying pan and pounded or ground to a fine powder. It is usual for the cook to do this on a curry stone, but it can be achieved, somewhat less finely, in an electric blender. The proportions are:

1 oz. (½ cup) dark cardamom seeds (used only in preparing masalas and savoury spices, not in sweet dishes, where the light varieties are preferred)

2 oz. (1 cup) cumin seeds
1 oz. (⅓ cup) cloves

Some Indian cooks also add cinnamon to their *garam masala*; it is, after all, a matter of individual taste.

Pass the *garam masala* through a sieve and store it in an airtight bottle.

AUBERGINE CURRY (*Baingan ki Curry*)

3–4 servings:

1½ lb. (about 4) small aubergines (egg-plants)
1 oz. (2 tablespoons) vegetable fat
1 teaspoon (1¼) turmeric
2–3 cloves
1 teaspoon (1¼) cumin seeds, ground
6 peppercorns
2 medium-sized ripe tomatoes, peeled and coarsely chopped

1 teaspoon (1¼) ginger, finely chopped
3 green chillies, seeded and chopped
¼ teaspoon (⅓) chilli powder
salt
juice of 1 lime or ½ lemon
2 tablespoons (2½) fresh coriander or parsley, minced
1 heaped teaspoon (1¼) ground coriander seeds

Peel the aubergines and cut into quarters; if using large aubergines, simply cut them into smaller pieces than quarters. Drop into cold water immediately they are peeled otherwise they will turn black. Heat the fat in a saucepan and when it is very hot add the turmeric, cloves, cumin seeds and peppercorns. Cook for 3 minutes, add the tomatoes, ginger, chillies, chilli powder, coriander seeds and fresh coriander. Cook over a medium heat for 8–10 minutes, stirring often to prevent burning. Add the aubergines, salt to taste and lime juice. Cover the pan and cook slowly, adding $\frac{1}{2}$–1 cup of warm water after the aubergines have been cooking for 10 minutes. Before serving sprinkle lightly with more chopped coriander or parsley.

Serve with rice etc.

PEAS AND CHEESE CURRY (*Matar Panir Curry*)

4 servings:

1 lb. (2 cups) peas, shelled	$\frac{1}{4}$ teaspoon ($\frac{1}{3}$) ground mustard seeds
1 lb. Indian-style cottage cheese (panir) (see page 28)	1 teaspoon ($1\frac{1}{4}$) ground poppy seeds
2 large onions, chopped	1 teaspoon ($1\frac{1}{4}$) ground cumin seeds
1 teaspoon ($1\frac{1}{4}$) fresh ginger, finely chopped	1 large cardamom pod, crushed
$\frac{1}{2}$ teaspoon ($\frac{2}{3}$) ground turmeric	1-in. piece cinnamon
$\frac{1}{4}$–$\frac{1}{2}$ teaspoon ($\frac{1}{3}$–$\frac{2}{3}$) chillies, ground and seeded	8 oz. (1 cup) vegetable fat
	2 cups ($2\frac{1}{2}$) water
	salt to taste

Cut the cheese into 1-inch cubes. Grind the onions with the spices (except the cinnamon), to a fine paste, without using any water. Heat the fat until it is very hot and quickly fry the cheese until a golden brown. Take out most of the fat, add the curry paste and cook this until it separates from the fat. Add the peas, cheese, salt and cinnamon, stir and cook for 10 minutes over a medium heat. Add the water, cover the pan and continue cooking until the peas are tender. Remove the cinnamon.

Serve hot with rice or *chapaties*.

VEGETABLE CURRY (*Subzi ki Curry*)

4–6 servings:

2 lb. mixed vegetables: potatoes, turnips, beans, peas, sweet peppers, vegetable marrow, etc.	1 onion, chopped
	6 chillies, seeded and chopped or cayenne pepper to taste
2–4 cloves garlic, coarsely chopped	3 tomatoes, peeled and coarsely chopped
$\frac{1}{2}$ teaspoon ($\frac{2}{3}$) cumin seeds	$\frac{1}{2}$ teaspoon ($\frac{2}{3}$) sugar
2 tablespoons ($2\frac{1}{2}$) coriander seeds	$\frac{1}{2}$ teaspoon ($\frac{2}{3}$) salt
4 tablespoons (5) butter or oil	

Clean the vegetables, trim and peel where required and cut into fairly small pieces. Pound the garlic with the cumin seeds and mix this with the remaining spice and a little water to make a paste. Heat the fat and fry the paste for 5 minutes, add the onion, chillies and tomatoes, stir gently and continue cooking for 3 minutes. Add the remaining vegetables, sugar and gently stir. Add salt and enough water to just cover. Cook over a moderate heat until the vegetables are tender but not soft.

Serve with rice and lentils.

PRAWN CURRY (*Jhinga ki Curry*)

6 servings:

24 large shelled fresh prawns (butterfly size)

1 small piece tamarind or 3 tablespoons ($3\frac{3}{4}$) lime or lemon juice

3 tablespoons ($3\frac{3}{4}$) water

8–10 dry red chillies

1-in. piece fresh ginger

1 teaspoon ($1\frac{1}{4}$) ground turmeric

$\frac{1}{2}$ teaspoon ($\frac{2}{3}$) cumin seeds, lightly roasted

6 peppercorns

2 teaspoons ($2\frac{1}{2}$) coriander seeds, lightly roasted

fresh coriander, chopped, or parsley to taste

4 cloves garlic or to taste

1 teaspoon ($1\frac{1}{4}$) dry mustard

3 oz. (6 tablespoons) ghee or other fat

salt

1 cup ($1\frac{1}{4}$) thick coconut milk (see page 238)

1 cup ($1\frac{1}{4}$) thin coconut milk (see page 238)

Soak the tamarind in the cold water. Prepare the curry paste; pound the chillies, ginger, turmeric, cumin seeds, peppercorns, coriander seeds, fresh coriander, garlic, mustard and the tamarind juice to a smooth paste. This should be thin, so add a little water if necessary.

Heat the fat, add the paste, stir and fry for about 5 minutes. Add salt and bring slowly to the boil. Add the prawns, stir and cook these slowly for 5 minutes, then add the thick coconut milk. Let all this cook until the milk has evaporated, then add the thin milk. If you prefer more gravy, add another cupful of water. Simmer for about 15 minutes. Serve with rice, chutneys and *pappadams* (*see* page 24).

FISH CURRY (*Machhi ki Curry*)

6 servings:

2 lb. fish, white and firm

3 onions

6–10 dried chillies, split and seeded

6 peppercorns, crushed

1 tablespoon ($1\frac{1}{4}$) ground coriander seeds

a small piece of tamarind or 1 tablespoon ($1\frac{1}{4}$) lemon juice

1 teaspoon ($1\frac{1}{4}$) ground cumin seeds

1 tablespoon ($1\frac{1}{4}$) ground turmeric

1 small piece fresh ginger, thinly sliced or chopped

3–4 cloves garlic, chopped

1 grated coconut or $\frac{1}{2}$ lb. ($2\frac{1}{2}$ cups) desiccated coconut

2 oz. (4 tablespoons) ghee or other fat

2 cups ($2\frac{1}{2}$) water

1 cup ($1\frac{1}{4}$) each thick and thin coconut milk (see page 238)

salt

Rub the fish with salt, leave it for 15 minutes then wash off the salt. Chop 2 of the onions and thinly slice the third. Pound the chopped onions, chillies, peppercorns, coriander, tamarind, cumin, turmeric, ginger and garlic together with the coconut to a paste adding the water as you pound. This makes a thin curry paste.

Heat the fat and fry the sliced onion, stir in the thin coconut milk and the curry paste. Simmer and bring it slowly to the boil. Add salt and continue to cook for about 10 minutes. Add the pieces of fish and cook slowly until tender. Add the thick coconut milk and continue to simmer for a further 10 minutes as boiling will curdle the milk. Serve with rice, curd, chutneys and *pappadams*.

CHICKEN CURRY (*Murghi ki Curry*)

4–6 servings:

1 large chicken, cut into serving pieces
1 tablespoon (1¼) lightly roasted coriander
  seeds
6–8 peppercorns
6 red chillies, chopped and seeded or
  chilli powder to taste
2½ oz. (5 tablespoons) ghee or vegetable fat
2 onions, thinly sliced

2–3 cloves garlic, thinly sliced
salt
1 small piece fresh ginger, finely chopped
1 cup (1¼) curd or yoghourt
1 teaspoon (1¼) garam masala (see page
  13)
a little coriander, finely chopped or parsley

Pound together the coriander seeds, peppercorns and chillies and mix with enough water to make a thin paste. Heat the fat and lightly fry the onions, stir in the paste and fry for a minute or two, then add the chicken pieces. Stir and fry the chicken until brown, add the garlic, salt and ginger. Stir the mixture, add water to cover and simmer until the chicken is tender. Add the curd and ½ cupful of water and continue cooking until the chicken is tender. Add the *garam masala* and the coriander and continue to cook slowly for another 10 minutes. Serve with rice, *pappadams* and *dahl* (*see* pages 21 and 24).

DUCK CURRY (*Badak Vindaloo*)

A dish from Goa. A *vindaloo* curry is distinguished by its sour-hot flavour also because it is prepared with plenty of gravy. There is a basic recipe for all of the *vindaloos* with slight variations here and there in quantities. As with all Indian curries, tender duck or other meat is not required; and the duck or whatever used, once seasoned and in the pan, can cook steadily until it reaches a fit state for eating.

3–4 servings: depending on size of the duck:

1 medium-size duck
2 tablespoons (2½) ground cumin seeds
12 dry seeded chillies or chilli powder to
  taste, but a vindaloo should be a hot
  curry
1 pod black cardamom, crushed
1 teaspoon (1¼) ground turmeric

2 cloves garlic
¼ cup (⅓) mild vinegar
4 tablespoons (5) ghee or other fat
1 large onion, chopped
1 tablespoon (1¼) coriander or parsley
  finely chopped
salt to taste

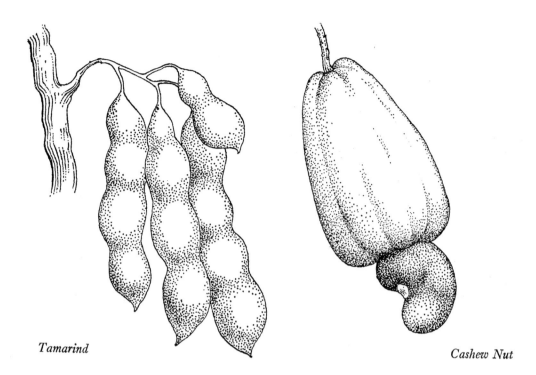

Tamarind   *Cashew Nut*

Cut the duck into serving pieces. Pound or grind together the cumin, chillies, garlic, cardamom and turmeric with the vinegar. This makes a hot curry paste. Heat the fat, add the onion and cook this until it is soft. Add the coriander, the duck, salt and cover the pan. Simmer, stirring from time to time, for about 10 minutes. Add the curry paste and 2–3 cupfuls (2½–3¾) of boiling water or stock. Cover again and cook slowly stirring from time to time to prevent burning.

To this is usually added potatoes, peeled and quartered and cooked in the pan on top of the duck or cooked separately and served with it. If using this dish as a party dish, with 2–3 duck, use discretion with the spices as doubling all of them would be too powerful.

MUTTON or LAMB CURRY (*Gosht ki Curry*)

4–5 servings:

2 lb. mutton or lamb
1 tablespoon (1¼) fresh coriander or
parsley, chopped
½ fresh coconut, finely grated or 4 oz. (1¼
cups) desiccated
2 teaspoons (2½) fresh ginger, chopped
1 onion, chopped
1 clove garlic
4 green or red chillies, seeds removed or
chilli powder to taste

1 teaspoon (1¼) ground turmeric
2 tablespoons (2½) curd (see **page 22**)
2 tablespoons (2½) vegetable fat
ground ginger
1 tablespoon (1¼) sesame seeds
1 tablespoon (1¼) coriander seeds
salt
1 cup (1¼) cashew nuts, finely chopped

Pound the coconut, fresh ginger, onion, garlic, green chillies, fresh coriander, turmeric and curd to a fine paste. Heat the fat, add the meat and sprinkle lightly with ground ginger. Cook until the meat is lightly browned, add the paste and cook for 10 minutes, stirring constantly. Crush the coriander and sesame seeds and 'dry fry' them. Dry-fried simply means frying without fat in a pan. This process enhances the flavour of any of the spices, especially sesame seeds. (*See* Korea, page 213.) Cook all these ingredients for a few minutes, add water or stock to cover, plus a little over. Add salt to taste and simmer until the meat is tender then add the cashew nuts. Serve with rice.

If cashew nuts are not available, try hazel nuts or other white nuts such as brazil nuts, or peanuts.

OTHER MAIN DISHES

FRIED FISH IN MUSTARD SAUCE (*Sarse Batar Machhi*) (Bengal)

2–3 servings:

1 lb. fish
1 tablespoon (1¼) mustard seeds
4–6 green chillies, seeded
4 red chillies, seeded

salt
4 tablespoons (5) cooking oil (mustard oil for Bengali taste)

Grind the mustard seeds, chillies and salt with a little water to a smooth paste and leave for 30 minutes. Cut the fish into slices of equal size, spread with this paste, put in a heavy frying pan, add the oil and more salt to taste, if liked. Put the pan on a quick fire for 2 minutes, lower the heat and cook until the fish is tender. No water or other liquid is required.

Instead of whole chillies, chilli powder may be used.

FISH MOOLIE (*Machhi Moolie*)

This is a mild curry from Goa and the Mangalore coast.

2–3 servings:

1 lb. filleted fish, cut into squares
1 teaspoon (1¼) ground turmeric
2 oz. (¼ cup) ghee or other fat
2 onions, sliced
6 thin slices ginger or 1 teaspoon (1¼) ground

salt
1 cup (1¼) thick coconut milk (see page 238)
2–3 green chillies, whole or chopped and seeded or cayenne pepper
1 tablespoon (1¼) vinegar
1 cup (1¼) fish stock

Heat the fat and fry half the onion to a light brown. Add the turmeric, ginger, salt and gradually the coconut milk. Cook all this for a few minutes, then add the chillies and the rest of the onion, stir well, add the fish and stock, and cook until tender, then add the vinegar a few minutes before serving.

CHICKEN MOOLIE (*Murghi Moolie*)

Made as fish *moolie* but using chicken stock. It is cooked for a little longer and the quantities of all ingredients should be doubled. This type of *moolie* can be made with either half-cooked or raw chicken.

EGG MOOLIE (*Baida Moolie*)

This requires hard-boiled eggs, about 6 to 8 for the quantity of ingredients used in the fish *moolie*, and chicken stock instead of fish stock. The eggs are added to the curry whole. This is one of the best of the egg curries.

CHICKEN MOGHLAI STYLE (*Moghlai Qorma*)

4 servings:

1 large chicken
1½ cups (2¼) grated or desiccated coconut
4 tablespoons (5) almonds, blanched and chopped
2 tablespoons (2½) pine nuts
3 tablespoons (3¾) poppyseeds
chilli powder to taste

3 tablespoons (3¾) ghee or butter
2 large onions, thinly sliced
6 cloves
6 cardamom seeds, crushed
1–2 pieces cinnamon
1 cup (1¼) curd or yoghourt
juice of ½ lemon

Clean and joint the chicken. Pound the coconut, almonds, pine nuts, poppyseeds and chilli powder to a paste, adding water as you pound. Heat the fat and fry the onions to a golden brown, add the paste, stir well, add the chicken, cloves, cardamoms, cinnamon and curd and simmer for 2 hours. Add the lemon juice and, if you feel there is not enough gravy, a little more water. Remove the cloves and cinnamon before serving. Serve hot with rice.

This dish is rich but not meant to have a lot of gravy and is served for special occasions with rice.

SPICED CHICKEN (*Murgh Mussallam*)

4–6 servings:

1 large chicken
1 teaspoon (1¼) ground turmeric
1 teaspoon (1¼) ground cumin seeds
2-in. piece cinnamon
4 cloves
2 cardamom pods, crushed
1–2 onions, chopped
1-in. piece fresh ginger, chopped

garlic to taste
6 large tomatoes, peeled and chopped
salt
a little jaggery, molasses or black treacle (see page 241)
red chillies, whole, to taste
a little butter

Cut the chicken into serving pieces and lightly pound them. Pound or grind together all the spices with the onion(s), garlic, ginger and rub this into the chicken pieces. Put the chicken, *jaggery*, salt and the ground spices into a heavy pan, add the tomatoes, chillies and enough water to cover. Tightly cover the pan and cook over a slow fire until the chicken is tender. Uncover the pan, add butter and continue cooking for a few minutes. Remove the chillies before serving.

SPICED LAMB ('*Bharuchi*' *Masalawala Gosht*)

6–8 servings:

3½ lb. lamb or mutton

½ lb. crisply fried onions

1 small piece fresh ginger, chopped

1 small clove garlic

seeds of 2 cardamom pods

1-in. piece cinnamon

8 oz. (1 cup) ghee or other fat

2 hot chillies, seeded and chopped

1 cup (1¼) coconut milk (see page 238)

2 cups (2½) milk

½ teaspoon (⅔) saffron, soaked in the juice of ½ lemon

salt

2 lb. potatoes

The onions should be so crisply fried that they can be crushed to a powder in the hand. Clean or trim the meat and cut it into 12–16 pieces. Grind the ginger, garlic and the crushed onion to a paste and rub this mixture into the meat. Put aside 1 hour. Boil the potatoes in their skins, then cool, peel and cut into halves and sauté until a golden brown. Grind the remaining spices. Heat the fat in a deep saucepan or braising pan and fry the pieces of meat in this, adding the chillies and the ground spices. When the meat is brown, take the pan from the heat, cool, and then add the milk and the coconut milk. Return it to the stove and cook over a moderate heat until the meat is tender. Add the saffron and salt to taste and serve hot, garnished with the potatoes.

RICE AND LENTILS

RICE (*Chawal*)

There are many different ways of cooking rice in India. The following method is probably one of the most usual.

Wash the rice at least three times (with clean and unadulterated rice the washing can be reduced to once) and steep it in cold water for 1 or more hours. Drain absolutely free of water. Three-quarters fill a large pan with water, bring it to a rapid boil and throw in the rice. Half cover the pot and let the rice cook so quickly that it dances and the water almost boils over. Stir the rice from time to time. In 15 minutes, at the most 20 minutes, it should be soft but not a pulp. Take the pan from the heat, throw several cups of cold water over the rice, then drain it again and put into a warm oven to dry and reheat.

It helps to add salt to rice when cooking to keep the grains firm; also a little lime or lemon juice added to it keeps it white and prevents the rice from breaking.

LENTILS (*Dahl*)

Usually *dahl* is made with red lentils, in Britain called Egyptian lentils, or the green lentils (*moong dahl*). Both types cook quickly without soaking.

6–8 servings:

8 oz. (1 cup) lentils, red or green	**2 teaspoons (2½) ghee or butter**
1 small piece fresh ginger	**salt and black pepper to taste**
1 onion, chopped	

Wash the lentils and cook them in about 1½–2 cups of water with the remaining ingredients until soft. Beat with an egg-beater a couple of times.

Indians always add fresh ginger to any type of lentils, which being gassy need the ginger to help the digestion. Failing fresh ginger, ground ginger may be added when beating, not when cooking. If less quick cooking lentils are used, more water will be required and this can be added as the lentils cook. There is always a cure for too little liquid but not for too much. This kind of purée is usually served as an accompaniment to curries, by Westernized Indians it is usually poured over the curry, otherwise served in a small bowl.

Garnish:

Heat a little butter or other fat and lightly fry some thinly sliced onions until brown. Add these immediately before serving.

LENTILS AND RICE KEDGEREE

In 1886 John Murray of Albemarle Street, London, published one of the most fascinating dictionaries I know. Its full title is *Hobson-Jobson: being a Glossary of Anglo-India Colloquial Words and Phrases, and of Kindred Terms; Etymological, Historical, Geographical and Discursive.* To happy owners it is known simply as *Hobson-Jobson.*

This is all to explain the kedgeree, for this is what Hobson-Jobson, my Bible on matters concerning Indian etymological affairs, has to say about this dish.

'Kedgeree, Kitchery, Hind. *Khichri*, a mess of rice, cooked with butter and *dal* (see *Dholl*), and flavoured with a little spice, shred onion, and the like; a common dish all over India, and often served at Anglo-Indian breakfast tables, in which a very old precedent is followed, as the first quotation shows.

'The word appears to have been applied metaphorically to mixtures of sundry kinds (*see* **Fryer** below), and also to mixt jargon or lingua franca.

'In England we find the word is often applied to a mess of re-cooked fish, served for breakfast: but this is inaccurate. Fish is frequently eaten *with* kedgeree, but is not part of it.'

4 servings:

8 oz. (1¼ cups) long grain rice	**2 cardamom, pods peeled**
4 oz. (1 cup) lentils	**1 teaspoon (1¼) ground turmeric**
1 onion, finely chopped	**1-in. piece cinnamon**
¼ teaspoon (⅓) cumin seeds	**salt, pepper**
2 cloves	**2 oz. (4 tablespoons) butter or ghee**

Separately wash and soak the rice and lentils for 30 minutes. Crush the cardamoms and cloves. Heat the butter in a saucepan and fry half the onion. Put this aside for later garnishing. Add the spices, salt and pepper to the pan and cook these for 2 minutes, add the remaining onion and cook this until it is a light brown. Drain the lentils and add to the spices, stir, add the rice, stir again and continue to cook until the rice begins to stick to the bottom of the pan. Pour in enough water to reach 1 inch above the level of the rice and lentils. Cook over a low heat until both are soft and serve hot garnished with the fried onion.

The usual type of lentils for this dish are reddish, small lentils which cook quickly.

CURD OR CLABBER *(Dahi)*

Curd is important in Indian cooking, especially in curries, but it is also served with *pilaus*. The best substitute in Britain and the United States is yoghourt, preferably the thick yoghourt and naturally the unflavoured variety.

In India the milk of the buffalo is used for making curd. In Britain the best milk is probably rich Jersey milk. Pasteurized milk curdles only with extreme difficulty.

The simplest way in which to prepare curd is to bring the milk to blood heat—say 1 pint (2½ cups)— and add to this the juice of 1 lime or half a lemon. Stir well, for the lime must be thoroughly mixed into the milk. Leave in a warm place for 12 hours, or according to the warmth of its resting place. If your home is centrally heated, the milk will set in some 12–15 hours, and most certainly within 24 hours, which is the outside limit, otherwise the curd will become sour, a different sourness to that of curdled milk. By set, I mean that the curd is so thick it can be positively cut.

When one batch of curd is made take a little of it, using 1 tablespoonful (1¼) of curd to 1 pint (2½ cups) of milk and curdle the fresh milk with it. This curd is a 'starter' and when making curd regularly one usually saves from each batch of curd just enough to get another batch going. In Indian homes a bowl of curd is available all the time, or it can be purchased in the bazaar.

A good quality yoghurt can also be utilized as a starter.

CLARIFIED BUTTER *(Ghee)*

Ghee is used considerably in Indian and Pakistani cooking, especially in the north, and is simple to make. Heat some butter in a saucepan over a moderate heat and stir it from time to time until it is completely melted. Throw in a few grains of rice and let the butter boil until these brown, this is the sign that the *ghee* has formed. Stir it well so that the froth at the top is all mixed up. Remove it from the heat and leave in the pan in a refrigerator. In a few hours a thick layer of clarified butter sets on the top and the undesirable residue sinks to the bottom. Take the solidified portion from the pan carefully with a spoon and knife in order not to disturb the residue at the bottom, which is discarded.

Ghee may be bought already prepared in tins in Indian and other shops selling Oriental foodstuffs.

INDIAN BREADS

PHULKAS

For both *phulkas* and *chapaties* the dough should be fairly soft. Make a flour and water dough with about 8 oz. (1 cup) of wholemeal flour (in all these bread recipes which follow, wholemeal flour (*atta*) is meant and not refined white flour).

Break off pellets the size of a walnut and flatten these between the palms of the hands. Dip in flour and roll out thinly on a floured board. (There are in India small round wooden *chapati* boards and short, rather squat, fat rolling pins used only for 'bread' making.) Brown both sides of the *phulka* very lightly on a griddle or thick frying pan over a medium heat, then hold over hot coals, or a gas flame to puff out.

CHAPATIES

Make a dough in exactly the same manner as for *phulkas*, break off the pellets—again walnut-size—and roll these out paper-thin 8–10 inches in diameter. These are cooked on a griddle turned upside down (unlike the Western griddle or frying pan, the Indian griddles are curved like saucers). They are not puffed up on hot coals and it needs expertise and practice to know exactly when to flip the *chapati* over with one twist of the hand.

PARATHAS

These are roasted on a griddle or in a heavy iron frying pan with *ghee* or vegetable oil. The traditional *paratha* is triangular in shape but since this is difficult to roll they can be rolled either as squares or rounds. Make a dough as for *phulkas*, roll out the pellets somewhat larger than the *phulka* on to a floured board. Brown on both sides on a dry griddle, then pour a little *ghee* or vegetable fat around. Press down with a spoon to brown, turn over and add some more *ghee* or vegetable fat. Press on both sides to puff up and when nicely browned on both sides the *paratha* is ready. They also can be made with white flour.

PURIS

These also belong to the Indian breads and there are many varieties, those made with plain flour and water dough; others with yeast with seasonings; some stuffed, others plain, and finally sweet *puris*. The kind one usually meets in India are the plain ones which, if well made, are very good. The more elaborate varieties are served for special and festive occasions. It is usual to eat several *puris* at a sitting and the cook sends out plate after plate of piping hot *puris*. They are eaten at once and if they become cold they are returned to the kitchen and a new batch called for.

12 oz. (2¼ cups) wholemeal flour   **water**
2–3 tablespoons (2½–3¾) ghee or vegetable fat

Rub the *ghee* into the flour and add enough water to mix this to a stiff dough. Knead thoroughly with the hands for about 10 minutes, or use an electric mixer. Break off pellets about the size of a ping-pong ball and flatten these into rounds with the palms of the hands. Now for the rolling out part of it. The correct way to roll the dough is to grease your pastry board and rolling-pin lightly and then brush the dough very lightly on both sides with melted *ghee* or other fat. Roll out thinly, not too thin or they will not puff up well. Turn once during rolling.

Fry in deep hot fat. Press down lightly with the back of a perforated spoon and as soon as it rises to the surface flip it over quickly and let it fry until a deep golden colour.

This recipe produces 24–28 *puris*.

PAPPADAMS

I do not suppose that even in Indian villages anyone but a *pappadam* professional makes these delectable 'breads'. They can be bought easily enough nowadays in Britain and America. In India they come 'penny plain and twopence coloured' with a variety of flavours, spices and seasonings. They are extremely simple to prepare. Put them under a grill, or over a high flame, or in a hot oven, or, perhaps best of all, fry them in deep fat. They become crisp whichever way they are cooked.

As soon as they change colour they are ready. They darken very quickly. Before cooking, *pappadams* are soft, thin rounds of dough. When cooked, they become crisp and snap easily.

CHUTNEY *(Chutny)*

It is interesting to note what Hobson-Jobson has to say on chutneys. 'A kind of strong relish, made of a number of condiments and fruits, etc., used in India, more especially by Mahommedans, and the merits of which are now well known in England.'

This is curious for today chutney is more used in Hindu cooking than Muslim.

But here we have also: 'The *Chatna* is sometimes made with cocoa-nut, lime juice, garlic, and chillies, and with pickles is placed in deep leaves round the large cover, to the number of 30 or 40.'

And, in 1820, we have: '*Chitnee, Chatnee*, some of the hot spices made into a paste, by being bruised with water, the "kitchen" of an Indian peasant.'

I am more inclined to believe that chutney is part of the Hindu or general Indian cooking, not Muslim. However, whatever else chutney is, it is not a mixture of apples and raisins, nor something which comes out of a jar. This does not mean that the chutneys in jars are not acceptable, but these are Anglo-Indian or British and not Indian. With a curry several chutneys usually are served, some hot, others mild.

AUBERGINE CHUTNEY *(Baingan ki Chutny)*

1 large aubergine (eggplant)	juice 1 small lemon
2 green chillies, seeded and finely chopped	salt to taste
1 onion, finely chopped	½ lb. grated or desiccated coconut

If possible roast the aubergine over gas or charcoal **or** under the grill until the skin is burnt and the flesh is very soft. Or it can be boiled in its skin until soft. As soon as it is cool enough to handle, peel and mash. Mix with the remaining ingredients. The flavour of a roasted aubergine is vastly superior to a boiled one.

COCONUT CHUTNEY (*Nariel ki Chutny*)

Pound or blend about 4 tablespoons (5) of freshly grated coconut (or desiccated) with 1 small piece of chopped ginger. Add some finely chopped, seeded green chillies to taste, or if these are not obtainable, use capsicums (sweet peppers) and enough finely chopped green coriander or parsley, to make the chutney a soft green colour. Add sufficient lime (or lemon) juice to make all this into a firm paste.

CUCUMBER CHUTNEY (*Kira ki Chutny*)

Peel and chop a very small cucumber. Mix this with an equal quantity of finely chopped onion, season with salt and pepper and sharpen the flavour with mild vinegar, or lemon juice.

GARLIC CHUTNEY (*Lasan ki Chutny*)

This is simply grated or desiccated coconut mixed with cayenne or chilli pepper and plenty of finely chopped or pounded garlic.

GREEN CHILLI CHUTNEY (*Mirchi Chutny*)

Slit as many green chillies as required, discard the seeds, cut the flesh into tiny pieces and mix with finely chopped fresh ginger, salt, lime or lemon juice and chilli powder.

MINT CHUTNEY (*Pudina ki Chutny*)

Every province in India has its own way of making mint chutney.

4–5 sprigs fresh mint
2 small green chillies, seeded and chopped
1 teaspoon (1¼) ginger, finely chopped
1 teaspoon (1¼) sugar

½ mild onion, finely chopped
juice of 2 limes or 1 lemon
1 clove garlic, finely chopped

Strip the mint leaves from their stems. Pound or blend with all the remaining ingredients to a paste; it should be somewhat looser than the coconut chutney. Failing green chillies, use any of the hot red peppers, or cayenne or chilli powder.

ONION CHUTNEY (*Piaz ki Chutny*)

Mince as many mild onions as required, add a few chopped mint leaves, add lemon juice to taste and leave for 1 hour. Use 1 tablespoonful (1¼) per person.

POTATO CHUTNEY (*Alu ki Chutny*)

Cooked, diced potatoes simply flavoured with chillies or a chilli pepper, salt, pepper and lime (or lemon) juice.

TOMATO CHUTNEY (*Tamatar ki Chutny*)

This is simply peeled and chopped raw tomatoes mixed with minced onion, some finely chopped mint and a few drops of lime or lemon juice.

SIDE DISHES

GENERAL RECIPE FOR A VEGETABLE SIDE DISH (*Raita*)

1–2 cups curd or yoghourt
salt, pepper
dry mustard to taste

fresh coriander or parsley, chopped
vegetables as required

If using curd, press out or let the excess water drip out. Thick yoghourt can be used as it is. Flavour this with salt, pepper, dry mustard and coriander. Then mix with any one of the following vegetables: skinned and chopped tomatoes; grated raw carrot; peeled and finely cut cucumber; seeded and chopped green chillies or capsicums (sweet peppers), and cooked, diced potatoes.

Raita is always served chilled and many people also add garlic, finely chopped or minced.

SPICED CURD (*Raita*)

4–6 servings:

4 cups (5) curd or yoghourt, well beaten
2 tablespoons (2½) ghee or other fat
6 cloves garlic, or to taste, thinly sliced
1 teaspoon (1¼) ground turmeric

1 teaspoon (1¼) salt
4 green chillies, finely chopped and seeded
2 tablespoons (2½) finely chopped coriander or parsley

Heat the fat until it is sizzling hot, fry the garlic, turmeric and salt for 2 minutes. When the sizzling has stopped, add the curd, chillies and coriander. Cook very slowly for 5 minutes, stirring all the while.

Serve with boiled rice or kedgeree or as a chutney. Failing green chillies, use dried chillies or chilli powder.

CUCUMBER WITH CURD (*Khira ka Raita*)

2 cups (2½) curd or yoghourt
salt
green chillies, finely chopped and seeded
½ teaspoon (⅔) chilli, powdered

1 teaspoon (1¼) coriander, finely chopped
1 level teaspoon (1¼) cumin seeds, roasted and powdered
½ lb. cucumbers, more or less

Mix all the seasonings, add the curd. Peel and grate the cucumber and add this to the curd. The proportion of curd or yoghourt is 1 cupful of either to 1½ cupfuls of cucumber.

BANANAS IN CURD OR YOGHOURT (*Kela ka Raita*)

4–6 servings:

3 bananas, thinly sliced
2 cups (2½) curd or **yoghourt**
salt, pepper

1 green chilli, seeded and finely chopped
fresh coriander or **parsley, finely chopped**

Mix the salt and pepper into the curd and whisk until it is smooth. Add the bananas and chilli. Serve garnished with coriander.

BOMBAY DUCK

This is a side dish not a chutney and is used mainly in the south and in Bombay, seldom in the north. Bombay duck is dried *bummelo* fish, plentiful on the west coast of India. These are small transparent fish which are hung out to dry on the beaches. Their presence to anyone within smelling distance is all too obvious. Bombay duck is available in Britain and the United States in tins. The *bummelo* when cooked fresh is a delicious little fish.

BOMBAY DUCK SALAD

Take 6 Bombay duck and either toast, fry or roast them and crumble into small pieces. Mix with finely chopped chilli pepper, thinly sliced fresh ginger, minced onion and a little mild vinegar.

AUBERGINE 'SALAD' (*Baingan Bhurta*)

Bhurtas have somewhat the same function in the Indian cuisine as western salads. They can also be used with curries as a side dish.

4 servings:

2 aubergines (eggplants)—about 1 lb.
2 tablespoons (2½) ghee or **other vegetable**
fat
¾ teaspoon (1) white cumin seeds
½ teaspoon (⅔) black cumin seeds

½ teaspoon (⅔) chilli powder
1 tablespoon (1¼) ground coriander seeds
¼ teaspoon (⅓) garam masala (see **page 13**)
salt to taste

Roast the aubergines in ashes or over a high gas flame until the skin burns, cracks and wrinkles. Leave for five minutes then pull off the skin and mash the pulp. Heat the fat and fry all the cumin seeds, when they turn brown add the aubergine pulp, the chilli powder, coriander, *garam masala* and salt. Cook until the pulp is nicely browned. This is a typical Indian *bhurta* and is a version of the 'poor man's caviar' of the Balkans.

POTATO 'SALAD' (*Alu ka Bhurta*)

Boil as many potatoes as required in their skins, peel and mash. Heat a little fat, add chopped onion and green, seeded chillies and salt to taste and cook for a few minutes. Then add the potatoes. Serve hot or cold.

SPICED CAULIFLOWER (*Masalawali Phulgobi*)

4–6 servings:

1 large cauliflower
3 tablespoons (3¾) oil
2 teaspoons (2½) fresh ginger, coarsely
   chopped
3 green chillies, seeded and halved (if not
   available use cayenne pepper)
salt to taste

1 teaspoon (1¼) sugar
1 heaped teaspoon (1¼) ground coriander
   seeds
juice of 1 lemon
½ teaspoon (⅝) garam masala (see page 13)
2 tablespoons (2½) fresh coriander or
   parsley, finely chopped

Cut the cauliflower into sprigs, discarding all the coarse parts. Soak the sprigs and tender stalks for 1 hour. Heat the oil and when this is hot add the ginger and chillies and cook these for 2 minutes. Add the cauliflower and salt. Cover and cook over a medium heat for 10 minutes. Add sugar, juice and the remaining spices and simmer until the cauliflower is tender, there should be enough liquid in the cauliflower to steam it if the pan is tightly covered. Just before serving, sprinkle with fresh coriander.

This dish can be served as a side dish to meat or vegetable curries, or with roasted or boiled meat.

CHEESE

WHITE CHEESE (*Chaaman, Paneer* or *Panir*)

This is somewhat similar to the Balkan goat cheese or Greek *feta* and is used a great deal in Indian cooking in the north. It is cooked as a vegetable, cut into squares and fried and eaten plain.

4 pints (10 cups) milk, unpasteurized
1 tablespoon (1¼) sour milk or curd

juice of 2 limes or 1 lemon

Bring the milk to boiling point and as soon as it boils lower the heat and add the curd and the juice. Stir to mix. It will curdle immediately. Cook for 3–5 minutes more. Strain through fine muslin

Do not throw away the liquid as this is usually kept for making another batch of cheese. Tie the cheese in a cloth and hang it to drain. When it is quite cool put into another clean piece of muslin and put into a refrigerator, weigh it down and leave until it is very firm.

SWEETS

ALMOND FUDGE (*Barfi*)

½ lb. (1⅓ cups) ground almonds   1 lb. (2 cups) granulated sugar
1 cup (1¼) water

Boil the sugar and water to the soft boil stage, add the ground almonds and cook it all for 5 minutes. Spread this mixture on to a lightly greased flat sponge cake pan, let it get cold and then cut into cubes or diamond shapes.

One of the simplest of the several varieties of Indian *barfi*.

RICE PUDDING (*Payesh*) (West Bengal)

4–6 servings:

2 pints (5 cups) milk   6 oz. (¾ cup) palm sugar or soft brown
2 oz. (⅓ cup) rice   sugar

Cook the milk and rice together until the rice is soft. Add the sugar and continue cooking until the rice is of a custard consistency. Pour into a bowl, cool and then put into a refrigerator. This dish is always served cold. Palm sugar also adds its own soft colour to the rice, but a good brown sugar would do the same, but then add a little rose-water and a few raisins.

PARSEE FOOD

The Parsees are well known in India for their delight in food and eating, and their dishes are quite different from the ordinary run of Indian cooking.

CHICKEN CURRY OF 100 ALMONDS (*Murghi ki Curry San Badam*)

6–8 servings:

1–2 chickens, depending on size   2–3 cloves garlic
2 cups (2½) grated or desiccated coconut   1 scant tablespoon (1¼) poppyseed
1 onion, spiked with cloves   4–6 oz. (½–¾ cup) butter
salt, pepper   1 cup (1¼) tamarind juice, or ½ cup (⅔)
100 almonds, blanched (¼–½ lb.) depending   lemon juice
   on size
15 chilli peppers, seeded or chilli powder
   to taste

Put half the coconut aside and use the remainder to make 2 cupfuls (2½) of milk (*see* page 238). Boil the chicken(s) in plenty of water until tender, adding the onion, salt and pepper. Be sure that at least 4 cupfuls (5) of water remain in the pot. Take out the chicken and joint it. Strain the stock.

Grind the almonds and pound them until smooth or use ground almonds. Add chilli peppers and garlic and continue pounding until a paste, adding the poppyseeds and grated coconut and, as you pound, a little water. If using a blender, put the whole lot into this adding of course some liquid.

Heat the butter and lightly fry the paste. Add the chicken stock and the coconut milk. Simmer gently until the sauce is thick and the butter rises to the top. Add the tamarind juice and the chicken. Simmer until the chicken has absorbed some of the flavour of the sauce. Serve the chicken in the sauce with boiled rice.

SCRAMBLED EGGS (*Ackoori*)

6 servings:

8 eggs	**1 lb. onions**
2 lb. potatoes	**8 oz. (1 cup) ghee or other fat**
3–4 green seeded chillies or chilli powder	**1 teaspoon (1¼) turmeric**
to taste	**salt**
1-in. piece ginger, finely chopped	**½ cup (⅔) coriander or parsley, finely**
1 clove garlic	**chopped**

Peel the potatoes and either coarsely grate them (which is easier) or cut them into match-size strips. Leave in a bowl of cold, slightly salted water for 30 minutes. Finely chop the chillies, ginger and garlic. Chop the onions coarsely and beat the eggs until frothy. Heat the fat in a deep frying pan and fry the potatoes to a golden brown. Take them from the pan, drain and put aside but keep hot. Pour off most of the fat leaving only enough to fry the onions and the garlic until brown; add the turmeric, ginger and finally the eggs and salt. Stir lightly until the eggs are set and mixed into the onions. Just before the eggs are cooked stir in the coriander. Turn the scrambled eggs and onions on to a hot dish and surround with the fried potatoes.

Ackoori can be served on buttered toast.

SPICED ONION SALAD (*Cachoombar*)

2–3 servings:

2–3 large white onions	**coriander or parsley**
3 large firm tomatoes	**1 teaspoon (1¼) salt**
1 very small cucumber	**½ cup (⅔) light vinegar**
4 green chillies, seeded or chilli powder	
to taste	

Peel and chop the onions, tomatoes and cucumber into small pieces, as near as possible of equal size. Finely chop the chillies and the coriander. Mix all these ingredients together, arrange in a shallow dish, sprinkle with salt, add vinegar and leave for 30 minutes before serving.

The chillies can be omitted but the flavour suffers.

Pakistan

Ask any Indian the difference between Indian and Pakistani food and he will admit to none. True they were a single country before Partition. But there is a difference, as the Pakistani is quick to point out. Pakistani food is never so heavily spiced as Indian food; there are none of the rich, yellow over-spiced curries of India and tears seldom course down the face of the unwary diner in Pakistan. Although rice is the staple food, in the form of pilaus and *biryanis*, Pakistan is a country of meat eaters, its people admitting of but one culinary taboo—as Muslims they do not eat pork.

There are four distinct schools of cooking in Pakistan; Pathan, Sindhi, Punjabi and Moghul. Pathan cooking is a man's cooking, for a virile people who stand no nonsense in the kitchen and eat meat all the time, basically despising vegetables. When they talk of meat they mean sheep, and the 'fat-tailed-one', a species of sheep with a heavy fat tail. They have terrific recipes for roasting a whole sheep, stuffing it tightly with a rich pilau. The sheep comes whole to the table for serving. Pathan cooking is close to Greek cooking with sizzling kebabs and a preference for mutton. There is, however, one big difference. The Greeks drink wine with their food, while the Pathans prefer buttermilk.

The whole flavour of frontier food comes from the smoke of the wood fires. When Pathans use spices and herbs, they do so sparingly. Mint and coriander are two favourites, aniseed and cloves are used, but never does one find a recipe (when there are recipes) with a long and complicated list of spices and herbs to bemuse the cook and change the flavour of the meat. When the Pathan cooks meat he wraps it up in its own fat, giving it a flavour unlike any other meat cooking.

Next we have Sindhi cooking, much influenced by Hindu rules. The Sindhis are, however, great fish eaters, unlike the Pathans who view fish with grave suspicion. The Sindhis use rather more spices than elsewhere in Pakistan and they have a particular fondness for fresh coriander.

Punjabi food is discussed in the introduction to the Indian chapter (*see* page 9).

Finally there is Muslim food much of which springs from the Moghul Courts. This cooking is not everyday cooking, 'better eaten but once or twice a month', I was warned. But not all of this is so rich and there is also plenty of simple food.

Much Pakistani food has an Arab heritage, pilaus, unleavened bread, kebabs and an extravagant use of nuts, almonds, pistachios and pine nuts which are found in abundance in the country.

Even so, probably the favourite form of cooking in Pakistan is *tanduri* cooking apart from kebabs. (For *tanduri* cooking *see* page 38.) It is simple cooking but even so requires an expertise for the swiftness of the hand saves many a nasty burn.

Very typical of the whole country, indeed of the whole sub-continent, are small portable iron stoves fuelled with coke, charcoal or wood. On such stoves the Pakistani cook can produce succulent pilaus, *biryanis*, *dopyazas* and *qormas*, the Pakistani version of the ragoût. Much of the family and all the roadside cooking is done on such a stove.

Roadside cooking is excellent, the best public cooking in a country which lacks good eating houses. Most of this cooking is done in deep bowls, blackened with the fuel of ages, containing sizzling hot fat in which all kinds of kebabs are cooked, as well as sweet *jalebies*, also a favourite sweet of the Bengali. A student's lunch in some parts of the country is a dish of kebabs covered with a type of soft omelette tossed from the pan on to a 'plate' of equally hot *nan* or frontier bread. This can be followed by a dish of *kulfi*, a sort of frozen cream, smothered with *falooda*, which looks like vermicelli, spread with a thick syrup and finally topped, in winter, with fresh snow or in summer with powdered ice.

The Pakistani is proud of the fruit of his country. There are peaches and apricots, both white, with a very sweet flesh, and yellow or golden; large grapes; melons, macron dates so rich in syrup, which they freely exude, that they have to be kept in jars; plums and pears; apples crisp and sharp in flavour; bananas and papaws; custard apples and cherries. The streets of Peshawar are lined with fruit trees. In the spring, smothered with blossom, they are a lovely sight against a background of snow-tipped mountains and tumbling streams.

Citrus fruits are especially good. There is a short season of wild strawberries and of raspberries and a Pakistani can grow lyrical on the quality, flavour and lusciousness of their mulberries.

Nuts there are in abundance, including the *chilgosa*, a long brown nut with a shell which cracks easily.

As in most countries of the East, food is seasonal and one enjoys each season with its blessings. Except in the main cities, many families in Pakistan live as their forefathers did before them, making their own white sweet butter, their unleavened bread and daily milking their own buffalo.

PLAIN PILAU (*Pulao*)

Proudly, a Muslim cook once said to me: 'There are many ways of making a pilau, as many as there are stars in the sky,' a splendid Eastern exaggeration. Even so, it is a pretty poor Muslim cook who cannot think up at least one hundred different kinds of pilau, naturally all variations on a basic theme.

3 servings:

8 oz. (1 cup) long grain rice	**salt, pepper**
3 tablespoons (3¾) cooking oil	**2 pints (5 cups) boiling water** or **light stock**

Heat the oil, preferably one with not too strong a flavour such as groundnut, add the rice and gently fry, stirring all the while. Add plenty of salt and pepper and, when the rice begins to look translucent, slowly add the liquid. The reason for this slow action is that the rice sizzles and bubbles alarmingly at first. When all the liquid is added stir the rice, cover the pan and cook over a very low heat for 15 minutes. Uncover and gently turn over the rice with a wooden spoon.

Indian Thali (*see page* 11)

If serving a plain pilau it can be garnished with a large chunk of butter or with roasted, blanched and slivered almonds; or raisins or currants and even chopped hard-boiled eggs. Other garnishes include fresh rose petals or gold or silver leaf (*see* page 246); crisply fried onion rings; grilled tomatoes, or fried or grilled fish. Pilaus also are served with kebabs, small grilled game birds, such as quail, with fried meat balls, strips of boiled chicken or duck or grilled lamb chops. Saffron is often added when cooking the rice to turn it yellow.

It is simply a matter of a fertile imagination—'as many pilaus as you have stars in the sky.'

CHICKEN PILAU (*Murghi Pulao*)

6–8 servings:

1 large chicken	2–4 onions, sliced
8 oz. (1 cup) ghee or other fat	salt
2 black cardamom pods crushed	2 lb. (5 cups) rice
4 pieces cinnamon	4 pints (10 cups) stock

Cut the chicken into 6 or 8 pieces. Heat the fat and fry the cardamom and cinnamon with the onions until browned. Take these from the pan, put aside but keep hot. Add the chicken and cook this, stirring from time to time until it is brown. Add the onions, spices, salt and rice, stir and cook for 5 minutes, add the stock, covering 1 inch above the rice, and cook over a low heat, tightly covered, for 30 minutes.

My recipe says now put live charcoal on top of the lid. If cooking the pilau in a dish which will also go into the oven then put it into a warm oven still covered and cook it until the rice is quite dry. It has roughly the same effect as piling live charcoal on the lid. If neither method of drying out the rice is possible, cover the flame with a piece of kitchen asbestos and let the rice remain on the stove until it is dry. A pilau must always be dry.

SPICED PILAU (*Yakni Pulao*)

12 servings:

Yakni:	Pilau:
1 tablespoon (1¼) coriander seeds	2 lb. (5 cups) long grain rice
½ tablespoon (⅔) cumin seeds	2 lb. breast of lamb
8 cloves	1 large onion
4 black cardamom pods, crushed	4 oz. (½ cup) butter
10 peppercorns, crushed	4 peppercorns
4 cloves garlic	4 cloves
1-in. piece fresh ginger, crushed	2 black cardamom seeds
2 bay leaves	salt
1 onion	2 cups (2½) curd or plain yoghourt
4 pints (10 cups) water	½ teaspoon (⅔) saffron, soaked

Tanduri Chicken with Onion Salad (see page 38)

First prepare the *yakni*, which means cooking a mixture of spices in water to be incorporated in the pilau. All the spices are tied in a muslin bag. The cardamoms must be crushed, otherwise the flavour will not emerge from the seeds inside. If fresh ginger is not available, use the dried variety, not the powder, and soak it first. Fewer cloves may be used if their rather pungent flavour is not liked. Put the water into a large saucepan, add the bag of spices, and the *yakni*, onion and cook over a low heat for 3 hours. Remove from the heat and strain. This liquid is the *yakni*.

After the *yakni* has been cooking for about 2 hours, wash the rice and leave it soaking for 1 hour. Wash the meat and cut it into cubes. Slice the onion. Heat the butter and fry the onion until it becomes soft but not brown; add the meat, stir, add the rice and fry for 5 minutes. Add the peppercorns, cloves, cardamoms, salt, curd, saffron and the *yakni*. Cover and cook over a good heat for 15 minutes. Lower the heat to simmering and continue cooking, tightly covered, for 30 minutes.

Pile the pilau on a large platter, put into a hot oven for 5 minutes to dry and serve generously garnished with crisply fried onion rings and strips of hard-boiled eggs.

CHICKEN BIRYANI (*Murghi Biryani*)

A *biryani*, very much like a pilau, is a meal in itself and does not require any accompaniment. There are no hard and fast rules for its preparation, some are rich, others are less so. The difference basically between a *biryani* and a pilau is that in the first mentioned the rice is first partially cooked on its own and then cooked further with the spiced meat.

4–6 servings:

1 large chicken
1 lb. (2½ cups) long grain rice
small piece fresh ginger, finely chopped
4 cloves garlic
1 small piece turmeric or about ¼ teaspoon
    (⅓) powdered
2 cups (2½) curd or plain yoghourt
4 cloves
3 cardamom pods

4 oz. (½ cup) ghee or other fat
4 medium-sized onions, coarsely sliced
a few threads saffron soaked in a little
    water
salt, pepper
4 oz. (⅓ cup) almonds, blanched and
    slivered
2 oz. (½ cup) seedless raisins

Cut the chicken into serving pieces. Clean the rice and soak in cold water for 3 hours. Pound the ginger, garlic and turmeric with 1 cupful (1¼) of the curd (the blender will do this). Marinate the chicken in this mixture and leave for 1 hour.

Drain the rice. Coarsely crush the cloves and the cardamom pods. Heat half the fat, fry the chicken pieces and simmer them until tender. In another large pan heat the remaining fat to boiling point and quickly fry the onions until crisp. Take these from the pan and keep hot. Put the saffron, salt, pepper, cloves, cardamom and rice in the same pan, stir for a moment or so to mix the rice with the spices, then add 1½ cupfuls (2) of boiling water. Cook rapidly until the rice is half cooked and all the liquid has evaporated.

Transfer half this rice to another saucepan, cover it with the browned onions, chicken, almonds, raisins, the remaining rice and the curd. Put the pan over a very low flame and continue cooking until the rice has absorbed the curd and each grain is dry and separate. Turn out on to a large hot serving dish and serve immediately. In Pakistan it is usual to decorate or garnish *biryani* with gold or silver leaf (*see* page 246) which looks very festive. Instead of chicken, the equivalent quantity of lamb or mutton may be used.

FISH IN CORIANDER (*Sail Machhi*)

This is a Sindhi recipe.

4 servings:

1 fish, weighing about 2 lb.	**green chillies to taste**
salt	**chilli powder to taste**
a large bunch of coriander	**1 tablespoon (1¼) ground coriander seeds**
1 onion	**½–1 teaspoon (⅔–1¼) ground turmeric**
1–2 heads garlic	**fat for frying**
1-in. piece fresh ginger	**lemon juice**

Any white fish, such as halibut, turbot or cod will do for this dish. Cut the fish into steaks and rub over with salt. Chop the coriander and the onion. Peel the garlic. Mix all the ingredients (except the fish, fat and lemon) and blend to a paste. Thoroughly wash the fish under running water to make sure that the salt is washed off. Rub the paste into the fish steaks. Put a little fat or oil into a pan, add the fish and cook it over a slow fire until tender. There should be no need for any liquid as the water which flows from the fish should be sufficient. When the fish is half cooked it can be placed in the dish in which it is to be served and put into a moderate oven and the cooking continued until it is ready. Just before serving sprinkle generously with lemon juice.

Thick slices of stale bread are cooked in the same manner but as this has no natural liquid, peeled and chopped tomatoes are added.

If the fish is dry, add a little water to the pan.

FRIED PRAWNS IN TOMATOES (*Bagari Jhinga Tomato*)

3–4 servings:

1 lb. fresh prawns, shelled	**chilli powder to taste**
4 oz. (½ cup) butter or other fat	**1 teaspoon (1¼) garlic, finely chopped**
2 large onions, thinly sliced	**½ teaspoon (⅔) fresh ginger, finely chopped**
salt	**2 teaspoons (2½) ground cumin seeds**
1½ tablespoons (2⅓) ground turmeric	**2 lb. ripe peeled tomatoes made into juice**
2 sprigs curry leaves (see page 239)	**fresh coriander, finely chopped to taste**

Heat the fat and fry the onions until brown. Take from the pan. When cool and crisp crumble them. Put aside. Add the prawns to the frying pan, salt lightly, add the turmeric and fry for 3 minutes, stirring all the while, add the curry leaves, stir-fry for 3 minutes. Add the chilli powder and again fry for 3 minutes, stirring as before. Add garlic and ginger together; stir-fry for 3 minutes more and then when all ingredients are mixed and there is no aroma of raw spices, add the cumin seeds. Stir-fry again for 3 minutes, then gradually start adding the tomato juice, ½ a cupful at a time. When this is half used, add the onions and the fresh coriander. Stir, add the remaining tomato juice and let this cook until it is thick.

POMFRET PESHAWAR STYLE (*Peshawari Pomfret*)

1–2 servings:

1 pomfret (see **page 243**) or plaice
3–6 cloves garlic, pulped
½ lemon
salt to taste
½ teaspoon (⅔) chilli powder
¼ teaspoon (⅓) black pepper

1 black cardamom pod, crushed
a little coriander or parsley, finely chopped
¼ cup (⅓) curd or plain yoghourt
oil
1 lemon, cut into wedges

Thoroughly wash and gut the fish; keep on the head but remove the eyes and clean well under the gills. Rub the fish with the garlic, the ½ lemon, salt, chilli powder, black pepper, cardamom, coriander and curd. Smooth this mixture over the fish and leave it for 1 to 2 hours. Grill it on both sides until brown and the skin begins to crust. Brush the fish with a little oil and then return it to the grill. Or it can be baked in a very hot oven until browned, rubbed with oil and returned to the oven again. Or grilled over charcoal on a spit. Serve with wedges of lemon.

FRIED FISH KEBABS (*Machhi Kebabs*)

3–4 servings:

1¼ lb. firm white fish
2 tablespoons (2½) flour
1½ cups (2) curd or plain yoghourt
2 teaspoons (2½) powdered coriander seeds
¼ teaspoon (⅓) powdered cloves

½ teaspoon (⅔) dry chillies or cayenne
pepper
crushed black cardamoms to taste
juice 1 lemon

Cut the fish into thick cubes. Mix the flour and the curd together. Add the spices and lemon juice. Coat the fish cubes with this mixture and leave for 30 minutes. Grill the pieces of fish until a golden brown, basting from time to time with the curd marinade.

TANDURI CHICKEN (*Tanduri Chirch*)

This internationally known and popular dish hardly needs an explanation. It is chicken roasted in an extremely hot primitive oven (a *tandur* from which it gets its name) which looks like one of the jars used by the forty thieves. It is heated by a fierce charcoal fire at the bottom. The chicken, which is marinated for 24 hours, is spiced and threaded on to a long skewer and thrust into the oven.

It roasts quickly so only tender chickens are suitable for this treatment. The chicken comes out looking rather fearsome and is eaten with *nan roti* (*see* below). *Tanduri* chicken is eaten with the fingers and served with an onion salad prepared from very strong onions.

The following recipe is for 1 chicken. It is, or was, usual to offer a whole chicken per person. Nowadays one often sees *tanduri* chicken cut into serving portions. Like the roti, *tanduri* chicken must be served piping hot.

1–2 servings:

1 chicken
Marinade:
1 small onion, finely chopped
garlic to taste
½ teaspoon (⅔) chilli powder
1 teaspoon (1¼) mixed ground black pepper and green cardamom seeds
juice 1 lemon or **2 limes**
½ cup (⅔) curd or **plain yoghourt**

Clean and skin the chicken and make cuts in the flesh with a sharp knife on the breast and legs but without separating the joints.

Grind the onion with the garlic to a paste. Mix this with the remaining ingredients into the curd and pour it all into a bowl. Rub this mixture into the chicken and leave it for several hours—it is usual to leave it overnight.

Now the chicken can either be roasted in a very hot oven without any fat or it can be roasted or grilled in a modern rotisserie, in which case it can be brushed with a little oil from time to time.

Serve the chicken garnished with coriander and a dish of sliced red peppered onion.

TANDURI FISH (*Tanduri Machhi*)

1 serving:

1 whole fish, approximately 1 lb.
1 cup (1¼) thick curd or **yoghourt**
salt
1 teaspoon (1¼) ground chillies or **chilli powder**
5 tablespoons (6¼) melted butter
1 teaspoon (1¼) cumin seeds, powdered and roasted

Clean the fish; do not remove the head but cut off the tail. Make deep slits in the flesh 1 inch apart. Mix the curd, salt and chillies and marinate the fish in this for several hours. Take it from the marinade and put it on a skewer. Roast in a hot oven or rotisserie for 7 to 10 minutes. Take it from the oven, brush with a mixture of melted butter and cumin and return it to the oven and continue cooking for another 4–5 minutes.

Garnish the fish with sliced lemon and serve with a green salad.

UNLEAVENED BREAD (*Nan roti*)

Nan roti is plain white bread which, when freshly made and served hot, is soft and pliable and very satisfying. Cold it is disastrous. Apart from being a bread and a staple item of food in Pakistan, it serves as a plate for kebabs. It is not a bread for the foreigner to make, not even overseas Pakistanis do this—even those who possess a *tandur* oven. A brushwood fire is lit in the oven and kept going briskly until the necessary fierce heat is obtained. When the fire dies down the women of the household stand ready, flapping the dough expertly from hand to hand until it is the required size. It is then inserted into the top of the oven and slapped heartily against the inner surface to which it sticks until it is cooked. The usual size is somewhat more than a foot in length and looks like an elongated bat.

In the country in Pakistan where there are still large joint families and at every meal some 24 people, the *tandur* oven is worked overtime. But in towns, where families tend to be smaller, and even in small houses there is neither space for nor sense in the primitive *tandur*. However, there are many *tandur* bakeries and usually someone to fetch the bread straight from the oven to the table.

WHOLE CHICKEN KEBAB (*Murghi Seekh Kebab*)

2 servings:

1 grilling chicken	salt
4–6 onions	chilli powder to taste
4 cloves garlic	6 tablespoons (7½) melted butter
8 cardamom seeds	

Mince the onions, crush the garlic and the cardamoms. Mix with the salt and chilli powder to a paste, adding a little water. (All this can be done in a blender.) Rub this mixture well into the chicken and leave it for 30 minutes. If any of the paste slips off, rub it back. Brush the chicken with a little of the melted butter. It must not be too dry.

Insert a long skewer through the centre of the chicken and grill it over a hot charcoal fire or in a rotisserie. From time to time brush it with the remaining butter and grill steadily but not too quickly until the chicken is tender. Turn the skewer from time to time to ensure even cooking.

KEBABS (*Pacinda Seekh*)

3 servings:

1 lb. lamb	¼–½ cup (⅓–⅔) cream or milk
1½ cups (2) curd or ½ cup (⅔) cottage cheese	2 oz. (½ cup) almonds, ground
1 tablespoon (1¼) ground coriander	½ teaspoon (⅔) each powdered cloves and
a good pinch saffron, soaked in water	cardamom seeds
1 onion, finely chopped	2 oz. (¼ cup) butter

Pacinda is a particular manner of cutting meat into thin slices. But nowadays few butchers, even in Pakistan or India, know how to cut meat in this way. However, cutting the meat into strips and then flattening them is almost as good.

Cut the meat into thin strips and beat them flat. Tie the curd in muslin and leave to drain until very dry. Mix the coriander, saffron and onion and rub this over the meat and leave for 30 minutes. Mix the dry curd (or cottage cheese) with the cream, almonds, cloves, cardamom and half the butter and pour this over the meat and leave another 30 minutes. Rub all the curd marinade into the meat. Heat the rest of the butter, and fry the meat with marinade.

The main distinction of this dish is that the meat used is so tender that no chewing is required. This is considered a Muslim party piece.

MUTTON WITH CORIANDER AND TWO ONIONS (*Kotmir ka Dopyaza*)

Dopyaza means two onions, and the original recipe, so I am told, was created at Akbar's Court, the invention of a well-known courtier. It became fashionable and since its modest beginning (which the following recipe resembles), the recipe has been enlarged upon, so much so that some recipes produce party pieces. Although the recipe is remembered, the courtier's name has been forgotten, except the name by which he became universally known, *Maulana Dopyaza* ('Teacher Two Onions).

2 servings:

1 lb. mutton or lamb	1 teaspoon (1¼) each fresh ginger and
2 large bundles coriander or parsley	garlic, finely chopped
3 tablespoons (3¾) ghee or other fat	salt
2 large onions, minced	1 teaspoon (1¼) cumin seeds
2 green chillies	1 lemon
ground turmeric to taste	

Finely chop the coriander, mix with 1 cup (1¼) of warm water, if possible put in a blender, blend for a minute or so, strain and squeeze out as much liquid as possible. Put this aside.

Heat the fat and fry the onions until brown, add the chillies, turmeric, garlic, salt, ginger and finally the meat. Add 2 cupfuls (2½) of hot water, stir well, add the cumin and simmer over a low heat until the meat is very tender and the liquid reduced by half. Add the coriander liquid and continue cooking until the liquid has been completely absorbed and the meat is very tender. Serve garnished with lemon slices.

If not using green chilli peppers, I advise some chilli pepper to add pungency to the dish.

SHEEP KEBABS (*Bara Kebabs*)

Bara means sheep meat. The meat for this variety of kebab is taken from the calf muscles and it is cut with some of the bone and the fat . . . the point being that the meat is cooked in its own fat. As far as the Pathans are concerned, and this type of kebab comes from their territory, the only meat suitable is the meat of the 'fat-tailed one' and this is so tender it cooks in 10 minutes. The meat is threaded on to skewers and grilled over charcoal, barbeque style.

This is the typical Peshawari '*bara kebab*' and Pakistani friends of mine when they cannot get the correct kind of meat for this, hunt and kill the barking deer—which they say makes excellent kebabs—but is also not exactly easily available in the West.

LAMB KEBABS (*Shami Kebabs*)

6 servings:

2 lb. minced lamb
3 tablespoons (3¾) split peas
1 medium onion, chopped
1 small piece fresh ginger
3 cloves garlic
3 cloves
4 large cardamom pods

2–3 pieces cinnamon
salt
pinch of nutmeg
2½ cups (3) water
1 egg
fat for frying

Wash the split peas and mix with the meat and remaining ingredients, except the egg and fat. Put into a saucepan and cook slowly until the meat is tender and all the liquid is absorbed. Take out the cinnamon, cloves, and cardamoms and grind the rest through the finest cutter of a mincer or, better still, put into a blender. The result should be a paste. Shape this into round flat kebabs (i.e. patties) not too small and make a dent with your thumb and stuff with the following ingredients: finely chopped mint, fresh coriander or parsley, finely minced onion mixed with enough curd or yoghourt, to make a paste. Close the kebabs and shape them into discs. Brush with the egg. Heat a little fat and fry the kebabs in this until they are brown on both sides. (It is usual to use *ghee* for frying, vegetable fat may take its place, but never oil.)

SIMPLE KEBABS or SHASHLIK (*Tikka Kebabs*)

The meat used for *tikka* kebabs must be tender. It should be either from the female goat or the fat-tailed sheep. An interesting piece of information but one which might bring a snort from our butchers if we insisted on such a choice. The cook is also advised 'string the kebabs on to a thin wire and hang them over a good charcoal fire'. Nowadays with so many charcoal grills, this is not such bad advice after all. It is usual during grilling to baste the kebabs with the sauce left over from marinating.

4–6 servings:

1–2 lb. good quality lamb
12 peppercorns
salt, garlic
2 small onions

6 cardamom seeds (optional)
½ cup (⅔) dry curd
a small quantity ghee or other fat

Wipe the meat with a damp cloth and cut it into cubes, without fat; score each piece fairly deeply. Pound the peppercorns, salt, garlic, one onion and cardamom with the curd and fat to a paste. Thickly slice the remaining onion and rub the meat with this until it absorbs the flavour. Coat each piece of meat with the paste and thread on to skewers. Slowly grill, turning frequently to ensure equal browning. Or equally, the pieces of meat can be fried in a thick dry pan.

Serve with finely chopped coriander or parsley, sliced onion and lemon.

FLAT or SANDAL KEBABS (*Chapli Kebabs*)

Chaplis in the frontier area are sandals and these kebabs are colloquially called this because they are flat. They are rather more like our fritters, except they are not fried in deep fat. They are usually served as large as possible and the cooks just manage to slap them on to a slab of hot *nan roti*. The perfect *chapli* kebab is crisp around the edges and soft in the centre.

3–4 servings:

1 lb. minced lamb	1 cup (1¼) milk
fat for frying	3 tablespoons (3¾) flour
salt, pepper	2 onions, finely chopped
2 eggs	coriander, finely chopped

Heat enough fat to fry the meat until it changes colour, add salt and pepper and continue cooking until the meat is tender—in the Pathan country this is a matter of minutes since the quality of their lamb is so good. Make a batter with the eggs, milk and flour. Add the onion and coriander, then the cooked meat. Drop this mixture into the pan in big 'blobs'. Fry until brown on both sides.

Serve very hot, straight from the pan. Next to the unleavened bread (*nan roti*), this is the most typical dish of the Pathan country.

MINCED BEEF (*Kima*)

4–5 servings:

1½ lb. lean beef, minced	2 cloves
3 tablespoons (3¾) ghee or other fat	4 tomatoes, peeled and chopped
2 cloves garlic, chopped	½ lb. peas, shelled
1 large onion, chopped	1 tablespoon (1¼) lemon juice
¼ teaspoon (⅓) each ground turmeric,	
black and red pepper	

Heat the fat in a pan, add the garlic and onion and fry until these are a golden brown. Add the meat and spices, stir and cook over a moderate heat for 15 minutes. Add the tomatoes, peas and juice. Continue cooking gently until all the liquid has been absorbed.

A dish usually served with *parathas*, but it can be served with rice or potatoes.

STEWED LAMB (*Qorma*)

4–6 servings:

2 lb. lamb	1 onion, sliced
salt	4 cloves
2 cloves garlic, chopped	coriander seeds to taste
1 small piece fresh ginger, bruised	3 black cardamom seeds, well pounded
1 cup (1¼) curd or yoghourt	black pepper
3 tablespoons (3¾) ghee or other fat	pinch saffron, soaked in lemon juice

Wipe the meat, cut it into small pieces and rub with salt, garlic and ginger. Mix the curd thoroughly with the meat. Heat the fat and fry the onion, when this changes colour add the meat and cloves.

In another small pan dry-fry the coriander and cardamom seeds and sprinkle these over the meat. When the meat is brown add 2 cupfuls of water, stir and simmer the meat until it is tender. Add the pepper and saffron and continue cooking gently until the liquid is absorbed and the meat very tender.

Serve with rice.

SPICED POTATO SALAD (*Alu Raita*)

A totally different conception of potato salad.

2–3 servings:

3–4 large potatoes
2–3 medium tomatoes
2 cups (2½) curd or plain yoghourt
½ teaspoon (⅔) cumin seeds, roasted

salt, pepper
chilli or cayenne pepper to taste
coriander leaves or parsley, finely chopped

Cook the potatoes in their skins until tender. Cool, peel and slice fairly thinly. Drop the tomatoes into boiling water to loosen their skins, peel and slice, discarding the seeds and core. Mix with the potatoes, do this carefully. Beat the curd until smooth, add cumin seeds, salt and pepper, and pour this mixture over the potatoes and tomatoes, stir lightly, add chilli and garnish with coriander.

I find it better to chill the salad in one bowl then, for serving, pour it gently into another, otherwise it comes to the table with most of the curd at the bottom of the dish.

Used as a side dish to curries but can also be served with cold meats.

SEMOLINA PUDDING or CAKE (*Sooji Halva*)

6 servings:

1 cup (1¼) semolina
4 oz. (½ cup) ghee or butter
1 oz. (1 tablespoon) almonds, blanched
 and slivered
1 oz. (1 tablespoon) shelled pistachio nuts
1 oz. (1 tablespoon) seedless raisins

2–3 cardamom pods, crushed
8 oz. (1 cup) sugar
cloves to taste
a small piece cinnamon
3 cups (3¾) water
rose-water to taste

Heat the fat and quickly fry the almonds and pistachio nuts separately. Take them from the pan as soon as they are faintly tinged with brown. Add the raisins and the semolina and fry these until the semolina is a golden-brown, stirring all the time. The semolina takes on a faintly nutty flavour at this stage, which is good. Add the cardamoms, sugar, cloves, cinnamon and water, and stir well. Cook gently for 15 minutes with almost continuous stirring. When the semolina is quite dry, remove the cloves and cinnamon.

Pour the semolina into a shallow glass dish and spread it evenly. Sprinkle with rose-water and decorate it with almonds. (This is usually done by sticking the almonds upwards into the semolina and leaving about three-quarters of each almond visible.) The pistachios are coarsely chopped and sprinkled over the top. Serve cold.

ROYAL BREAD PUDDING (*Shahi Tukaras*)

4–6 servings:

4–6 thick slices white bread
4 oz. (½ cup) butter
4 oz. (½ cup) sugar
¼ cup (⅓) water

1 cup (1¼) double cream
12 whole almonds, blanched and slivered
cardamoms, coarsely ground

Cut the bread into uniform cubes and fry these in butter to a golden brown. Boil the sugar and water for 10 minutes. Pour this syrup over the bread cubes and leave to soak for 15 minutes. Put into a glass dish, add the cream, spread it evenly and let it soak into the bread, then add the remaining ingredients as a garnish. Serve very cold.

There are variations of the recipe. Many cooks add ground almonds with more cream or saffron. This latter adds flavour, also colour. Some add peeled and slivered pistachio nuts with the garnish, fried sultanas or seedless raisins, or silver or gold leaf.

CARROT HALVA (*Gajjar Halva*)

The correct type of carrot for this sweet is a translucent red carrot, indigenous to the sub-continent. What is important is the shredding of the carrots, for the shreds should be as long as possible. It is usual to make fairly large batches of this *halva* which keeps at least 7 days in a refrigerator.

6–8 servings:

1½ lb. carrots
8 cups (10) milk
good pinch saffron, soaked in milk for 30 minutes (optional)
¾ lb. (1½ cups) granulated sugar

sultanas (optional)
2–3 oz. (4–6 tablespoons) unsalted butter
blanched almonds or cashew nuts to taste
2 cardamom seeds, crushed
silver or gold leaf (optional)

Scrape the carrots and shred them into long thin strips. Bring the milk to the boil in a large saucepan, add the carrots and saffron. Cook this over a low heat until the carrots are thick and soft and all the milk has been absorbed. Stir from time to time; the more one stirs the better. Add the sugar, sultanas and the butter. Now stir well and pour this mixture into another hot and dry pan and boil, stirring constantly until the mixture begins to solidify and change to a deep red colour. Turn it out on to a dish and garnish with silver or gold leaf as well as almonds or cashew nuts and crushed cardamom seeds. Carrot *halva* is served both hot and cold. It reheats easily.

VERMICELLI PUDDING (*Savain*)

4–6 servings:

1 cup (1¼) fine vermicelli, broken into bits
1 oz. (2 tablespoons) butter
4 cups (5) milk

4 tablespoons (5) sugar
sultanas, pistachio nuts and crushed white cardamom seeds for garnishing

In the sub-continent of India vermicelli is sold already roasted. But it is obtainable in many Indian stores outside Asia. However, roasting vermicelli is not a difficult task.

Heat half the butter in a saucepan and 'roast' the vermicelli until it becomes a golden brown colour, about 5–7 minutes. Add the milk and boil vigorously. Lower the heat but continue to gently boil for 10 minutes. Add the sugar and continue boiling for another 10–15 minutes, stirring frequently. Heat the remaining butter and fry the sultanas until they plump up; add the nuts and, just before serving, sprinkle the pudding with the cardamom seeds. *Savain* is served either warm or cold and is very pleasant after spicy food.

Kashmir

A land of milk and honey.

Kashmiris drink a mixture of milk and honey as the Frenchman drinks wine. Or they drink milk and saffron or simply just milk. It is a lovely country often likened to Switzerland. Its capital, Srinagar, is entirely medieval, its population mixed, Hindus and Muslims.

There is not, however, as much difference between the cooking of the two communities as one might imagine. The Hindus have retained their religious individuality by sheer force of circumstance, both culturally and economically and they have absorbed much of the Muslim manner of cooking and eating.

There are, intermingled, in the Valley three types of cooking: that of the Kashmiri Pundits, i.e. Brahmins with their Brahminical restrictions; Kashmiri Muslim cooking, with its Persian influence, and Dogra, which is Indian Rajput, the food of the warrior castes and less restricted.

It is one of the curiosities of the Hindu Kashmiris that, although Pundits, they are great meat eaters. But they will not eat beef of any kind, and in the days of the Maharajahs the import of beef was severely punished. Today these rules are somewhat relaxed. But pork, naturally, is not eaten by the Muslims. The Pundits also will not eat sheep; they prefer goat and preferably young goat. Mutton is the favourite meat of the Muslims. Neither will the Pundits eat garlic nor onions. This is not so much for religious reasons but simply because they like their food to be mellow. This restriction, they insist, has given more variety to their dishes since they have made up for this lack. Instead, however, they always add a small quantity of asafoetida.

It is fair to say that the Muslims are the poorer section of the population and possibly this is one reason why they are less choosey about what they eat. But it is basically because their religion imposes fewer restrictions. Their diet is dictated by their pockets rather than their palates.

The Muslims like their daily quota of mutton, pilaus and spicy *biryanis*. No Kashmiri Muslim feels that he has eaten properly unless he has consumed a pound of rice a day. They are not fond of vegetables and their diet would appear somewhat on the dull side.

Both communities eat a lot of fruit, much of which was introduced into Kashmir by the British. Among the temperate fruits which flourish in Kashmir are loganberry, blackcurrant, raspberry, apple, plum, cherry, walnut and almond.

Kashmiri dishes are usually cooked in a sauce which they call a *yakni*, in cream or in curd. Pundits always, but always, cook meat in curd. On the whole it is a fairly mildly spiced diet. A favourite Muslim dish is *gushtaba*, which is mutton, rubbed rather than pounded, on a stone until it is shredded and then shaped into meat balls. It is then cooked in a *yakni* sauce and is curiously tasty despite this description. Both communities eat *abgost*, with its Persian influence; it is a dish of lamb chops cooked in milk and flavoured with onions and a little sugar. Both the Pundits and the Muslims are fond of sweet-sour dishes.

Both communities eat a lot of kebabs, a favourite is the so-called *seekh* kebab. This is mutton pounded until almost shredded and threaded on to a long skewer (or *seekh*), moulded until it looks like a slim sausage, grilled over charcoal and served with raw onions which have been dyed scarlet.

Although the Kashmiri Muslim uses garlic and onion, he is sparing of both. Both communities use spices but usually in the dried form, even powdered ginger is accepted since there is no fresh ginger. Spices are not grown in the temperate climate of Kashmir, except chillies, which the Kashmiri considers are unrivalled anywhere in the world.

Sweet dishes are common to both communities although the Hindus eat rather more than do the Muslims.

There is small game in plenty and good freshwater fish, especially trout. A type of salmon, with a faintly pink flesh, is quite good. Wild duck is a speciality of the area.

Kashmiris drink tea in vast quantities. There is the so-called Persian spiced tea *kahwa* in which cardamoms and cinnamon are important spices. Then there is salt tea or *sheer chai*, made with plenty of tea and water, baking soda and salt. When all this has been stewed for 25 minutes, milk is added. The end result is a pale pink brew which is a culinary shock for most of us. It is another item of diet given to Kashmiri women in childbirth (what a lot of nonsense the world over is served to women in childbirth). Salt tea is also recommended for insomnia and exhaustion and is the general household drink.

The Kashmiris are inordinately proud of their saffron, claiming it to be the finest in the world. No one can convince them otherwise. But even in Kashmir saffron is an expensive commodity, despite its universal use in the cooking of the country.

MUTTON WITH TURNIPS (*Shaljam Salam*)

4 servings:

2 lb. lean mutton, cut into serving pieces with or without the bone

2 oz. ($\frac{1}{4}$ cup) ghee or vegetable fat

1 teaspoon ($1\frac{1}{4}$) ground ginger

1 cup ($1\frac{1}{4}$) curd

4 small turnips, peeled and quartered

salt

2 heaped teaspoons ($2\frac{1}{2}$) ground coriander

1 level teaspoon ($1\frac{1}{4}$) garam masala (see page 13)

1 level teaspoon ($1\frac{1}{4}$) turmeric

$\frac{1}{2}$ teaspoon ($\frac{2}{3}$) chilli powder

4 green chillies, sliced and seeded (optional)

1 teaspoon ($1\frac{1}{4}$) sugar

handful fresh coriander

Wash the meat and wipe it dry. Heat the fat in a heavy saucepan and when smoking hot add the meat, ginger and curd. Cook over a high heat to seal the flavour, then lower the heat to medium and cook until the meat is nicely browned. Add ¼ cupful (⅓) water and scrape the sides of the pan to loosen the reddish sediment. (This is the curd which scorches during cooking and sticks to the pan. It gives colouring and a rather piquant flavour to the meat.) Bring to boiling point, add turnips, salt, spices and green chillies with enough water to cover, plus another ½ cupful (⅔). Cook over a medium heat until the meat is tender, add sugar and half the fresh coriander. Just before serving, add the remaining coriander.

Serve with plain boiled rice or chapaties.

One of the secrets of Kashmiri cooking is that the meat is turned again and again during the firs 30 minutes of cooking to ensure that it browns and also does not burn.

LAMB CHOPS IN BATTER (*Kamargaah*)

4 servings:

2 lb. small lamb chops (about 8–10)
1½ cups (2) milk
1½ cups (2) water
3–5 cloves
10 peppercorns, coarsely crushed
salt
1 teaspoon (1¼) aniseed, crushed
ground ginger to taste
fat for deep frying

Batter:
4 oz. (1 cup) gram or white flour (see **page 246**)
salt
1 tablespoon (1¼) softened fat
a pinch chilli powder
a little curd or yoghourt (optional)
a little garam masala (see **page 13**)

Sift the flour and seasonings into a bowl, add enough water (and curd if using) to make a thin batter. Whisk this until air bubbles rise; add the fat and let the batter rest before using.

The chops should have the fat left on. Wipe them with a damp cloth and put into a pan with the remaining ingredients, except the fat. Cook over a very low heat until the meat is tender and the liquid absorbed. Dip each chop into the batter and fry these in hot fat until the batter is a golden brown.

White flour is not the same by any means as *gram* flour, but it makes an adequate substitute.

FRIED AND SPICED LAMB (*Kaliya*)

4 servings:

2 lb. lamb, cut into serving pieces
2–3 oz. (¼–⅓ cup) ghee or vegetable fat
½ teaspoon (⅔) ground ginger
4 cloves
10 peppercorns, crushed
salt

¼ teaspoon (⅓) chilli powder
2 teaspoons (2½) ground coriander
2 teaspoons (2½) aniseed
½ cup (⅔) hot water
1 cup (1¼) curd

Wash and trim the meat, heat the fat and cook the meat with the ginger, cloves and peppercorns until the meat loses its rawness and is slightly browned. Add salt, chilli powder, coriander, aniseed and the hot water. Simmer until the meat is almost tender, add the curd and cook until the meat is very tender.

Three cardamom seeds may also be added. Failing aniseed, caraway would be a good substitute in this recipe.

Serve with plain boiled rice.

SPICED LAMB (*Roghan Josh*)

4–6 servings:

2 lb. lamb, cut into pieces
12 almonds, blanched
2 tablespoons (2½) thick cream
½ teaspoon (⅔) ground ginger
2–3 oz. (¼–⅓ cup) ghee or vegetable fat
2 teaspoons (2½) ground coriander seeds

1 teaspoon (1¼) garam masala (see page 13)
½ teaspoon (⅔) chilli powder
salt
slivered almonds and pistachio nuts as a garnish

The quality of lamb in Kashmir is poor, so that the cheapest cuts of European lamb can be used with good effect for this recipe.

Pound the whole almonds to a paste using a little iced water to prevent oiliness. Mix this with the cream and put aside. Wash the meat and wipe it dry. Heat the fat in a saucepan and when hot add the meat and the ginger and cook over a high flame to 'seal the flavour' then lower the heat to medium and cook the meat until it is nicely browned. Add all the spices, salt and about 1½ cupfuls (2) of water and when the meat is almost tender add the almond and cream mixture. Continue cooking until the meat is tender and the liquid is absorbed.

The secret of this preparation, and indeed all Kashmiri dishes, is the slow cooking and the almost total absorption of the liquid. When the meat is ready for serving only a little thick gravy should remain. Before serving sprinkle generously with almonds and pistachio nuts.

This is a special version of a popular Kashmiri dish.

Serve with rice.

POT ROAST LEG OF LAMB (*Raan*)

6–8 servings:

1 3–3½ lb. leg of lamb
1 teaspoon (1¼) ground ginger
8–10 cardamom seeds
12 peppercorns, crushed
6–8 cloves
1½ teaspoons (2) cumin seeds, ground
1½ teaspoons (2) coriander seeds, ground
2 1-in. pieces cinnamon or 1 teaspoon (1¼) ground cinnamon

¼ teaspoon (⅓) ground mace or nutmeg
1 teaspoon (1¼) poppyseeds
saffron to taste, soaked in milk and pounded
1 cup (1¼) curd or yoghourt
4 oz. (½ cup) ghee or vegetable fat
20–30 almonds, blanched and slivered
salt

Nepalese Street Market

Pound the spices and peppercorns with the curd to a paste and wipe the meat with a damp cloth, trimming off any excess fat. Coat the meat with this paste and put it into a wide shallow pan. Using a two-pronged fork, prick the meat deeply and thoroughly, turning it over every now and then. Continue this process for 15 minutes then leave it to marinate for 2 hours. Heat the fat in a deep vessel and when really hot add the meat with its marinade. Cover the pan and brown the meat, turning often until it is evenly browned. This process takes some 30 minutes. When the meat is nicely browned, add 4 or 5 cupfuls (5–6¼) of warm water, the almonds and salt. Cover the pan and seal the lid with a flour and water dough or put a really heavy weight on top. Cook very slowly until the water is absorbed, about 1½ hours. Do not uncover during cooking time.

I do not seal my pan with dough as my pans have tight-fitting lids, but it is true there is no need to uncover the pan. Also the meat in Kashmir is less tender than in the West, therefore probably our meat will take less cooking than this recipe suggests so that a little testing is permissible after 1 hour of cooking.

SWEET-SOUR PILAU (*Mutanjan*)

4 servings:

½ lb. (1¼ cups) long grain rice
¾ lb. lamb, cut into cubes
6 cloves
1 teaspoon (1¼) fresh ginger, finely chopped
2 teaspoons (2½) ground coriander seeds
3 1-in. pieces cinnamon
salt

} loosely tied in a bag

¼ lb. (½ cup) sugar or to taste
juice 3 limes or 1½ lemons
1½ oz. (3 tablespoons) ghee or other fat
4 cloves
8 peppercorns
3 cardamom pods, crushed
20 almonds, blanched and slivered
¾ teaspoon (1) saffron, pounded in a little milk

Wipe the meat with a damp cloth and put into a saucepan with the bag of spices. Add salt to taste and 3 cupfuls (3¾) water. Cook until the meat is tender and 1 cupful (1¼) of liquid remains. Remove the spices, squeezing the cloth bag out over the pan to draw out all the flavour. Add sugar, two-thirds of the lime juice and cook slowly until the sugar is dissolved. In another pan boil the rice in water and the remaining juice until almost tender. Drain. Heat the fat and add the remaining spices. Cook until the cloves 'pop', add the rice, meat and its stock, the almonds and saffron. Toss with a fork to mix and cook slowly until the liquid is absorbed and the rice tender. Put on the middle shelf of a medium oven for 30–40 minutes to dry out. Remove the cloves before serving.

LIVER KEBABS (*Dahi Kaleji*)

A Muslim dish.

2–3 servings:

1 lb. liver
1 oz. (2 tablespoons) fat
¾ lb. onions, sliced

6 oz. (¾ cup) curd or yoghourt
3 teaspoons (3¾) ground ginger

Ta Pin Lo (*see page* 112)

Heat the fat, when this is hot add the onions and cook these until they begin to soften, but do not let them brown. Add the liver, stir this into the onions, add the curd and ginger, again stir and cook gently, covered, for 15 minutes.

SPICED POTATOES (*Dam Alu*)

3–4 servings:

10–12 whole potatoes of equal size; this is important
oil for deep frying
1½ oz. (3 tablespoons) ghee or other fat
salt

½ teaspoon (⅔) chilli powder
2½ teaspoons (3) ground coriander seeds
½ teaspoon (⅔) powdered ginger
1 teaspoon (1¼) garam masala (see page 13)

Cook the potatoes in their skins until half tender. Peel. Prick each potato with a fine knitting needle through and through—right through each potato, this makes them spongy. They should, however, not be broken. Fry in hot oil until a light brown. Drain.

In another pan heat the *ghee* until it is smoking. Add the potatoes, salt, chilli, coriander and ginger and cook over a low heat, turning the potatoes around for a minute or so. Add about ½ cupful (⅔) water and the *garam masala*—and it is usual to add here a little more coriander as this is a mild and popular spice—turn the potatoes around and about until well coated with the spices, put the pan into the oven, cover and cook until the potatoes are really tender but not too soft.

STUFFED PEPPERS (*Bhari Mirch*)

3–6 servings:

6 evenly sliced green or red sweet peppers
4 tablespoons (5) ghee or vegetable fat
¼ lb. minced meat
1 teaspoon (1¼) ground coriander
½ teaspoon (⅔) garam masala (see page 13)
¼ teaspoon (⅓) chilli pepper
¼ teaspoon (⅓) turmeric
1 potato, peeled and diced

1 teaspoon (1¼) fresh ginger, finely chopped
2–3 chillies, seeds discarded (optional)
juice 2 limes or 1 lemon
1 tablespoon (1¼) fresh coriander, chopped or parsley
salt

While the Kashmiris would use mutton in this recipe we can use beef or pork or veal.

Cut a thin slice from the top of each pepper and remove the core and seeds. Drop the peppers into boiling water for a few minutes, take from the pan and peel. (The skin comes off thinly, but the peeling can be omitted.) Heat half the fat and brown the meat, add all the spices, except ginger, and ¼ cupful (⅓) water. Cook until the liquid is absorbed and add the remaining ingredients.

Taste and correct for seasoning, stir and cook until the potato is fried. Stuff this mixture into the peppers. Return the matching top slice to each pepper. Heat the remaining fat and cook the peppers on top of the stove for about 5 minutes, turning once. Add about 1 cupful (1¼ cups) warm water and simmer until the peppers are tender and the liquid is almost absorbed.

GROUND RICE PUDDING (*Phirni*)

This is served on festive occasions, weddings, dinners etc., in fact, it is essential at a Kashmiri wedding. If given any other sweet dish than *phirni* the guests would be incensed. It has a distinctly Middle Eastern flavour and is very pleasing after a spicy meal.

6–8 servings:

4 oz. (¾ cup) ground rice
2 quarts (10 cups) milk
6 oz. (¾ cup) fine sugar

rose-water to taste, be generous
silver leaf (see **page 246**)
finely grated almonds and pistachio nuts

Mix the rice with enough milk to make a thin paste. Bring the remaining milk to boiling point over a high heat then lower the heat and stir in the rice paste. Stirring constantly continue to cook over a low heat until the mixture is fairly thick. Add the sugar and continue cooking until the desired consistency is obtained. *Phirni* should not be too thick. Pour the mixture into a bowl and beat it until it is cool. Add rose-water to flavour, stir this thoroughly into the rice, and pour the rice into small glass or earthenware bowls. Cover each pudding with silver leaf and generously sprinkle with nuts.

In the original recipe twice as much sugar is used as the Kashmiris are very sweet toothed.

SWEET RICE PUDDING (*Mehta Chaval*)

6 servings:

½ lb. (1¼ cups) rice
½ lb. (1 cup) sugar
6 cups (7½) milk
12 white cardamom seeds

24 almonds, blanched and slivered
30 grains saffron, soaked in milk and
   pounded
2 oz. (¼ cup) butter

Dissolve the sugar in 1 cupful (1¼) water and cook slowly until a thin syrup forms. Cook the rice in the milk until tender but not too soft. Drain thoroughly, pour the syrup over the rice, add the cardamoms, almonds, saffron and butter. Put this all over a low flame and cook slowly until the liquid is absorbed. Put into a medium oven for 30 minutes.

This glorified rice pudding is served on festive occasions in Kashmir and served in small, shallow earthenware pots, each portion covered with silver leaf as well as finely chopped pistachio nuts and almonds.

The Kashmiris, instead of putting the rice into an oven, put the pot on a bed of glowing coals and live coals on the lid. This method causes the bottom of the rice to catch and this layer of rice, which has to be scraped off the pan, is greatly appreciated for its burnt-sugar flavour.

KASHMIRI TEA

The real Kashmiri tea is made from pressed blocks of Ladakh tea. Since these blocks are not easily obtained outside of Kashmir, a substitute must be found. To try this tea, the best substitute is probably a mixture of green tea and Darjeeling or Orange Pekoe blend, in the proportion of three parts green tea to one of the Darjeeling or Orange Pekoe. With this one uses half milk, half water and the tea is made in large quantities.

To make 4 cups (5) of tea, use $2\frac{1}{2}$ cups (3) of milk and the same quantity of water, 3 level teaspoons ($3\frac{3}{4}$) green tea, 1 teaspoon ($1\frac{1}{4}$) of Darjeeling or Orange Pekoe, 6 green cardamom seeds, 6 blanched and slivered almonds, 1 teaspoon ($1\frac{1}{4}$) shelled pine nuts, 1-inch piece of cinnamon, 1–2 cloves and sugar to taste, and this means plenty. Put all the dry ingredients into a muslin bag and stew gently in a pan for 35 minutes. Lift out the bag, squeeze it hard back into the pan to extract all the flavour, and serve the tea piping hot.

This tea is very sweet and rich. Not all Kashmiris bother with the muslin bag and one is apt to find bits of tea leaves and spices floating around in the cup. Kashmiris usually make their tea in a type of samovar, rather like the Russian samovar and it does seem that there is tea to drink all the livelong day.

Nepal

Kathmandu is the picturesque capital of Nepal, the only Hindu Kingdom in the world. Called 'the Valley' it is the heart and soul of the country, backed by peaks of the majestic Himalayan range and surrounded by wooded hills.

Flying into Nepal over the foothills of the Himalayas, a rolling mass of gorges, monstrous ripples of nature, thickly covered hillsides with only here and there open spaces where man has carved his mark and terraced the slope for rice cultivation. Rice, as in so many countries of this area, is the staple food of the Nepalese.

The houses in Kathmandu are doll's houses. On their roofs grow grasses and flowers, or are piled high with chillies put out to dry. The top floors are usually homes, while the lower floors are shops or eating-houses. Some of these are little more than holes in the wall. Ancient women crouch on the blackened floors cooking over charcoal, using pots which have not changed since the beginning of time. Interspersed between the shops and houses are shrines and small temples, Hindu and Buddhist, and Tibetan prayer wheels, all mixed up higgledy-piggledy, and with ochre-splashed Gods at every point. There are fierce wild stone animals of the jungle and the imagination, leering dragons and monsters with great lolling scarlet tongues.

I went in search of the markets, only to discover that the city is one vast market with squatting vendors at every street corner patiently selling their rather pathetic piles of fruit and vegetables. Here there is nothing of the lusciousness of the usual Eastern bazaar for Nepal is not a rich country agriculturally. Lucky is the vendor with a tree for his pitch; luckier still he who has a platform round a tree, meant in fact for itinerant holy men, in which Kathmandu abounds. There is also a small enclosed market for general fruit and vegetables.

For most people the market or shopping centre, starts from the square in the old part of the town, with its narrow streets, so narrow that opposite balconies often meet. On either side are two-storied houses of brick and wood, some with lovely carvings on doors and window frames or with carved pillars, the work of the Newars, earlier inhabitants and rulers of the valley. As a result Kathmandu still remains medieval. Its streets are cobbled, its houses warped with age and leaning like so many bedizened warriors at rest after a hard campaign. The men wear soft pixie-like caps, set at a jaunty angle, cotton trousers baggy at the top but tight from the knee down, over which they wear a European-style jacket.

It is a jostling, clattering jungle of men, women and thieving cows, running children and wandering, hapless dogs, a world of green-eyed yellow gods, fascinating and so absolutely different from any other city in the world. Here are both the sacred and profane, and no one minds the little shop built just inside the temple gates.

There is never much interesting food to buy in Kathmandu or other Nepalese bazaars. Rice, wheat, very small potatoes, ground nuts, maize and sugar, chillies galore (great heaping mounds of them spread out throughout the city), pulses and buckwheat—these are the main produce of the bazaar. There is a certain amount of fruit, apples in season, oranges and peaches, as well as bananas and several varieties of persimmon.

Fish comes only in the evenings, mountain fish and then not in great variety. Meat is of poor quality and what one sees in the butcher shops hardly encouraging. Sheep are butchered on the day of selling and eating, the heads are 'decorated' with a yellow substance, probably turmeric, and the painted head is then cheerfully exposed to the public gaze, I assume to show that this is sheep-mutton and not goat-mutton.

Here in the same market one can buy round balls of soap but it is not easily recognizable, being of a dirty grey colour, and cooking pots, sold by the weight. There are mysterious spices, kerosene, lentils and matting to protect the porters who scale the mountains, for almost everything is carried on someone's back. There are sacks of coarse rock salt, and even coarser sugar, *ghee* for frying and great black umbrellas for protection during the monsoon rains. What is lacking in quantity and quality in the Khatmandu market is made up for in antiquity and entertainment.

I remember my first visit well. I had returned to my hotel after a hard day's sightseeing, exhausted and ready to stretch myself on my bed. But no. 'Come and meet the Princesses,' I was told. 'The Second Princess is the finest cook in the Valley.'

What could be better, I told myself, as visions of the horizontal position faded. I went downstairs to squeeze myself in between the Second and Third Princesses, to whom I was introduced and with whom I chatted until we came to the question of food and eating.

'Your Royal Highness,' I began, 'I am told that the best food in the Valley is served in your house. May I come and talk to you about food?' Somewhat surprised she nevertheless agreed to see me the following day.

Therefore, the next day the Princess and I sat down to talk on her verandah. Sitting there in her comfortable chair, sweet peas in her hair to match her sari, she did not look as though she ever went into a kitchen.

'There is,' she explained, 'little difference between our food and Indian food, at least as eaten by the ruling classes in the Valley for, after all, we are of Rajput [Rajasthan] origin. We use rather more chillies,' she added.

'We have an unusual spice called *timur* which comes from the Himalayas. I will fetch some for you.' And she went herself to the kitchen. The spice came, rather large, like peppercorns, with an elusive flavour quite unknown to me, which is not surprising since it is exclusive to the Himalayas.

The Princess talked of the eating habits of the Nepalese. She explained that although Hindus they are not vegetarian, since they are of the warrior caste who are permitted to eat meat in order to be healthy and strong to fight. 'For example, we are very fond of wild boar. This is a particular favourite of the Nepalese and we serve it in a number of ways, in curries or as dried meat kebabs, heavily spiced with chillies. We like dried meat of all kinds, drying it until it is so brittle that it can be crumbled until it looks like small grain. It is then mixed with crushed chillies. This is served often with drinks, for the Nepalese are a drinking people.

'We are also fond of *chura*, a type of raw or uncooked rice.' And at the sight of my doubtful expression, she continued: 'You can only judge Nepalese food by eating it. Come and dine tomorrow and I will give you those dishes which are truly Nepalese.'

So my husband and I dined with the Second Princess who took me in hand as we walked round the table, insisting that I take something of each dish. I piled my plate with wild boar curry, wild boar and chicken kebabs, chicken curry and several kinds of vegetable curry, a thick black lentil purée —very good indeed—and finally the *chura*, the flavour of which was lost in such a splendid mixture of dishes that I never discovered whether it was really good or not.

When I had finally devoured all this, and devour is the only word for such eating, I was offered a dish which looked like soft fudge but is simply dried curd, in flavour not unlike the Russian Easter *pashka*.

After dinner, over *café brûlé* and liqueurs, we talked of food; of a pâté made from the barking deer; of the excellence of peacock pilau. Rhino meat, someone volunteered, is good, for the beast is sluggish and his meat tender. Tiger meat makes good steaks, something between veal and chicken; one can cut it into a sort of Chateaubriand steak, grill it over charcoal, adding as a flavour some Marsala. They are fond of mountain goat, barking deer and musk, for there is plenty of game in the forests.

So, finally, what can be said of Nepali food? Not one of the fine cuisines of the world but in some Nepalese homes one eats meals which are well remembered.

Measurements for cooking have not yet been standardized in Nepal. This does not make Nepali food less interesting but it does increase the difficulty in writing about it. More or less I have given the ingredients as they were given to me, but occasionally acted upon my own taste regarding the quantities of hot chillies usually suggested. Even some of my Nepali friends blanch at three tablespoonfuls of hot chillies. Therefore, I can only advise, 'Use discretion'.

EGG SALAD or CHUTNEY (*Phool ka Achar*)

This is called a chutney in Nepal but, I feel, the use of this name might confuse people preparing this dish for the first time. It should be served as a side dish to a curry. It does, however, make an interesting opening to a meal, served with a salad of chopped (not sliced) very ripe tomatoes. The red and white compliment each other.

6 servings:

12 hard-boiled eggs, shelled and halved
1 tablespoon (1¼) butter
1–2 teaspoons (1¼–2½) chilli pepper or to taste
1 teaspoon (1¼) cumin seeds, pounded
¼ teaspoon (⅓) cardamom seeds, pounded (optional)

2 cups (2½) thick curd or plain yoghourt
½ cup (⅔) coriander or parsley, chopped
1 small lime or half a small lemon, finely chopped with the skin

Heat the fat and fry the spices; do this with care as they burn easily. This frying is to rid the spices of their 'raw' odour.

Beat the curd, add the coriander, the lime and finally the spices. Mix all this thoroughly then drop in the egg halves. Combine gently so that the eggs do not break, turn into a glass dish and serve cold.

For those with a real interest in herbs, try and get coriander for this recipe, rather than parsley, although the latter is a fair substitute.

SCRAMBLED EGGS (*Khuras ko Anda*)

4 servings:

8 eggs
1 onion, finely chopped
4 dry red chillies, seeded and finely chopped or chilli powder
1 tablespoon (1¼) fresh ginger, finely chopped or 1 teaspoon (1¼) ground

1 teaspoon (1¼) green coriander or parsley, finely chopped
2–3 tablespoons (2½–3¾) butter
salt

Heat the butter and fry the onion and chillies until soft but not brown. Break the eggs into a bowl, whisk, mix the remaining ingredients together, pour the beaten eggs over them, add the mixture to the pan, stir well and cook until set, in the usual manner of scrambling eggs. Serve hot.

POTATO KEBABS (*Alu ko Kufte*)

These little fried potato kebabs or croquettes are extremely popular in Nepal and are offered as snacks with drinks.

6 servings:

12 large potatoes
oil
Stuffing:
4 spring (green) onions, finely chopped
2 cups (2½) cooked cauliflower

1 cup (1¼) chopped coriander or parsley
1 cup (1¼) peeled and mashed tomatoes
juice of 1 lime
salt

Mix the stuffing ingredients together.

Peel the potatoes and cook them in salted water until very soft. Mash until smooth. Divide the mashed potatoes into small portions each large enough to make a fairly small potato ball. Roll into balls and make a hole in the middle. Fill each with some of the stuffing, close up the hole and slightly flatten. Heat a little oil and fry the potato balls until brown.

These kebabs are served hot.

CHICKEN CURRY (*Kukhoora ko Tarkari*)

4–6 servings:

1 large chicken
2 onions, thinly sliced
2 cups (2½) curd or plain yoghourt
1-in. piece fresh, or 1 teaspoon (1¼) ground
 ginger
4 cloves garlic, pounded
salt

½ cup (⅔) butter, plus 1 tablespoon (1¼)
½ tablespoon (⅔) ground turmeric
½ tablespoon (⅔) each ground cumin,
 poppy and mustard seeds, crushed
2 cardamom pods, crushed
1 cup (1¼) water

Mix half the onions with the curd and add the ginger, garlic and salt. Mix well. The chicken should be cut into smallish serving pieces; in Nepal they get 12 pieces from one chicken. Add the chicken pieces to the mixture and turn these about until well coated with the curd. Leave for 30 minutes to marinate.

Heat the ½ cup butter and brown the remaining onion. Add the turmeric, cumin, mustard and poppy seeds and fry these for a moment, then add the chicken and its marinade and cook over a low heat until the curd is dried out. Add the remaining butter and the cardamom seeds, shake the pan to ensure that all the ingredients are well mixed, add the water, cover the pan and cook gently until the chicken is tender. Add more water if required but the curry is meant to be fairly dry.

Nepali chickens are usually as tough as the Gurkhas so they take a lot of slow cooking to become edible. Serve with rice or a pilau.

MIXED VEGETABLE CURRY (*Masmas*)

6 servings:

¼ cup (⅓) each vegetable oil and butter
1 bay leaf
a pinch of timur (see **page 58**) (optional)
4 red chilli peppers, seeded and split
5 green chilli peppers, seeded and sliced
 (optional)
6–8 cloves garlic or to taste, chopped
1 large piece ginger, finely chopped
1–2 large onions, coarsely chopped
8 medium-sized potatoes, peeled and
 thickly sliced

½ teaspoon (⅔) powdered turmeric
salt to taste
1 cauliflower, cut into flowerets
spring (green) onions to taste
2 cups (2½) shelled green peas
5–6 ripe tomatoes, peeled and quartered
fresh coriander or parsley, finely chopped
2 teaspoons (2½) ground coriander seeds
1 tablespoon (1¼) cumin seeds
1 cup (1¼) water

Heat the oil until smoking and bubbles begin to form. Add the butter and mix well. Add the next 10 ingredients or as many of them as are being used. Cover the pan and cook gently for 20 minutes. Add the remaining ingredients and continue to cook gently until all the vegetables are tender.

Carrots and turnips can be added to this list and firm French beans, snapped into halves. Such vegetables take well to this sort of treatment.

Most Nepalese would also add at least 1 tablespoonful (1¼) of chilli powder to this curry.

PORK CURRY (*Songoor ko Tarkari*)

4–6 servings:

3–4 lb. pork, cut into cubes
½ cup (⅔) cooking fat
2–3 cups (2½–3¾) water
1 cup (1¼) curd or plain yoghourt
Curry:
½ cup (⅔) chives, finely chopped
2 large onions, minced
8 cloves garlic, minced

2 teaspoons (2½) ground cumin
12 dry red chillies or substitute cayenne pepper
1 teaspoon (1¼) ground cinnamon
3 teaspoons (3¾) ground turmeric
3 teaspoons (3¾) ground coriander
2 teaspoons (2½) salt

Heat the fat in a large pan and lightly fry all the curry ingredients, adding them to the pan in the order given. Add the pieces of pork, let these brown, add the water, stir this into the curry, add the curd and continue cooking until the meat is tender. Serve with rice.

FRIED or CURRIED MUTTON (*Bhutuwa*)

4 servings:

2 lb. mutton cut into small pieces
¼ cup (⅓) cooking oil
¼ cup (⅓) ghee
½ teaspoon (⅔) ground coriander
6 red chillies, seeded and chopped
1-in. piece chopped ginger

1 teaspoon (1¼) ground turmeric
½ tablespoon (⅔) chilli powder or to taste
1 tablespoon (1¼) ground cumin seeds
6 cloves garlic, pounded
salt

Heat the oil and *ghee* together until it bubbles. Add the meat and the next 6 ingredients and cook over a gentle heat until the meat is tender. Add garlic and salt and continue cooking another 20 minutes. Serve hot with rice.

This dish of mutton would be served as one of several curry dishes.

I do not know why the garlic is added so late, but there it is. This curry is rather too hot for most Europeans. So use the chilli powder with discretion. The 6 red chillies will be hot enough for most people. Otherwise a good curry.

SWEET PILAU (*Guliyan Pulow*)

6 servings:

6 tablespoons (7½) butter
1 lb. long grained rice
3–4 light cardamom seeds
4–6 cloves
½ cup (⅔) seedless raisins
½ cup (⅔) almonds, blanched and slivered

sugar to taste
¼ teaspoon (⅓) saffron, soaked in rose-water
3 cups (3¾) water
2 pieces cinnamon
pinch of salt

Heat the butter and fry the rice until it is brown but take care it does not scorch. Add the cardamom seeds, cloves, raisins, almonds, sugar and saffron (with the rose-water). Stir well and add the water. Add the cinnamon and salt and bring this to the boil. Boil for 10 minutes. Reduce the heat and continue to cook for 30 minutes. Remove the cinnamon and cloves before serving.

This pilau can be served both hot and cold, plain or with soft brown sugar and thick cream.

RICE PUDDING (*Kir*)

This is very much like the Norwegian Christmas rice porridge.

4–6 servings:

1 cup (1¼) pudding or Carolina rice
2¼ teaspoons (2⅔) butter
5 pints (12 cups) milk
sugar to taste
1 heaped cup (1¼) of the following mixed:

fresh chopped coconut, raisins, almonds, pistachios and cashew nuts
1 teaspoon (1¼) vanilla essence or rose-water

Stir the rice with the butter and put it with the milk into a thick pan and bring to a gentle boil, stirring frequently. The rice is cooked slowly until it is very soft—it takes about 1 hour. The chopped sweetmeat and flavouring are added just before serving. Take from the heat and serve cold.

There are several *kir* or *kheers*, all are simple dishes but extremely pleasant and do match the spicy heavy dishes after which they are served.

CURD PUDDING (*Shrikund*)

This is the recipe of the Princess Princip Shah of Nepal and is somewhat reminiscent of the Russian Easter *pashka* and, for my taste, one of the best of the Oriental curd puddings.

6–8 servings:

2 lb. dry curd cheese, cottage cheese or ricotta

$\frac{1}{4}$ teaspoon ($\frac{1}{3}$) saffron

1 teaspoon ($1\frac{1}{4}$) rose-water

1 cup ($1\frac{1}{4}$) sugar

powdered cloves, cinnamon, cardamom and black pepper

Dissolve the saffron in the rose-water and beat it into the curd. Add the remaining ingredients and again beat thoroughly. Serve cold in a glass dish.

Ceylon

Ceylon is a beautiful island, variously called 'The Isle of Spices' by the Dutch, the 'Isle of Rubies by the Ceylonese-enamoured, and the 'Island of Sea and Palms' by the Sinhalese themselves who think of it as the 'Garden Isle of Asia' or as the 'Isle of Flowers and Perfumes'.

Three-quarters forest covered, the main economy of the island depends on three exports, tea, rubber and coconut. Probably nowhere else in the world does the palm flourish as in Ceylon. Of these the coconut palm is indubitably the most useful and one of the most wonderful trees in the world. It is the tree of life, providing food, drink, housing and clothing. The scraped flesh of the nut goes into curries; the cabbage or small leaves are pickled or made into salads, and the green young nuts are used as medicines and in sweet preparations. The more mature nuts provide milk (*see* page 238), while the sap of the tree gives toddy, distilled in Ceylon to become *arrak* which, at its best, can be described as a form of whisky.

Apart from the usual brown coconut, there is another interesting variety, the *coco-de-mer*. This is supposed to have floated from the Seychelles and is allegedly the fruit with which the Devil tempted Eve, thus strengthening the Seychelles' claim to be the original Garden of Eden.

Many are the legends concerning the history and the shape of the *coco-de-mer*, or double coconut. There was an ancient belief that the fruit was produced on a palm which grew below the sea. Many virtues are ascribed to it as a medicine and at one time great prices were paid for it. One Malay prince coveted the *coco-de-mer* greatly and, it was recorded, would exchange a laden junk for a single nut. One writer wrote: 'Its fruit is shaped like a human heart . . . when the husk is taken off, the inner double nut is like the thighs of a woman. It is taken to India for the harems. Its shell is used in the Well of Knowledge in Banaras. If this is the tree which was used to test our mother Eve, then this isle (Seychelles) should be the Garden of Eden. . . .'

On the whole the Ceylonese are vegetarians, especially so in the country districts. Their taboos naturally include meat or poultry, often eggs and fish. In the towns people are less strict and there are many Buddhists who will eat meat, provided they have not been instrumental in killing the animal.

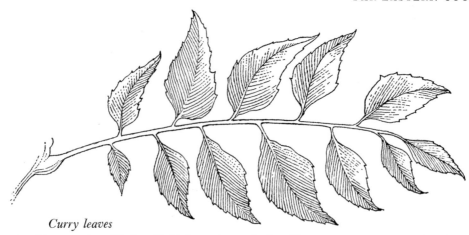

Curry leaves

But in the villages, where life is still fairly unchanged, the villagers are vegetarian. They have their small houses, and gardens. In each garden will be a betel nut vine (*see* page 236), a pepper vine, a chilli pepper bush, a patch of lemon grass (*see* page 241) and gourds. They will have, if possible, a jackfruit tree, a mango and a papaw tree and naturally a few banana leaves. There is a saying that if a man has all these things in his garden he needs nothing more in this world.

It is hard to define what is true Sinhalese food. Religions, intermarriage, foreign occupations (i.e. Portuguese, Dutch and British) and large inroads of Indian indentured labour, have all made their mark on the cooking of the island.

Briefly, the Ceylonese eat curries of all kinds and often with a greater variety of spices than are usual in Indian curries. They have their own special flavourings, one of which is lemon grass. Then there are *hoppers* which can only be described as a sort of ground rice pancake. They eat a lot of fish, much of which is pickled or dried, in particular Maldive fish. There is a fair variety in sweet dishes and numerous pilaus.

Of the spices, cinnamon is Ceylon's most important. It was the spice which Moses was ordered to use but it no longer commands the world's markets as it did. Even so, there are several acres of cinnamon trees in the island and the most elegant district of the capital is Cinnamon Gardens. In January, when the trees are in full bloom, it is a lovely sight. By April the bark is ready for peeling and cutting. Removing the bark in long strips is a skilled process and even more skilled is the process of skinning the bark, for the outer cover is not required in the finished product. The skinned bark is left for a while to ferment and dry, then it is rolled into quills for the market. From these quills is also distilled cinnamon oil.

An important tree for the village is the jackfruit, the fruit of which can grow to a monstrous size. It is a relative of the breadfruit, a splendid-looking tree prolific of fruit. When this is cooked it is a valuable source of food. It does not taste like bread but, correctly dealt with, it is good eating, especially when roasted whole in hot coals.

There is the usual variety of tropical fruit in the island, with a profusion of mangoes, papaws, really juicy pineapples, mangosteens, which are fairly acid, cool and fragile. There is the smelly *durian* which takes so much courage to try for the first time. Some people never recover from its horrible smell, but those who do become addicts. There is the *pomelo* and the usual citrus, and cashews —so many people know only the nut which grows at the end of a pear-flavoured fruit, so seldom used. The loquat, a small apricot-skinned fruit, native to China which has become naturalized in India and Ceylon and the Levant (it is called the Japanese medlar in southern Europe where it also grows), is pleasing though with not much flesh and a lot of stone. There are varieties of plums, sour-sop, which makes an excellent drink as well as ice-cream, the custard apple proper with its thick creamy pulp, of almost the same consistency as custard. It has a lot of pips but is good eating for the patient. There is the *rambuttan* (*see* page 89) and rose apple, a fruit with a variety of names, a stone like an olive, somewhat resembling a grape and not very good, but used for making jam.

There are excellent fish. A favourite is *seer*, the salmon of Ceylon, then mackerel and sole, pomfret of course, crabs, prawns, lobsters.

Finally there is, and most surely not for eating, the *dugong*, bearing a curious resemblance to a woman, and reputed to be the creature which has given rise to the stories of mermaids.

Yes, Ceylon is a lovely island fringed by palms and white sands where elephants go down to the sea to bathe and fish 'sing' in the lagoons.

YELLOW RICE (*Kaha-Buth*)

One of the important festive dishes of Ceylon. It is tinted with saffron, cooked in coconut milk and comes generously garnished to the table on a large platter. The exact quantity of spices used varies with individual cooks.

6 servings:

1 lb. (2⅓ cups) long grain rice
½ teaspoon (⅔) saffron, dissolved in a little water
3 heaped tablespoons (3¾) ghee or other fat
8–10 small red onions or 2 large onions, finely sliced
10–12 curry leaves (see page 239)

1½ pints (3¾ cups) each thick and thin coconut milk (see page 238)
12 peppercorns
3–6 cloves
6–10 cardamom pods, crushed
salt

Clean the rice. Pound the saffron with the water until the colour runs deep (more saffron can be used if a very vivid colour is preferred). Heat the fat in a deep saucepan and fry the onions and the curry leaves for a few minutes; the onions should be soft but not brown. Add the rice to this and let it fry for 4 or 5 minutes. Blend the saffron with the combined coconut milk so that this turns a rich yellow colour. Pour this over the rice in the saucepan and stir well. Add the peppercorns, cloves, cardamoms and salt. Stir well, let the mixture come to the boil, lower the heat and simmer the rice until it is tender. Reduce the heat to almost nothing and continue cooking until the rice is dry and fluffy. Before serving, remove all the whole spices.

Garnish with thin strips of potato, sliced tomatoes and sultanas, all fried; roasted cashew nuts coarsely chopped and thinly sliced hard-boiled eggs.

SPICED SCRAMBLED EGGS (*Egg Roloung*)

3–4 servings:

8 eggs, yolks and whites separate
salt, pepper to taste
a few curry leaves (see page 239) (optional)

1 teaspoon (1¼) finely chopped fennel
a little butter
1 tablespoon (1¼) finely chopped onion

Beat the egg yolks until smooth and the whites until stiff. Whisk together, adding salt and pepper. curry leaves and fennel. Heat the butter, add the onion and cook until it is soft but do not let it brown Pour in the whisked egg, let it begin to set and then gently stir until the mixture is quite set.

CUCUMBER CURRY (*Pipinge Hodi*)

4 servings:

2 large cucumbers
1 large onion, chopped
½ teaspoon (⅔) powdered turmeric
2 green chillies
1 sprig curry leaves (optional)

¼ teaspoon (⅓) dill seeds
salt to taste
2 cups (2½) thick coconut milk (see page 238)

Thinly peel the cucumbers and cut each one into 3 pieces and each piece into 2 pieces lengthwise. Put the cucumber into a saucepan, add the onion and the remaining ingredients (except the coconut milk) with a little water, cover the pan and bring to the boil. Stir, lower the heat and add the coconut milk and let it cook gently until the cucumber is tender. Do not let the coconut milk boil or it will curdle.

BEEF CURRY (*Harak Muss*)

4–5 servings:

2½ lb. stewing beef, cut into small pieces
1½ cups (2) thin coconut milk (see page 238)
½ tablespoon (⅔) chilli powder
a pinch turmeric, for colour
4 cloves garlic, finely chopped
a small piece fresh ginger
1 small onion, sliced

1–2 pieces lemon grass or lemon rind
salt
1-in. piece cinnamon
½ tablespoon (⅔) fenugreek seeds (see page 239)
½ cup (⅔) thick coconut milk (see page 238)
1 tablespoon (1¼) ghee or other fat
juice of ½ small lemon

Put the thin coconut milk into a saucepan, add the meat, chilli, turmeric, garlic, ginger and half the onion, lemon grass, salt, cinnamon and fenugreek. Bring all this to the boil and cook steadily until the meat is tender. Add the thick coconut milk. In the meantime, heat the fat, add the remaining onion and the juice and stir this into the beef curry 10 minutes before serving. Remove the ginger.

More onion than the recipe suggests may be used, it is all a matter of personal taste. The above recipe, which produces a kind of well-spiced stew (as indeed do most of the Ceylonese curries), does well for stewing steak. Serve with rice.

WILD BOAR CURRY (*Val-Ooru-Muss*)

6 servings:

3 lb. wild boar
2 tablespoons (2½) mixed roasted, chopped chillies
6–8 small onions, sliced
½ teaspoon (⅔) dill or fennel seeds
6 cloves garlic, chopped

1-in. piece fresh ginger, finely chopped
1 tablespoon (1¼) mild vinegar
½ teaspoon (⅔) turmeric
salt
1½ cups (2) water
juice ½ lime or small lemon

Wash the wild boar and cut it into cubes. Put into a pan with the remaining ingredients, except the lime juice. Add sufficient hot water to cook the meat without burning—but do not smother it. The finished curry should be dry. However, take care that the liquid does not completely dry out, add more hot water if necessary. Cook steadily, stir from time to time and add the juice shortly before serving.

There is a lot of wild boar in Ceylon, used in a number of ways and considered a great delicacy. Wild boar tends to be indigestible so note the counteracting spices, ginger, dill and garlic. A very hot curry, although one can reduce the quantity of chillies or use chilli powder.

CHICKEN CURRY (*Kukul Muss*)

4 servings:

1 large roasting chicken
3 small pieces cinnamon
6 cloves
2 tablespoons (2½) coriander seeds
½ tablespoon (⅔) cumin seeds
¼ teaspoon (⅓) fenugreek seeds
½ teaspoon (⅔) fennel seeds
12 cardamom seeds
6 small onions or 2 large
1 teaspoon (1¼) chilli powder
peppercorns

1 cup (1¼) thin coconut milk (see page 238)
¼ teaspoon (⅓) ground turmeric
2 tablespoons (2½) vinegar
salt
1 cup (1¼) thick coconut milk (see page 238)
For tempering:
1 level teaspoon (1¼) ghee or other fat
6 small red onions, sliced or 1 large
a good pinch of dried mustard
6–8 curry leaves (see page 239)

This curry should also include some interesting leaves and local herb flavours, but as these are not available, either in Europe or the United States, I have perforce omitted them in order not to confuse.

For tempering: this is an expression often used in Ceylon. It means to blend or mix and it is always done in the manner described in this particular recipe.

The chicken should be jointed into 2 breasts, 2 wings, 2 legs, the backbone and the neck. But joint it as you wish, much depends on the size of the bird. Split the gizzard and remove the white skin. Use the liver, heart and gizzard in the curry. Leave all this aside until required.

Break the cinnamon into small pieces and crush the cloves. Lightly crush the seeds, this brings out their full flavour. Slice the onions lengthwise.

Fry in a deep, thick frying pan the chilli, coriander, cumin, fennel, fenugreek and peppercorns (this is called roasting them). Stir all the while to avoid burning, and cook for about 2 minutes. Put aside. Put the chicken pieces, heart, liver etc. into another saucepan. Add the cinnamon, cardamoms, onions, cloves and the thin coconut milk. Add the fried spices and the turmeric, stirring all the while with a wooden spoon. When all is blended, add the vinegar (or lemon juice) and salt.

Cook the curry over a moderate heat so that the chicken simmers steadily until it is tender. Add the thick coconut milk and continue cooking for another 10 minutes, or until the gravy is thick and oily. Turn out the curry into a bowl, put aside but keep hot.

Heat the tempering fat in another saucepan, add the sliced onions and mustard, also the curry leaves and cook until the onions are brown. Pour the curry on top, let it simmer a few minutes longer, stir well and serve with rice, chutneys or *sambols*. Remove the cinnamon before serving.

FISH CURRY

4 servings:

2 lb. firm white fish	**1 cup (1¼) each thin and thick coconut milk**
1 teaspoon (1¼) powdered turmeric	(see **page 238**)
salt, black pepper to taste	**4 tablespoons (5) oil**
1 teaspoon (1¼) chilli powder	**1 onion**
1 teaspoon (1¼) cumin seeds	**4 cloves garlic** — all sliced
1 tablespoon (1¼) coriander seeds	**1 small piece ginger**
1 piece cinnamon	**1 tablespoon (1¼) vinegar**
4 cloves	**coriander leaves or parsley, finely chopped**

Clean, wash and cut the fish into serving pieces. Mix the turmeric, salt and pepper and rub this mixture into the pieces of fish.

Pound or grind (or use a blender) the remaining spices, adding a little of the thin coconut milk to make this into a thin paste. Heat the oil, fry the fish until brown and put aside. Add the sliced ingredients to the pan and fry these until soft, then add the paste, stir and cook for 5 minutes. Add the remaining thin coconut milk. Bring to the boil, add the fried fish and continue to cook until it is reheated. Lower the heat, add the thick coconut milk and simmer until this is hot. Finally add a little more salt and the vinegar. Serve in the sauce, garnished with coriander.

FISH WITH TURMERIC SAUCE (*Fish Mouille*)

4 servings:

1 hot poached fish, about 2 lb.	**1 teaspoon (1¼) cornflour (cornstarch)**
1 oz. (2 tablespoons) butter	**¼ cup (⅓) coconut milk** (see **page 238**)
a piece of cinnamon	**1 teaspoon (1¼) powdered turmeric**
1 cup (1¼) fish stock	**chillies** or **chilli powder to taste**
salt, pepper to taste	**3 cups (3¾) hot cooked rice**

Heat the butter in a saucepan, add the cinnamon and fry it for a few moments. Add the stock, salt and pepper. Mix the cornflour with the coconut milk and turmeric to a paste. Add the paste and the chillies to the pan and stir until the mixture thickens. The sauce must be stirred continuously or the coconut milk will curdle. Arrange the fish on a plate, surround with rice and pour the sauce over the top. Discard the cinnamon.

The name of this dish is rather a mystery. It could be of French origin, since the sauce has a French consistency, but the flavour is definitely Eastern. Instead of coconut milk, cow's milk, flavoured with grated or desiccated coconut, may be used.

FISH SMORE (*Fish Simore*)

2 servings:

2 thick fish

2 teaspoons (2½) curry powder (see page 13)

½ teaspoon (⅔) chilli powder

salt

a good pinch saffron, soaked in water

2 tablespoons (2½) oil

1 large onion, finely sliced

2 cloves garlic, thinly sliced

2–3 thin slices fresh ginger or ½ teaspoon (⅔) ground

2 cloves and 2 cardamom pods, crushed

1-in. piece cinnamon

2 bay leaves

1 green chilli (optional)

2 tomatoes, peeled and finely sliced

1 cup (1¼) coconut milk

lemon juice and rind

Wash the fish and rub it well with the inside portion of the lemon rind. Mix the curry powder, chilli powder, salt to taste and saffron. Coat the fish in this and put aside. Heat the oil in a pan and fry the onion and garlic until a light brown. Add the remaining spices, green chilli, bay leaves and the fish and fry for another 5 minutes. Add the tomatoes and continue cooking a further 5 minutes on a slow fire. Add the milk and cook slowly until the fish is done. Add lemon juice just before serving. Remove any whole spices. If using thick coconut milk take care that it does not curdle.

SHREDDED CABBAGE (*Gova Mellung*)

4 servings:

1 small firm cabbage, finely shredded

½ teaspoon (⅔) saffron, soaked in water

4–6 small onions, sliced

1 teaspoon (1¼) cumin seeds

salt

2 tablespoons (2½) coconut, grated or desiccated

½ tablespoon (⅔) lime or lemon juice

Wash the cabbage and put it into a pan with the saffron, onions and cumin. Add 2 tablespoonfuls (2½) water with salt to taste. Cover and cook gently until the cabbage is tender. Stir in the coconut, let this cook for a while, add the juice, mix it well and serve hot.

A *mellung* is a dish of shredded vegetables and the Sinhalese do not consider a meal complete without a dish of shredded greens or other vegetables.

TOMATO SAMBOL (*Thakkali Sambol*)

This is a very simple recipe for which there are no exact ingredients, they are 'as required'.

Take some peeled tomatoes and cut them into small pieces. Add a little thick coconut milk, some crumbled Maldive fish (*see* page 241), a few sliced onions, sliced green chilli peppers or capsicum (sweet peppers), a squeeze of lime or lemon, a little salt and mix well together.

CUCUMBER SAMBOL (*Pipinge Sambol*)

Sambols are side dishes to rice and similar to *sambals* in Malaysia and Indonesia, and play the same role as chutneys in Indian cooking.

1 cucumber
1 teaspoon (1¼) crumbled Maldive fish (see **page 241**)
1 small onion, finely chopped
2 green chillies or a little sweet pepper, finely sliced

2 tablespoons (2½) thick coconut milk (see **page 238**) (optional)
salt and sharp vinegar to taste

Thinly pare the cucumber and cut it into half. Then cut both pieces thinly, cutting round and round the flesh until the seed part of it is reached. Roll up the 2 long pieces together and cut into strips. Put all this into salt water, let it remain for a few minutes, then squeeze out all the liquid and put the cucumber into a glass dish. Add the remaining ingredients, mix well and serve.

Ceylonese vinegar is rather sharp. Extremely popular is a coconut vinegar which is prepared in various strengths.

Cucumbers in Ceylon are small, as usual in the East. For this *sambol* half a Western cucumber is enough.

ONION SAMBOL (*Loonu Miris Dehi Ambul*)

This is simply finely chopped onions mixed with finely chopped and seeded red chillies or chilli powder, a little crumbled Maldive fish (*see* page 241), lime or lemon juice with salt to taste and curry powder.

Instead of serving this *sambol* raw it can be fried. It is served with milk-rice as well as with curries. Some cooks also use dried prawns with onion *sambol*. Maldive fish is optional.

STUFFED SAVOURY PANCAKES (*Albassara*)

12 servings:

Filling:
1 medium-sized chicken
4 oz. (½ cup) butter
2 onions, finely chopped
salt, pepper
a little ground ginger
stock or water

Pancakes:
3 oz. (scant ½ cup) flour
salt, pepper
4–5 eggs
1 pint (2½ cups) milk
butter

The filling should be prepared first. Joint the chicken. Heat the butter and lightly fry the onions, then brown the chicken pieces. Sprinkle with salt, pepper and ginger. Add enough stock to cover the chicken and cook gently until it is tender. Take it from the pan, strip the flesh from the bones and cut it into very small pieces. Return these to the pan and continue cooking until thoroughly reheated. Take from the heat and keep hot until required.

Sift the flour, salt and pepper into a bowl and add the eggs, one at a time, beating well between each addition. Add the milk and beat the whole to a thin batter. Heat a little butter in a pan, pour in a small quantity of the batter and fry on one side until a pale brown; turn and brown on the other side. Repeat this procedure until all the pancakes are made.

Arrange the pancakes in batches of 6, one on top of the other, each pancake spread with some of the chicken mixture, the top pancake being left plain. It is important to work quickly and serve the *albassara* as hot as possible. If the pancakes become cold, put them into a hot oven for a few moments to reheat.

A Muslim recipe.

POTATO PANCAKES (*Aardapplen Koek*)

makes 10 pancakes:

$\frac{1}{2}$ **lb. potatoes**	**sugar to taste**
4 oz. (1 cup) sifted flour	**pinch of salt**
2–3 eggs, beaten	**butter**
1$\frac{1}{2}$ cups (2$\frac{1}{4}$) coconut milk (see **page 238**)	

Peel the potatoes and cook them in salted water until very soft. Drain entirely free from water and mash them until absolutely smooth. Alternately add the flour and eggs, beating the mixture well after each addition to ensure creaminess. Gradually thin this to a batter consistency with the coconut milk. Add sugar and salt. Heat a little butter in a frying pan and pour the mixture in small amounts into the hot fat and fry on both sides until brown.

This recipe is from the Burger community of Ceylon with its strong Dutch influence and is very much a part of the Ceylon cuisine. The pancakes are very light and can be served in any of the usual pancake ways, but probably butter and soft brown sugar is the best accompaniment.

COCONUT BREAD PUDDING

4–6 servings:

$\frac{1}{2}$ **lb. stale bread**	**4 oz. ($\frac{1}{2}$ cup) granulated sugar**
2 cups (2$\frac{1}{2}$) milk	**vanilla flavouring to taste**
4 oz. (1 cup) grated or desiccated coconut	**3 egg whites, beaten until stiff**
3 egg yolks, well beaten	**butter**

Break the bread into small pieces and put these into a basin. Boil the milk and pour this over the bread. Let it soak for 30 minutes. Beat it lightly with a fork and add the coconut. Beat the egg yolks with the sugar and vanilla flavouring and add this to the bread mixture and when blended fold in the egg whites. Pour this into a buttered baking dish and bake in a moderate oven for around 40 minutes, or until the pudding is brown. Turn out to serve, sprinkled with soft brown, sieved sugar, cream or a jam sauce.

The cook of a friend of mine in Colombo was famous for this pudding. He also added nuts, such as cashew, and raisins or sultanas. The pudding should be firm enough to turn out but even so have a light spongy texture.

MALAY PUDDING (*Wattalappam*)

This pudding, of Malay origin, has become so much a part of the Ceylon kitchen that it was served to Her Majesty Queen Elizabeth II on her state visit to the island. It is rich, spicy and basically a steamed egg pudding which can be served both hot and cold. It is often served after yellow rice.

6–8 servings:

6 egg whites
6 egg yolks
**8 oz. (1⅓ cups) jaggery, molasses or soft
   brown sugar**
1 cup (1¼) thick coconut milk (see page 238)
pinch of powdered cardamom

**a dash each of ground cinnamon and
   nutmeg**
pinch of salt
1 tablespoon (1¼) rose-water
**2 tablespoons (2½) each cashew nuts and
   sultanas**

Beat the whites and the yolks separately. Scrape the *jaggery* with a knife and dissolve it in the coconut milk. If using sugar or molasses, simply mix this into the cocunut milk. Strain through a fine cloth. Fold the whites into the yolks and whisk in the sweetened coconut milk. Add the spices, salt and rose-water and pour the mixture into a greased mould. Cover with greased paper and steam for about 1¼ hours, or until the pudding is firm. Halfway through, remove the paper, drop in the nuts and sultanas and continue cooking. Or the custard can be baked in a water bath in a low oven.

It is usual to serve the pudding in the mould in which it is cooked. Instead of one large mould, several small ones may be prepared.

Burma

It is trite but accurate to describe the Burmese as friendly, politics apart. They took me to their hearts, showed me all I wanted to see and not the least of my pleasures was eating Burmese food with Burmese both in their homes and gaily at night in the many eating stalls of the capital.

I was taken to the house of a Burmese woman who had the reputation of being the best cook in Rangoon. The day happened by fortunate chance to be one when she was preparing food for a public banquet. 'She is so good,' said my introducer, 'that she prepares food for all distinguished gatherings.'

Her house was one of the old homes of Rangoon, a type which is fast giving way to modern white-washed houses. This was large and one-storeyed, black and brown with the ageing of its timbers and with a verandah which ran right round the house. We stepped into the main room, lofty as a barn and raftered. At one end of the room was a shrine. It was sparsely decorated and the bamboo walls were movable, dividing the rooms as occasion demanded; 'instant rooms', no less. Outside in the surrounding garden there were many flowering trees and bushes, the fruit and leaves of them all being edible. There was a small kitchen garden in which my hostess grew, it seemed to me, every possible vegetable, from East and West, providing her inspiration.

We sat on a low divan-cum-bed and all around were similar beds. She had a large family, not all intimately connected but joined in the haphazard friendly way of the East. As she talked with me in excellent English she also threw gems of advice to the many servants, some of whom had been in her family for a long time, others seemingly quite young and new. 'They will marry soon and go; but they will go as good cooks,' she said.

My roving eye alighted on the many silver bowls and mugs, the iron pots, the earthenware dishes, most of them filled with sauces of varying descriptions. I was shown one which held edible leaves, another flowers, a third with *ngapi* (*see* page 242), the famous Burmese paste which no Burmese likes to be without. We took a small trot around the garden—one does appear to trot in the East with small precise steps—and she pointed out the lemon grass, which is grass-like as its name suggests and is strongly flavoured of citronelle. She explained the uses of the leaves, all of which were either used in soups or to make their distinctive type of salad, *thanthat*.

Burmese food is interesting and very pleasing, quite different from Indian and Chinese. Indeed there seems to be less of either of these influences than elsewhere in Asia. As we inspected the pots of simmering riches she talked of Burmese cooking in general and expressed her opinion that the West had not truly explored its full possibilities, its richness and variety.

Most of the cooking was being done on charcoal, on a raised stone fireplace which looked somewhat like a table. On this everything was cooking, curries, meat and vegetable dishes, and soup.

Most foreigners living in Burma know the main dishes, *Mohinga* and *Kaukse-Hin*, and those who have lived there long are familiar with the fish sauces so appreciated by the Burmese gourmet. Their curries are called curries only for the want of a better name, for, as the Indians understand curries, what the Burmese eat is not curry. They use less spice, add lemon grass to all their dishes and, basically, the Burmese eat something they call 'sour curries' to which they add a fair amount of oil and salt.

Rice is of major importance, being the staple diet and usually served plain. It is surely some of the finest rice in the world, with long fine grains. Noodles of the thin vermicelli type come next, a good second, and are used in many of the festive dishes and, of course, in all Chinese inspired dishes. But it is rice which is important and there are endless varieties. Among the popular types used in the country is a glutinous rice called *pittu* or black rice, which is by no means bad eating. Then there is 'winged rice' and 'buffalo grain' and a type of sticky rice which is used at harvest festivals. There is a local saying: 'His rice and his pot do not agree,' in other words, he does not cut his coat according to his cloth.

The daily meals of the Burmese are simple. Morning, in the towns, brings bread and coffee; the midday meal is of fruit and a meat dish. But in the country there is no difference between the two main meals of the day. The best urban meal of the day is the evening meal, and here the menu is fairly set. It starts with a soup, which is quite different from Western soups. Various flowers or leaves, as well as vegetables, go into the light stocks which are usually of fish. There is always a dish of salad, again leaves and flowers, all very crisp. Then there will be either a meat or fish dish, but preferably fish, for the Burmese love fish of all kinds. At one meal there might be several kinds of fish, depending on the style of the meal. One of these is almost bound to be prawns, cooked in their shells. Other fish is served dried or salted, soused or curried. One favourite fish is soused for so long that all its bones soften. If there is not a dish of fish, there will be one of meat and then a dish of lightly cooked vegetables some of which will be soaked in vinegar or dressed in garlic and any of the traditional Burmese sauces, such as *ngapi* with its almost evil smell, and salty but agreeable flavour. Much of the food is dipped into this particular sauce. If guests arrive unexpectedly another easy dish can be added, some more salad or *thanthat* or perhaps a dish of tomato curry.

There is a standard meal for entertaining which I soon discovered. A clear soup, delicately flavoured, fish dish, usually a prawn curry, then a plate of cooked vegetables and one of raw vegetables, a chicken curry and all this followed by semolina halva. If not a chicken curry, pork or duck is used.

Vegetables of all kinds are extremely popular among Burmese, both those we know as European plus the many Oriental varieties. I have already mentioned the fondness for what is collectively called 'leaves' and these include tamarind, mango leaves, and even the leaves of the *neem* tree. The last are so bitter that they require to be rubbed heavily in salt to rid them of some of their bitterness—but they are good against fevers. Roots, such as the lotus root, as well as the roots of several other aquatic plants, are everyday items of diet and so are field mushrooms which appear after the monsoon rains. How these vegetables are all cooked depends on their texture. Some are served raw but they are never overcooked as the Burmese prefer them crisp and crunchy in the Chinese manner.

Burma's coastline and its rivers seem to be teeming with fish of all kinds. There are shellfish, crabs and crayfish, prawns and shrimps—prawns are as much a part of Burmese eating as say herrings are of the British. Roasted turtle and iguana eggs and dried fish in purified ginger are gourmet's delights.

Soups are always clear, never thick purées. Many are plain but all are flavoured with prawns in some form or another, with fish stock and *ngapi*, garlic and onion. Stock is made freshly for each batch of soup and when it comes to the boil prepared vegetables are thrown into it, and these are cooked only for a matter of minutes. The favourite vegetables or leaves for such soups are those with a sour flavour, lemon grass, tamarind, *neem*, mustard greens, drumstick leaves etc. None of these greens is mixed without pattern. Calabash goes with peppercorns, green chillies are married to sorrel. Each soup has its own distinctive flavour and, even when sieved, the flavour can still be clearly detected. For festive occasions a richer soup is demanded and usually made with pig's trotters, chicken or duck, to which dried mushrooms, sweet-smelling flowers or leaves, as well as the finest quality vermicelli, are added.

Sweet dishes as we know them in Western meals have no place in Burmese menus. After a meal the Burmese prefer to serve fruit, and their favourite is mango. During a meal they will often serve something sweet which, they explain, is 'food for the saliva' and not so much for enjoyment as nourishment. However, if they do not have puddings, the Burmese have a large variety of unusual sweetmeats, many of them with delightful sounding Burmese names. They come in a variety of colours. There are rich cakes with raisins and nuts, or some soaked in coconut syrup.

A popular afternoon treat among Burmese is the eating of sour fruits spread with *ngapi* and chilli sauce. Green mangoes are one of the chief fruits used in this manner, also another extremely sour fruit, so sour that it causes one to shiver when eating it. This, aptly, is called 'The shiver-sour fruit'.

Burma is a tea-producing country and tea is the national drink, not the heavy black tea of the West but plain or green tea which is drunk at any time of the day. Then there is the so-called pickled green tea, flavoured heavily with garlic and spices. This, too, is offered in the country at all times of the day in keeping with the hospitable traditions of the people.

COOKING RICE IN THE BURMESE FASHION

The old-fashioned Burmese cook still uses an earthenware pot for rice cooking, one reserved for rice and rice only. Modern Burmese women now use modern cooking utensils, especially aluminium ones, but still one pot is used exclusively for rice.

According to the Burmese, the rice pot should be of a particular size, that is, large enough so that when the rice is cooked it will rise to the top of the pan. Rice, say the Burmese, must be cooked immediately before eating, otherwise it becomes unpalatable and indigestible.

Although the quality of Burmese rice is good, like Indian rice, it is also pretty dirty and so instructions for cooking rice are thus: 'Clean and dry, pick out all grit, paddy and other grain. Measure about 4 tins (cups) and put into a medium-sized *dekshie* (saucepan) or aluminium pot. Half fill this with cold water and briskly but gently swish it round the vessel and pour off the dirty water. Repeat this a second time. Then fill the vessel with clean drinking water rising to 2 inches above the rice.

Set on a moderate heat. Cover until it boils over, then cut off the scum, half cover and allow to simmer till a grain or so dissolves when pressed hard between finger and thumb. By this time most of the liquid has been absorbed and what remains must be drained off. Return the pot to a gentle heat. Every 2 minutes hold a cloth over the cover and around the brim, firmly but completely turning the pot upside down, shaking strongly. This process is repeated 2 or 3 times until all the grains are fully swollen and entirely separated.'

COCONUT RICE (*Ohn-Hta-Min*)

6 servings:

2 cups (2½) long grain rice	1 onion, chopped
2 large coconuts	½ teaspoon (⅔) sugar
½ tablespoon (⅔) vegetable oil	salt

Grate the flesh of the coconuts. Put the grated coconut into a bowl, add a little warm water, squeeze to get out as much thick coconut milk as possible. Add more warm water to the coconut, squeeze again as hard as possible. Repeat this process until you have in all 6 cupfuls of coconut milk. To each cup of rice, there should be 3 cupfuls of coconut milk.

Wash the rice thoroughly (this process may well be omitted if the rice is clean). Put the rice into a large pot, add the coconut milk—there should be enough liquid for its level to be 1 inch above the rice. If there is not enough coconut milk, then add water. Add the oil, onion, sugar and salt. Mix thoroughly and cook over a moderate heat until all the liquid has evaporated and the rice is tender and the grains separate.

Coconut rice is accompanied by many and sometimes curious side dishes. Here are some of the more usual suggestions: fried fresh prawns; devilled livers; pork or beef curry; chicken *doopia* or double onion chicken; duck *vindaloo* or kebabs. In Burma there would also be mangoes pickled in brine and chilli-fry, which is very hot red chillies, seeded and coarsely pounded, fried in oil and mixed with powdered dry shrimps, salt and fish paste.

Milk generously flavoured with desiccated coconut may be used instead of coconut milk, but it must be strained.

I was told coconut rice is eaten by the Burmese when 'they feel like it'. Not every day; not even every week. It is considered something rather special and offered at large parties.

BURMESE PILAU (*Biriani*)

6 servings:

1 cup (1¼) long grain rice	4 each cloves and cardamon seeds
2 lb. chicken or lamb	1 piece cinnamon
½ cup (⅔) ghee or butter	chillies, salt, turmeric and peppercorns to
6 large onions, 3 sliced and 3 minced	taste
6 cloves garlic, minced	6 eggs, fried
1 tablespoon (1¼) each ground cumin and	
coriander seeds	

Joint the chicken into fairly small pieces or, if using lamb, cut into 1½-inch squares. Heat the fat and fry the sliced onions until a golden brown and crisp, take from the pan and keep hot. Add the garlic, the ground onions and the spices, fry until fragrant, i.e., a few minutes, stirring all the while, then add the meat and salt. Continue cooking until the meat is three-quarters cooked. Add half the browned onions and 1 cupful (1¼) of water, cover the pan and simmer for 10 minutes. Add the rice, stir it well into the meat etc., and add enough hot water to cover 1½ inches above the rice. Cook over moderate heat until all the liquid has been absorbed. Place the pan with the rice and meat in a warm oven and leave until the rice is quite tender and the grains separated. Serve garnished with fried eggs and the remaining onions.

The type of pan required for this dish is one that can be used both on top of the stove and in the oven.

VEGETABLE SOUP (*Hincho* or *Hingyo*)

6 servings:

mixed vegetables
6 cups (7½) water
pepper, salt
½ cup (⅔) dried prawns or 4 large fresh ones

1 teaspoon (1¼) blachan (see page 237)
2 cloves garlic, finely chopped
2 onions, finely chopped

Put the water into a large saucepan with the pepper, salt, prawns, fish paste, garlic and onions and bring to the boil. Clean and trim the chosen vegetables and cut into fine strips. Add these to the pan and continue cooking until the vegetables are tender.

The soup is served in a bowl alongside rice which it is meant to moisten. *Hincho, Hinjho* or *Hingyo* is the Burmese national soup.

The Burmese choice of vegetables would be the tender shoots of pumpkin or other gourds, drumstick leaves, tamarind leaves, thinly sliced marrow, cabbage or any other edible leaves.

CHICKEN or LAMB CURRY WITH NOODLES (*Kaukse-Hin*)

6 servings:

1 chicken or 2 lb. lamb
cooked noodles, served hot
1 coconut, grated or 4 oz. (1¼ cups)
    desiccated
a handful coriander or parsley

6 cloves garlic
6 small onions, sliced
½ teaspoon (⅔) ground turmeric
salt and a squeeze of lemon or lime

Cut the chicken into serving pieces or the lamb into small pieces. Extract 1 cupful (1¼) of thick milk from the coconut (*see* page 238), then a second extract with 3 cupfuls (3¾) warm water. Put the chicken or lamb into a pan, add second or thin extract of coconut milk, the coriander or parsley, garlic, onions and turmeric. Cook gently uncovered for 1½ hours or until the meat is tender. Ten minutes before serving, add salt, the remaining coconut milk and the lemon juice. Allow to cook for a few minutes, then serve hot.

The serving of this dish is more or less classical. Each person should have a bowl of noodles (the Burmese use *tha saing*, a cross between vermicelli and spaghetti) and over this the curry gravy and meat is poured. Side dishes are offered in some variety; chopped hard-boiled eggs; grated fried fresh coconut mixed with fresh, finely chopped coriander; crisply fried cloves of garlic; chopped spring (green) onions or crisply fried onion rings; sliced lime or lemons; *ballachow* pickles and, finally, chilli powder. Each person takes a little of all these side dishes, adding them to the curry in his individual bowl.

Instead of chicken or lamb, prawns or firm white fish may be used.

In Burma this dish, of Chinese origin, is a favourite. Apart from the side dishes suggested, *kaukse* may be made as simple or as rich as desired. Crabs, flaked fish, liver, preferably chicken livers, certain sausages, mushrooms, dried flowers, which the Burmans like to use in their cooking, as well as vegetables such as peas, may all be added.

NOODLES WITH A FISH SAUCE (*Mohinga* or *Mon-Dee*)

This dish is a national favourite and prepared with rice noodles, a type of very fine noodles which are not prepared in the house but are professionally made. However, when this is not obtainable Chinese rice noodles can be substituted, or even the finest Italian vermicelli.

With the noodles is served a gravy or sauce, plus side dishes. At first it may seem confusing but the recipe I have given shows that it is not difficult.

6–12 servings: depending on how much vermicelli each person takes.

1–2 lb. cold cooked vermicelli or **Chinese noodles**

2 lb. white fish

½ cup (⅔) sesame oil or substitute

4 shoots lemon grass (see **page 24**)

salt

1 teaspoon (1¼) ground turmeric

2 tablespoons (2½) soy sauce, mixed with a little anchovy essence (a substitute for blachan

1½ in. fresh ginger or ½ teaspoon (⅔) ground

4 each pounded garlic cloves and onions

1 lb. mixed, quartered onions and chopped cauliflower

Side dishes:

pulped and squeezed tamarind, when not available use mild vinegar

chilli powder

spring (green) onion, finely chopped or a non-curled parsley or English parsley

hard-boiled eggs, preferably duck, cut into quarters

very small fried fish cakes

wedges of lime or lemon

Clean the fish and cook it in lemon grass or lemon rind flavoured water until it is just tender. Drain and keep the liquid. Remove all the bones from the fish, drop these into the fish liquid and continue cooking it to make a fish stock, adding at least another 8 cupfuls (10) of water.

Heat the oil, add salt and turmeric and fry the fish pieces until lightly browned. Take from the pan and keep hot. Strain the fish stock and pour this gradually into the pan in which the fish was cooked. Add the soy sauce and anchovy mixture, ginger, then the pounded ingredients. Mix these well, finally add the quartered onions and cauliflower and cook these over a moderate heat until tender.

Return the fish to the pan, reduce the heat to simmering and leave until ready to serve with the cold vermicelli and a variety of small side dishes which are served in small bowls to be taken at will. Serving:

The cold noodles are served in bowls, a bowl per person, and the hot fish and vegetable sauce or gravy is served in a large bowl. One takes the sauce and pours it piping hot over the cold noodles and adds as much from the side dishes as desired. The hard-boiled eggs are sometimes added to the sauce in the pan at the same time as the pieces of fish which, I think, is nicer as they are then served hot. Where lemon grass or substitute is not available, increase the quantity of ginger and use the extra quantity in cooking the fish. Whiting is a good fish for this recipe.

PRAWN SAUCE (*Blachan*)

½ lb. dry prawns or shrimps
3 tablespoons (3¾) sesame or vegetable oil
10 cloves garlic, sliced lengthwise
2 onions, sliced

1 tablespoon (1¼) chilli powder
1 teaspoon (1¼) anchovy essence or 1 tablespoon (1¼) soy sauce
1 tablespoon (1¼) salted fish (optional)

Pound the prawns. Heat the oil and fry half the garlic; when they are a light brown colour take them from the pan and put aside. In the same oil fry the onions, when brown take them from the pan and put aside. Pound the remainder of the garlic, add the chilli powder and the pounded prawns and sauce. Finally the salted fish. Mix well. Fry together until the mixture is dry, then add the fried onions and garlic.

Without *blachan* there is no Burmese cooking. It is eaten as a chutney or pickle but can also be used as a sandwich filling. Dried prawns are often available at Orien al grocers.

MINCED FISH CURRY (*Sha-nga-Boung*)

3–4 servings:

2 lb. firm white fish
1 teaspoon (1¼) chilli powder
4 cloves garlic
1 teaspoon (1¼) powdered ginger
1 short stalk of lemon grass or substitute (see **page 241**)

2 onions, 1 finely minced
1 tablespoon (1¼) ground rice
½ cup (⅔) vegetable oil
3 cups (3¾) coconut milk (see **page 238**)

Clean, wash and fillet the fish. Finely chop or mince it. Put aside. Pound the chilli powder with the other flavourings and the minced onion (the blender will do this). Mix this paste with the minced fish and the ground rice. Break off pieces of the mixture and shape into small flat pieces like cutlets. Slice the remaining onion thinly.

Heat the oil until smoking hot and fry the sliced onion until brown. Take it from the pan. In the same oil fry the fish cutlets on both sides to a golden brown. Lift the cutlets carefully from the pan and cut each piece into thick slices. Pour off most of the oil.

Pour the coconut milk into the pan and bring gently to boiling point. Lay the fish in this, cover the pan, lower the heat and let it cook slowly until the fish is reheated. Serve with a garnish of sliced fried onions (also sliced raw onion can be added). Serve with rice.

STEAMED FISH IN BANANA LEAVES (*Nga-Baung-Doke*)

This is a *must* in Burmese cooking and not at all difficult to prepare. In place of edible *yai-yo* leaves, use leaves from a Chinese-type cabbage, tender cabbage or lettuce. In place of the banana leaf wrapping, aluminium foil or parchment cooking paper can be used. Allow one or two packages per person.

5–10 servings:

2 lb. firm white fish, filleted
1 teaspoon (1¼) salt
1 teaspoon (1¼) ground turmeric
pinch of chilli powder
2 cloves garlic
1-in. piece fresh ginger or 1 teaspoon (1¼) ground
6–8 medium onions, sliced

1 tablespoon (1¼) flour
1–2 tablespoons (1¼–2½) thick coconut milk or milk flavoured with coconut (see page 238)
1 tablespoon (1¼) sesame or other oil
15–20 yai-yo leaves
banana leaves or aluminium foil
tooth picks

Wash and clean the fish, make sure there are no bones left. Cut into pieces about 3 × 1½ inches. Rub these pieces with half the salt and turmeric. Pound or blend the chilli, garlic and ginger with 2 of the onions to a paste, adding the flour, the coconut milk, oil and the rest of the turmeric. Slice the remaining onions and combine these with the paste.

Cut the banana leaves (or the foil) into 6-inch squares. On each square first place a *yai-yo* leaf (or substitute), on this a spoonful of the paste, then a piece of fish. On top of the fish put another spoonful of the paste and cover this with another leaf. Fold the banana leaf into a neat bundle and secure it with a toothpick (in Burma they use thin bamboo sticks). Cook these bundles in a steamer for about 30 minutes, by which time the fish will be cooked.

Foil requires no bamboo stick or even string.

FISH CURRY (*Chin-Ye*)

3 servings:

1½ lb. fish
1 large onion, chopped
1 small piece fresh ginger
3 red dry chillies, seeded and chopped or ¼ teaspoon (⅓) chilli powder
10 cloves garlic or to taste
salt

good pinch saffron, soaked in a little water
1 lb. white pumpkin or marrow
1 tablespoon (1¼) sesame, vegetable or peanut oil
soy sauce to taste
3 tomatoes, peeled and coarsely chopped
1½ tablespoons (2) tamarind or lemon juice

Pound or grind the onion, ginger, chillies and garlic, adding a little water to a smooth paste. A blender will do this. Cut the fish into medium-sized pieces and mix well with salt and saffron. Slice the pumpkin—more or less any type of gourd or squash may be substituted. Heat the oil, add the paste, stir well and fry this for a few minutes. Add the soy sauce, again stir, then add the fish, tomatoes and the sliced pumpkin. Stir gently, add tamarind juice, plus 3 cupfuls (3¾) water. Bring to a gentle boil,

add salt to taste and continue cooking gently for a few minutes longer or until the fish is tender.
An every day people's dish. In Burma *seinzangapi* paste would be used and not soy sauce.

MEAT CURRY (*A-Tha-Hin*)

4–5 servings:

2 lb. beef, lamb or pork	salt
2 onions, finely chopped	good pinch turmeric
2 cloves garlic	chilli or cayenne pepper to taste
1½-in. piece fresh ginger or 1 teaspoon (1¼) ground	2 oz. (¼ cup) cooking oil
	1½ tablespoons (2) soy sauce

Cut the meat into strips. Grind the onions with the garlic and ginger. Mix the salt, turmeric and chilli
pepper. Heat the oil in a saucepan and when hot add the ground ingredients and seasonings. Add
the meat and cook this until it is evenly browned. Add the soy sauce, water to cover and cook slowly
until the meat is tender. Serve with rice.
The result looks not unlike a *boeuf Strogonoff* and does not have what is considered a 'curry' flavour.

PORK CURRY (*Wet-Tha-Hinlay*)

There are many different Burmese recipes for pork curry; this is one of the simpler ones, but dry.

6–8 servings:

3–4 lb. pork, cut into serving pieces	4 tablespoons (5) sesame or vegetable oil
10 medium onions	1 teaspoon (1¼) salt
3 cloves garlic, pounded	1 tablespoon (1¼) soy sauce
4 large dry chillies, seeded and split or 1 teaspoon (1¼) chilli powder	a good pinch turmeric
	vinegar

Mince or pound the onions, garlic and the chillies. Heat the oil until smoking hot, add the pork,
brown it, add the remaining ingredients (except vinegar), mix thoroughly, lower the heat and cook
steadily but carefully until the pork is tender. When almost ready, add a little vinegar.

GOLDEN PORK (*Wet-Thani*)

This is a traditional Burmese dish about which expatriate Burmese dream. It should keep for months
if bottled and sealed and doting Burmese mothers send jars of 'golden' pork to sons and daughters
studying overseas.

3 lb. pork cut into 1-inch squares	6 oz. (about 1 cup) ginger, minced
1 lb. onions, minced	1 cup (1¼) oil
1 large head garlic, minced	salt to taste

Grind (in a blender) or pound the onions with the garlic and ginger to a paste. (This is a lot of garlic but it is Burmese taste.) Put the paste in a piece of thin cloth and squeeze it tightly over a bowl to extract as much juice as possible.

Mix the juice with the pork, oil and salt and put into a hot saucepan. Cook over a medium heat until the pork is almost cooked. Take out half the meat and mince it. Mix this with the garlic, onion and ginger mixture and put it all back into the pan. Stir and cook until everything is a golden brown.

Many Burmese cooks add a little vinegar to counteract the rich flavour of the pork.

CUCUMBER SALAD (*Thanthat*)

6–8 servings:

3 medium-sized cucumbers
3 tablespoons (3¾) vinegar
salt
½ cup (⅔) sesame or vegetable oil
1 large onion, finely chopped

20 cloves garlic or to taste
1 teaspoon (1¼) ground turmeric
2 tablespoons (2½) mixed roasted black and white sesame seeds (see page 213)

Peel, remove seeds and cut the cucumbers into strips, about ¾-inch long. Put these into boiling water adding the vinegar. Bring to the boil, cook the cucumbers but remove them as soon as they are transparent. Drain and lightly sprinkle with salt. Heat the oil and when really hot add the onion and garlic, but each separately and fry until a golden brown. Take from the pan, add the turmeric and colour the oil, it becomes a bright yellow. Add salt, half the sesame seeds and fry for a few minutes or until fragrant. This forms a dressing. Take the pan from the heat and cool. When ready to serve, add vinegar to the dressing, not too much. Drop the parboiled cucumbers into this dressing, then pile pyramid-shape on a plate, sprinkle with the remaining sesame seeds and surround with the fried onion and garlic. Pour the dressing over the lot or serve it separately, as you wish.

Other vegetables can be prepared in this manner; cabbage, cauliflower, carrots, beans and extremely good cooked in the same manner are bean sprouts.

SPICED MUSHROOMS (*Taung-Bho-Hmo*)

2 servings:

1 lb. field mushrooms
1 large onion
4 cloves garlic
2 blades lemon grass (see page 241)
4 tablespoons (5) vegetable oil

1 teaspoon (1¼) powdered turmeric
salt to taste
1 large onion, sliced
1 tablespoon (1¼) lemon juice

Clean and thickly slice the mushrooms, discarding the stems (these can be used to flavour a soup). Mince the whole onion, garlic and lemon grass. Bring the oil to the boil, add the turmeric, salt, the minced ingredients and the sliced onion. Cook for a few minutes, add the mushrooms, stir and cook over a low heat until they are tender. Sprinkle the lemon juice over the mushrooms just before serving. Serve with boiled rice or a plain pilau.

As a substitute for lemon grass, the leaves of lemon balm or verbena would be the best in this recipe, otherwise use strips of lemon peel.

BURMESE HALVA OR CAKE (*Sanwin-Ma-Kin*)

12 servings:

2½ cups (scant 3) semolina
3 large coconuts
3 eggs
1¾ cups (2¼) fine sugar
1 teaspoon (1¼) salt

2 oz. (4 tablespoons) butter
¾ cup (1) seedless raisins
slivered almonds, roasted sesame or poppyseeds (see page 243)

Grate the coconuts and make 8 cupfuls (10) of coconut milk (*see* page 238). Dry-fry the semolina in a frying pan until it begins to brown and has a pleasant odour. Beat the eggs and sugar together in a large bowl until light and frothy. Gradually add the semolina, mixing it in well. Add the coconut milk and salt, stirring all the while. Pour into a thick-bottomed pan and cook over a slow heat until the mixture boils and thickens. Add the butter. Take the semolina from the heat, add the raisins and pour the mixture into a lightly greased, fairly deep baking tin. Sprinkle the slivered almonds, sesame or poppy seeds over the top. Bake in a moderate oven until the top is well browned. Leave until quite cold before slicing and serving.

This is a favourite Burmese cake for festive occasions and resembles Greek halva or semolina cake. It can be made richer by adding more eggs, say another 2, also more fruit.

SWEET SAGO WITH COCONUT (*Tha-Gu*)

1 cup (1¼) sago
4 cups (5) water
1 cup (1¼) sugar

red or green colouring
1 cup (1¼) grated or desiccated coconut

Bring the water to the boil, add the sugar and slowly dissolve this. Bring again to the boil, cook for 10 minutes, then add the sago. Cook this until it becomes transparent. Add colouring and pour the sago into a shallow pan to cool. When quite cold and set, cut into squares or diamonds, roll in coconut and serve.

Or divide the sago into two portions and colour one half red and the other half green. I experimented successfully with Crême de Menthe.

This sweet is not unlike the Turkish Delight (*lokum*), and the recipe makes a fairly large quantity of sago 'sweets' or candies.

BANANAS IN COCONUT MILK (*Nga-Pyaw-Thi-Ohn-No-San*)

6 servings:

18 small bananas
¾ lb. (1½ cups) granulated sugar or **to taste**

1 large coconut or **substitute** (see **page 238**)
pinch salt

Peel the bananas and place them in a deep, rather large frying pan. With the eye measure enough water to come about half way up the bananas. Mix this water with the sugar and cook it to a syrup in another pan. Make 2 cupfuls (2½) of thick coconut milk from the coconut. Add a pinch of salt. Pour the syrup over the bananas and cook them over a low fire. When the syrup boils, add the coconut milk. Turn the bananas carefully so they do not stick together and continue cooking until the bananas are dry and pink. Serve cool. Excellent with cream.

There are in Burma small, finger bananas. If using the type usual in Britain (in America there is more variety) cut them into halves.

Thailand

I remember well my first visit to Thailand, to the capital city of Bangkok, then a city of *klongs* (canals), an exotic Venice of the East. I had arrived by plane and by one of those delightful chances of aeroplane travel, was invited by a fellow passenger to dine that same evening in an old house by the river.

The dining table had been set in the garden. As we were eating Siamese style, it meant a spoon and fork but no knife, for a knife is no more needed for Siamese food than for Chinese or Japanese. We had a soup, deliciously flavoured and piping hot, as all Siamese soups must be, and served in a charcoal burning dish. There was rice, steaming, white and fluffy, the basis of our meal. Explained my host, 'When we invite someone to a meal, we say: "Come and eat rice",' adding, 'all other dishes are called collectively "with the rice" and are to be tasted and enjoyed with the rice.'

All the flavours were new. I was promised recipes and explanations on the morrow, 'Tonight,' smiled my host, 'enjoy your rice.' I did, plus the tingling peace of the tropical night, the delight of the lovely table setting and the life of the river below.

Next day I consulted my letters of introduction, without which no one in the East travels, and let me say here, the hospitality of the East is all it is said to be. I telephoned Prince Prem, a member of the Royal Family and a journalist. He seemed somewhat surprised when I mentioned my mission, although not less surprised than any member of any royal family might be, and certainly far less formal, about it. However, hastily defending himself behind his telephone, he said, 'Come and talk to my sister, I am sure she can help you, but I. . . .'

I trekked through Bangkok in a cycle rickshaw (taxis are usual nowadays) and found the Prince and his sister waiting for me; she had already arranged I should visit the Princess Sibpan Sonakul (who has since died), for she had written the then only book on Siamese cooking. The Princess was charming, happy that I should take all her recipes. 'But I am not good at cooking,' she said, 'go and see Mom Klong.'

Mom Klong was an expert on Thai food but a modest woman. 'I am not a cook,' she said. 'I know only a little gardening.' She had a small wooden house overrun with bougainvillaea with a *klong* running alongside and a stream slipping through the garden over which was a small russet 'Chinese willow-pattern' bridge. We started to drink tea and eat crisp pork, its skin like parchment, brittle enough to break. We talked a little and Mom Klong asked me to return the next day and sample a real Thai curry.

When I arrived, Mom Klong was sitting in her garden, filled with lilies and perfumed trees. We sat in the shade of a flowering tree and plunged into 'food'. A silent, young and barefooted servant came in with a tray of local vegetables and dropped on her knees in front of me. It is not a gesture that we in the West care about, but there it is, gracefully achieved and a sign of the deepest respect.

On the tray, just to show me, were some small tomatoes, an aubergine no larger than a pea, a small wild fig, green and without flavour until cooked and used much in hot Thai curries. There were also various leaves, a type of sweet basil, English mint and crushed coriander root. 'We use a great deal of root life,' explained Mom Klong. The list goes on, Chinese celery, with the pure celery flavour but not looking like celery, some sour fruit with the flavour of green gooseberry; another which grew by the sea and a favourite with fishermen because of its salty flavour.

A second girl came with another tray, dropped on her knees and offered me 'sandwiches' or *Khal Gleeb Pak Maw*. They are not sandwiches at all but steamed packets of flour pastry with a stuffing of pounded fish, crushed coriander leaves and onion. We also ate little fried dishes, a splendid black rice pudding, some orchids and finally a dish of something which looked like a kind, but only a kind, of caviar. 'It is ant's eggs,' explained Mom Klong. 'Would you care to try?'

Care? Well, that was not exactly my reaction but I tried. And my report is that doubtless one could acquire a liking for it, but it is hardly worth it. A curious crunchy nothing seemed to be in my mouth, nothing more than that.

'Thai food,' said Mom Klong, 'is rich, varied and of strange flavours. Our best Thai food is the Royal cooking. Because our climate is hot and humid, we do not have much appetite to eat, so much thought has gone into dishes which titillate the appetite—all the fish of the seas and rivers, birds of the air, leaves and flowers, and spices and herbs. We make a sauce called *Nam Prik Maeng* from a perfumed part of the electric beetle—it is often mistaken for the cockroach.'

I often went to Mom Klong and from her learnt much of what I know about Thai food. I discovered how fond they are of sauces, some very hot which send the newcomer shuddering for water, others mild, some sweet-sour. Thais are masters in the art of frying, are very fond of noodles, and cannot live without rice.

Like the Japanese, the Thais demand that their food should please the eye, the nose and the taste buds. A great deal of attention, therefore, has been given to the study of beautifying food. There are schools where girls are taught 'root or flower and vegetable sculpture', or how to carve roots and vegetables, especially ginger, into exquisite flowers. In a country where orchids are two-a-penny, a table decorated with them shows no extra thought, not like 'flowers' beautifully carved from edible roots. In Thailand you do eat the daisies.

Obviously where there is such a choice of eating the markets must be fabulous. The many markets of Bangkok are just that. The two most famous are the Sunday market and the floating market.

One does not attempt to hurry in the market—it would not be much use if one did. Shoppers are there not only to buy but also to enjoy their buying. Some stop and buy a cup cake from an old woman who mixes her batter as she squats on the ground at the same time keeping a wary eye on a small primitive oven perched on the top of an earthenware charcoal fire. She can produce these little yellow cakes as light as any cook with a modern thermostatically controlled stove. Next to her sits another cook, deftly picking up grilled bananas with long tweezers; another fills little packages of green banana leaf with cooked sweet glutinous rice to make another local favourite. Nearby, neatly piled, are her green banana leaves.

Past these one is in the main hub of the market, in the vegetable section. Here they sell an endless variety of vegetables, most of which many of us have never seen before. All kinds of pumpkins, including the sponge or loofah gourd; drumsticks and water chestnuts; Chinese lettuces, cabbage and aubergines, from the large purple kinds to the small and green ones like unripe tomatoes. Wild figs, mild and pale green chillies and scarlet hot ones. Varieties of cucumbers, strange little green fellows with a sour flavour, and others which taste as though salted.

There are roots of all kinds, large and small; great chunks of *taro* used in so many ways and excellent to make chips or crisps for cocktails; yams and bamboo shoots, beans from China, black beans and chick peas, winged beans which look as though they have flown off the end of a dart; red and white beans, all are there. Garlic is sold in the market fresh or pickled in a mixture of vinegar, salt and a little sugar. The Thais like a sweet-sour flavour. There are chives and onions, shallots and spring (green) onions, a lemon grass which vaguely resembles the onion but has the flavour of the lemon bush. There are jelly mushrooms, fragrant mushrooms and just plain mushrooms. As for leaves, it needs a botanist or a herbalist to understand the cooking of this country. Green leaves and brown; they even eat the flower of the begonia, and why not? There is a story of the princess who introduced a new flower to Thailand—it smelt good, it looked good and for the Thais it also tasted good.

The Thais take their food from the earth and the water. The many *klongs* which used to criss-cross through the town (alas, not many are left now) supplied the people with all kinds of food and medicine —and doubtless malaria as well.

Running through the seasons is an enormous variety of fruit. The Thais make fantastic 'natural' models of the local fruits and pile them together in exotic array in wicker baskets. There is the red, prickly-looking *rambuttan* with its lichee-like exterior (but its 'prickles' are soft); the café au lait coloured *chickoo* with its flavour of fudge; the *durian*, vile of smell but ambrosial in flavour; the custard apple, so aptly named, and mangoes, sweet as a peach but which while still green are sliced and eaten smeared with a fishy sauce, as in the Philippines. There is the papaw, wet and ripe, and the golden-yellow *mapron*. How shall I describe this fruit? It has a large stone, is usually eaten stewed as a *compôte*, the stone carefully removed and the peel skilfully taken off to make a pattern on the fruit when cooked; the peeling is as much an art as the cooking of it. For one month only the *mapron* finds its place in the market, then it disappears for another year. Pineapples and bananas have a longer season, as do the dark red apples, which look better than they taste. There are lichees too which look like round strawberries and *wampis*, a citrus fruit the size of a marble, the flavour a cross between a grape and a gooseberry.

From fruit to spices, those we know and many more. Star anise, favourite of the Chinese and Thais alike; poppyseeds and cumin; coriander and peppercorns. There are piles of crystallized or rock sugar, mounds of white palm sugar which looks like thick, sweet condensed milk; ginger and limes; dried chillies and mounds of thick, rich smelling sauces and fish pastes, the basis of so many Thai sauces and, of course, fresh juicy coconuts.

Great slabs of red meat, thin smoked beef, like the Balkan *pasturma*, and spicy sausages are there. There is smoked and dried fish, some looking like overfed kippers, some like small mackerel. Thailand's coastline and rivers provide plenty of fish, with prawns, shrimps, lobsters, and black turtles with vicious-looking tails. The favourite local fish is the thin silvery *tu*, some five inches long. There is also the true herring. Fish is cheap. Snobs in Bangkok have told me they never eat fish just because it is so cheap. There is a saying: 'In the water we have fish, in the fields we have rice,' denoting the prosperity of this country. If someone is sick, they say: 'He cannot eat fish and rice.'

Also there are mounds of dead electric beetles which find their way into many a dish. But it is not likely that the kindly 'Thais will mention this fact to the enquiring foreigner, unless persistent. One might recognize the bowls of ants' eggs, pickled with onions, salt and sugar, and very much appreciated. There are edible frogs, smoked lizard and roasted lizard eggs, very rich and full of vitamins; quails' eggs as well as the lowly ducks' and chickens' eggs.

The floating market is unique. Up and down the wide river go the freighters and storeboats, sampans, up-country boats, rice boats and floating restaurants. The waterways are narrow, lined with godowns, with houses, perhaps a temple and shops jutting over the water. Here are hundreds of small craft; whole families live and die, work and love, in these small boats and houses on the river. Orchids crowd the fences, great brown jars gleam in the sunlight and people, indifferent to the visitor's prying eye, go about their ways.

THAI SAUCE (*Nam Prik*)

Nam prik is a spicy sauce made of chillies and garlic and is eaten with side dishes of raw vegetables, blossoms, including orchids, eggs, fish, cooked vegetables and lotus stems. It is the most favoured dish among the Thais and can lay claim to being the national dish of Thailand, as it is the food of all classes. However, *nam prik* is not always the foreigners' favourite dish. It can be likened rather to a cross between the French hors-d'œuvre and a salad served with a pungent sauce.

It is an inexpensive dish eaten with everyone sitting around the table or on the floor, with a plate of rice in front of each person. A bowl of *nam prik* is placed in the centre of the table with all the side dishes around it. The food is eaten with a little of the *nam prik*, followed by a spoonful or handful of the rice. Each one selects the item of food he likes and combinations can be made by placing different bits of food on a lettuce leaf, adding a few drops of the *nam prik* sauce, then folding the leaf into a bite-size package. This is placed whole in the mouth.

As with most sauces, *nam prik* has its variations. Some of these are so hot that the unfortunate newcomer to the *nam prik* scene dashes off for the nearest tap of cold water to quench the burning fire. Often it is the large number of chillies which scare away the non-Thai. But it is the mark of a good cook to make a good *nam prik* sauce, and probably no two cooks make it in the same manner. Basic recipe of the Princess Sibpan Sonakul:

1 tablespoon (1¼) dry salted shrimps (smoked boneless herring can take the place of the shrimp)	a little brown sugar
	1–2 tablespoons (1¼–2½) lime juice or lemon
3–5 cloves garlic, coarsely crushed	½–1 teaspoon (⅔–1¼) soy sauce
½ tablespoon (⅔) shrimp or anchovy paste	hot chillies or tabasco to taste

All these ingredients are pounded in a mortar or in a blender until fairly smooth, but never absolutely so as little bits of the garlic and chillies should be observed when the sauce is served.

With the *nam prik* are served as side dishes roasted, fried, fresh or salted fish; raw cucumbers and small aubergines; any raw or pickled vegetables except mustard pickles; boiled shrimps or smoked fish; cooked green beans; hard-boiled eggs, shelled and fried in deep fat until they are crisp and puffed on the outside; lettuce leaves and other green, leafy vegetables, and spring (green) onions, raw or fried; omelette, especially one flavoured with green herbs.

Salted crabs, salted fish, are also used with *nam prik*.

CHICKEN, SHRIMP, PORK AND CUCUMBER SOUP (*Kang Ron*)

8 servings:

1½ tablespoons (2) each raw chicken, shrimps and pork, chopped
1 cup (1¼) cucumber, peeled and chopped
2 tablespoons (2½) fat or oil
garlic to taste, chopped
1 onion, finely chopped
1 teaspoon (1¼) ground coriander seeds
pepper
2–3 teaspoons (2½–3¾) nam pla (see page

242) or soy sauce flavoured with anchovy essence
4 pints (10 cups) stock
3–4 tablespoons (3¾–5) mushrooms, chopped
dash of monosodium glutamate
2 eggs, beaten
fresh coriander or parsley, finely chopped

Heat the fat and fry the garlic, onion, coriander and pepper. Cook over a slow heat until the onion is soft but not brown. Add the *nam pla*, then the chicken, shrimps and pork. Fry over a high heat, stirring all the while until the meat is just browned. Add the stock; the cucumbers, mushrooms and monosodium glutamate, cover the pan and bring all this to the boil. Lower the heat and cook gently for 20 minutes. Immediately before serving pour in the beaten eggs and slowly stir into the stock. Serve the soup generously sprinkled with coriander or parsley.

NOODLE SOUP (*Kang Wunsen Chud*)

This is rather more than a soup, it is almost a main course.

10–12 servings:

1 lb. rice noodles or vermicelli
1 chicken, the flesh stripped from the bones
salt, pepper and monosodium glutamate to taste

a few celery leaves, finely chopped
2 cups (2½) bean sprouts
2 spring (green) onions, finely chopped

Put the chicken carcass, skin and any spare bits of the chicken into a large saucepan, add 2 quarts of water (10 cups) and bring this to the boil. Lower the heat and simmer for an hour. Drain the stock and return it to the pan. Bring again to the boil. Put the raw chicken meat twice through the fine blade of a mincer. Mix with salt to taste, break off small lumps and form into small balls.

Add salt, pepper and monosodium glutamate to the chicken stock and when the stock is boiling drop the chicken balls into it. Cook slowly for about 10 minutes. In the meantime break the noodles into small pieces and add these to the soup. Bring again to the boil, add the celery leaves, the bean sprouts and the onions. Simmer for a few minutes longer as the vegetables should be only half-cooked.

Rice noodles cook in a few minutes. If using vermicelli, cook this in boiling water until tender before adding it to the pan.

MIXED VEGETABLE, PORK AND PRAWN SOUP (*Kang Chud*)

6 servings:

½ cup (⅔) mixed vegetables, diced
½ cup (⅔) lean pork, diced
½ cup (⅔) prawns or shrimps or chicken
   meat, diced
3 pints (7½ cups) water

salt, pepper
soy sauce
monosodium glutamate
spring (green) onions, finely sliced

Bring the water to the boil, add salt and pepper and the remaining ingredients with soy sauce and monosodium glutamate to taste. Boil until all the ingredients are cooked and serve garnished generously with spring onions.

PRAWN SOUP (*Tom Yam Goong*)

6 servings:

4 large prawns, peeled and cut into small
   pieces
3 pints (7½ cups) chicken stock
2 stalks lemon grass (see page 242)
1 teaspoon (1¼) nam pla (see page 241) or
   soy sauce mixed with anchovy essence

1 teaspoon (1¼) chilli paste (nam prik)
   (see page 90)
3–4 chillies or cayenne pepper
1 teaspoon (1¼) monosodium glutamate
fresh coriander or parsley, finely chopped
   as a garnish

Heat the stock to boiling point, add the lemon grass and simmer for several minutes. Add the remaining ingredients, except the garnish, and stir well. When the prawns are red the soup is ready. Serve sprinkled with coriander or parsley.

   Failing large prawns, use the equivalent in small prawns or shrimps.

   If using ready-cooked prawns, put these into the soup almost immediately before serving.

   Usually served in a charcoal heated brazier of the steamboat type.

STUFFED CRABS (*Poo Cha*)

6 servings:

6 cooked crabs
1 teaspoon (1¼) each of pounded garlic,
   pepper and coriander seeds
½ cup (⅔) coconut or cow's milk
1 large egg, yolk and white separated

nam pla (see page 242) or a mixture of soy
   sauce and anchovy essence to taste
coriander leaves or parsley, coarsely
   chopped
fat for deep frying, preferably pork fat

Take all the meat from the crab shells and put it in a bowl. Mix the pounded ingredients with the milk and the egg white. Add this to the crabmeat and flavour with *nam pla*. Fill the crab shells with this mixture. Beat the egg yolk and with this paint the crabmeat stuffing. Garnish with coriander. Fry in deep hot fat until brown, 3–5 minutes.

FISH IN A RED SAUCE (*Pla Num Deang*)

2 servings:

1 lb. fish
4–5 tablespoons (5–6¼) cooking oil
1 onion, chopped
1 tablespoon (1¼) tomato paste

½ cup (⅔) water
1 tablespoon (1¼) mild vinegar
salt, pepper

Heat the oil and brown the onion, add the tomato paste and the water, vinegar, salt and pepper and stir to a sauce. Add the fish, cover and cook until tender. Serve hot. In Thailand they use *pla kapong* for this recipe, a fish similar to mullet.

CURRY PASTE (*Kaeng Ped*)

A number of Thai recipes call for curry paste. Here is a recipe from the Princess Sibpan Sonakul. It is a bit fiery but it can be modified simply by using less peppercorns or chillies. I give the paste as she does, and where ingredients are called for which we are unable to obtain, omit. It will still be a good curry paste.

7–10 dried chillies, split and seeded or chilli powder
1 teaspoon (1¼) salt
1 teaspoon (1¼) peppercorns
2 teaspoons (2½) cumin seeds
2 teaspoons (2½) fresh coriander, chopped
½ teaspoon (⅔) lemon or lime peel, grated
2 tablespoons (2½) lemon grass, finely chopped

1 tablespoon (1¼) finely shredded kha (soapnut, see page 246)
2 tablespoons (2½) each garlic and shallot, finely chopped
1 teaspoon (1¼) salted shrimp paste or soy sauce

Soak the chillies in water (this makes them easier to pound) and then pound together with salt to a paste. Add the remaining ingredients in the order given. The idea of this is that you pound away until the paste is very fine. This is normally done in a mortar with a pestle. It can be achieved easily in a blender. Each cook makes curry paste according to his own inclination.

CHICKEN CURRY (*Kai-Ped*)

6 servings:

1 large chicken, cut into serving pieces
7 cups (8¾) coconut milk (see page 238)
curry paste (see page 13)
2 tablespoons (2½) nam pla (see page 242)
1 teaspoon (1¼) salt

pepper
1 cup (1¼) sweet basil
10 fresh chillies, seeded and split or chilli powder

To make the coconut milk, use 2 whole grated coconuts or 1 lb. desiccated coconut. Pour the coconut milk into a saucepan, bring it to a gentle boil and stir. Let it boil gently for 5 minutes. Take out half and put aside. Continue gently boiling the remainder in the pot for anther 15 minutes. Add the chicken pieces and continue to gently boil for another 10 minutes. Add the curry paste, the *nam pla*, salt and the remaining coconut milk. Let it cool until the chicken is tender. Add pepper to taste, basil and the chillies. Cook another 5–10 minutes and serve with rice.

The quantity of chillies can be reduced. A Thai curry is meant to be hot but tempered with the coconut milk. The addition of basil is very unusual.

GRILLED MARINATED CHICKEN (*Gal Yang*)

3–4 servings:

1 3-lb. chicken	Sauce:
1 lb. grated or desiccated coconut to make	½ cup (⅔) roasted, unsalted peanuts
3–4 cups (3¾–5) coconut milk	1 red chilli or cayenne pepper
pinch ground turmeric	3 cloves garlic
8 cloves garlic or to taste	½ teaspoon (⅔) salt
½ teaspoon (⅔) ground coriander seeds	1 tablespoon (1¼) soft brown sugar
10 chilli peppers or chilli powder	¼ cup (⅓) wine or cider vinegar
salt	

Make a thick coconut milk (*see* page 238) from the coconut. Cut the chicken into pieces for grilling.

Dust with turmeric, not too much or it becomes curried chicken. Mix the garlic, coriander and peppers and salt together. Put into a mortar or a blender, add some of the coconut milk, and pound this mixture to a paste. Add the remaining coconut milk, pour everything into a bowl, add the pieces of chicken and leave it several hours or overnight. Drain and dry the chicken and grill in any of the usual ways, preferably over charcoal and serve with the sauce. To prepare this, pound all the sauce ingredients together in a mortar or blender, mix with the vinegar to a paste and pour the sauce over the hot grilled chicken.

PEPPERED CHICKEN (*Kai Yang*)

2–4 servings:

1 tender chicken	6 cloves garlic, crushed
1 tablespoon (1¼) crushed peppercorns	a few coriander roots and leaves or
2 tablespoons (2½) salt or to taste	parsley, finely chopped

Blend all the flavouring ingredients thoroughly and rub these well into the chicken. Leave for an hour, rub any of the seasonings back which might have fallen off the chicken, then roast or grill it in the usual manner.

So many recipes in the world are reminiscent of others. This is similar to the highly garlicked grilled chicken eaten in the Middle East and served with watercress. Small grilling chickens can be treated as above and grilled instead of being roasted.

PIGEON IN A PUNGENT SAUCE (*Nok Pilap Priew-Hwan*)

2–4 servings:

4 pigeons, plucked and cleaned
2 tablespoons (2½) mild vinegar
1 tablespoon (1¼) sugar
2 tablespoons (2½) soy sauce
½ tablespoon (⅔) flour
2–3 tablespoons (2½–3¾) fat for frying

2–4 cloves garlic, crushed
1 small cucumber
1 onion, chopped
2–3 tomatoes, peeled and chopped
1–2 sweet peppers, seeded and chopped
coriander or parsley, finely chopped

Cut each pigeon into half.

Mix the vinegar, sugar, soy sauce and flour to a paste. Heat the fat, fry the garlic until brown, add the pigeons and fry them for a few minutes. Add the vegetables and finally the paste. Stir well and cook gently until the pigeons are tender. Serve garnished with coriander.

THAI CRISPY NOODLES (*Mi Krob*)

This is a dish of rice noodles fried until crisp and garnished generously with a mixture of prawns, pork and vegetables.

4–6 servings:

1 lb. Chinese rice noodles or vermicelli
1 small onion, finely chopped
5 cloves garlic
½ yellow bean cake, thinly sliced (optional)
8 oz. lean pork, thinly sliced
1 lb. chicken meat, thinly sliced
3–4 large shelled prawns, thinly sliced
2 tablespoons (2½) sugar

6 tablespoons (7½) vinegar
4 tablespoons (5) soy sauce (if possible fish soy) or add anchovy essence to regular soy sauce
a little lime or lemon juice
4–5 chicken or duck eggs
fresh bean sprouts, as desired
pork fat for deep frying

Scald the noodles in rapidly boiling water, drain and leave to dry out on a platter. Drying takes about 30 minutes.

In a large, deep frying pan put plenty of pork fat, let it cook until hot but not too hot. Fry the noodles until they are crisp and light brown. Take from the hot fat and put aside to drain.

Pour out most of the fat from the pan, leaving only enough to cook the remaining ingredients. First add the onion and garlic, stir well and when these are brown add the bean cake, pork, chicken and prawns. Continue stirring until these ingredients are cooked. Add the sugar, vinegar, soy sauce and juice and stir all the while. When all this is cooked the result should be salty, sweet and sour. Now break in the eggs, stir and cook until these become a thick layer. Slowly add the fried noodles and bean sprouts and stir until all are well mixed together.

This is *mi krob*. It is garnished with finely chopped fresh coriander, finely chopped chives, chopped red chillies, and grated orange peel, which is the nearest we can get to the local *soma*, a tiny bitter orange like the *kumquat*. Instead of cooking the bean sprouts with the noodles, they can be cooked separately and used as a garnish.

BEEF WITH CORIANDER SEEDS (*Nue Luk Pukchee*)

4–6 servings:

2 lb. beef
¼ cup (⅓) coriander seeds, toasted
⅓ cup (scant ½) soy sauce
1½ teaspoons (2) salt
1¼ teaspoons (1¾) pepper or to taste

1½ tablespoons (2) sugar
½ cup (⅔) oil
3–4 potatoes, peeled and diced
1 cup (1¼) onion, diced
⅓ cup (scant ½) water

Thinly slice the beef into 2 × 4-inch pieces. Rub the coriander seeds, soy sauce, salt, pepper and sugar into the beef slices. Let this stand for about 1 hour. Heat the oil over a good heat in a frying pan or skillet. Add the beef and let it brown fairly well. Arrange the pieces of meat in the centre of the pan, mix the potatoes and onion together and put this mixture on either side of the meat. Add the water, cover the pan and simmer for about 30 minutes or until the meat is tender.

The beef should be served in the dish in which it is cooked.

SWEET-SOUR BEEF (*Pad Preny Van*)

4–5 servings:

1½–2 lb. fillet beef, thinly sliced
1 tablespoon (1¼) garlic, finely chopped
4 oz. (1 cup) lard or pork fat
1 large onion, finely chopped
1 cup (1¼) cucumber, peeled and chopped
1 large tomato, peeled and finely chopped
2–6 red chillies, seeded and sliced or chilli powder

1 tablespoon (1¼) each sugar, soy sauce and vinegar
pepper
1 tablespoon (1¼) cornflour (cornstarch)
6 spring (green) onions, cut into strips
fresh coriander or parsley, chopped

Heat the fat and fry the garlic until brown. Add the beef and as it browns add the onion, stir, add the cucumber, tomato and chillies in this order. Stir well. Make a sweet-sour mixture from the sugar, soy, pepper and vinegar. Add this to the pan and stir well. Mix the cornflour with enough water to make a thin paste. Add to the pan and stir until the sauce thickens. Add the spring onions and coriander. Continue cooking for 30 minutes.

SWEET PORK AND EGGS (*Mu Wan*)

4–6 servings:

2 lb. pork
6 hard-boiled eggs, whole or halved
2 tablespoons (2½) oil or lard
3 tablespoons (3¾) brown sugar

¼ cup (⅓) nam pla (see **page 242**)
2 cups (2½) water
sliced fried shallots, spring (green) onions
   or onions

Cut the pork into pieces. Heat the oil, add sugar and *nam pla* and cook until this is thick and dark, like caramel. Add the water, bring this to the boil and add the pork. Cook uncovered over a low heat until the pork is tender. Add the eggs and continue cooking until these are hot. Arrange in a serving dish sprinkled with the shallots. Serve with rice. This is a kind of stew.

CUCUMBER SALAD (*Yam*)

The Thais have a number of pleasing salads which they call *yam*; they are quite unlike our Western salads. Among the *yam*, pronounced 'yum' by the way, is one of meat and roses. Another, called Galloping Horses, with oranges and pork.

2–3 servings:

2–3 small cucumbers, peeled and shredded
2–3 teaspoons (2½–3¾) onion, minced
1¼ tablespoons (2) salted dry shrimps,
   pounded
Dressing:
1 tablespoon (1¼) each lime or lemon juice

and soy sauce mixed with anchovy
   essence
Garnish:
red chillies, finely chopped and seeded or
   chilli powder

At the point of serving, mix all these ingredients (except garnish) together. Sprinkle the red chillies on top. Failing dried shrimps use potted. One medium-sized European cucumber approximates 2–3 small Eastern.

GREEN MANGO or APPLE SALAD (*Yam*)

2–3 servings:

2 big green mangoes or 3–4 green cooking
   apples
1 teaspoon (1¼) salt
¾ tablespoon (1) peanut or vegetable oil
¾ tablespoon (1) each shredded garlic and
   shallots
½ cup (⅔) lean pork, finely chopped
¾ tablespoon (1) dried salted shrimps,
   pounded

¾ tablespoon (1) soy sauce flavoured with
   anchovy essence
¾ tablespoon (1) peanuts, roasted and
   crushed
½ teaspoon (⅔) soft brown sugar
pepper

Grate the mangoes or apples into long strips, mix with the salt to remove some of the sour taste, then wash the pieces and squeeze gently to dry. Put into a large bowl.

Heat the oil and fry the garlic and shallots separately and when crisp take from the pan. Put aside; in the same fat quickly fry the pork, add the shrimps, the sauce, peanuts and sugar and stir well. Just before serving the salad, mix this sauce thoroughly into the grated fruit. Add salt and pepper, a little more sugar, if taste demands, the garlic and shallots. The Thais sprinkle finely chopped red chillies over the top.

Instead of dried salted shrimps, potted shrimps could be used, and spring (green) onions in place of shallots.

THAI CUSTARD (*Ma Praw Sankaya*)

Thai sweets are interesting and good but not easy to explain without going into considerable detail. The following custard should be steamed in small green coconut shells but, failing these, a pumpkin may be used.

4–6 servings:

1 pumpkin about 9–10 in. in diameter	½ cup (⅔) scalded cream
1 package shredded coconut or 1 whole coconut, grated	6 eggs, lightly beaten
1 cup (1¼) milk	½ cup (⅔) soft brown sugar

Cut off the top of the pumpkin and scoop out the seeds and pulp; leave the sides fairly thick. If necessary wash and drain well. Mix the coconut and milk, bring to a boil and cook. Squeeze all the milk from the coconut, strain it and discard the coconut—this will give 2 cupfuls (2½) of thick, rich liquid. Combine the coconut milk with the cream. Add the eggs and sugar and whisk until blended. Pour the custard into the pumpkin and put it in a steamer, arranging it carefully so that it cannot fall over. Cook over a very low heat until the custard is set. When set, and this can be tested with a knife inserted into the custard, take the pumpkin from the pan and put it aside to cool. It can be sliced in the same manner as one slices a pie if the pumpkin is shallow, otherwise the custard is taken out as from a dish.

If green coconuts are available, cut off the tops and then pour the mixture into 3 or 4 of these and steam in the same manner.

Malaysia

I flew from Singapore in a tiny aeroplane over lush, green paddy fields to Malacca which I shall always remember for its warm reception, my entry into several Malaysian homes and the quantity of food consumed.

Malay food is not easy to find except in Malay homes. As far as hotels and restaurants are concerned there are usually dining-rooms for European-style food and another for Chinese. This could not be adequately explained except that the Malay cooks do not care to share their recipes. I was told that many Malay culinary secrets are dying out, their owners preferring to die with them. Ah well, this is not unusual in other countries.

There are three main types of cooking in Malaysia—Malay, Chinese and Indian. The Malays are Muslims and they have but one religious taboo—they do not eat pork. The Chinese in some parts of the country refuse to eat beef or mutton on religious grounds, and the Indians, as always, retain their own eating taboos and their own style of cooking.

Formerly the three types of cooking remained distinct, as did the communities. But modern conditions, re-thinking and higher education among the young is changing all this. In cities like Kuala Lumpur and Penang these changes are very noticeable. As an example there has come to be a Malaysian-Chinese style of cooking where far more spices and chillies are used than is usual in orthodox Chinese cooking.

By and large three meals daily is the usual quota and the Malays like to eat rice three times a day too. It is an important feature in the Malay diet and is usually served with a variety of exotic additions. Two favourite spicing agents are ginger (both fresh and the dried root) and red chilli pepper. Other favourites are turmeric, giving a yellow tone to food, especially rice, cloves, coriander, tamarind and fenugreek; saffron, mustard, poppyseeds, onions. Garlic and pungent roots find a place in most dishes.

Generally speaking the Chinese community in Malaysia eats very well and thoroughly enjoys eating. I would say this applies equally to the Malays, judging from my own experience. The Chinese, too, consume vast quantities of rice but it is fair to say that all communities are deserting some of the

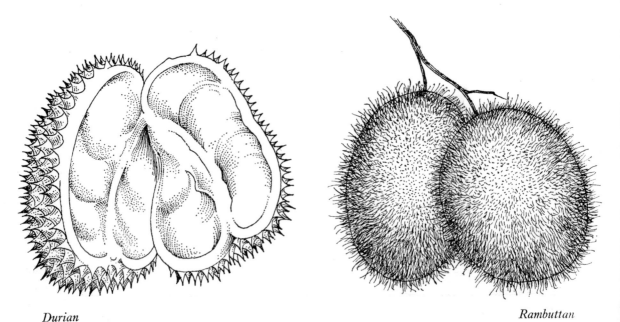

Durian   *Rambuttan*

old-fashioned meals of their ancestors and tending to adopt those of the West. One example is the Western-style breakfast. No longer does the day inevitably start with rice and maybe a light soup. Instead it is rolls and butter or toast and even cereals.

Malaysia is a country of plenty. Plenty of fish, much of it exotic, sea snails, sea slugs, limpets, crabs, oysters and splendid prawns, the latter in such quantities they are the cheapest fish on the market. A Malaysian can hardly conceive of a dish of vegetables without it being flavoured with prawns.

Vegetables and fruits are also plentiful, much of it indigenous. Most shopping is still done in the large central markets where the Malaysian housewife not only buys in the smallest possible quantities, as do the Chinese, but also where everything is fresh. Spices are ground under her enquiring nose, so is the fresh coconut. Coconut is so important to the Malaysian cooks that most of what we are sold here in Britain, and even the United States, is regarded as rancid. It certainly lacks the clean fresh smell of the coconut from Malaysia. Around the market are the dry goods or grocery stores so that shopping is as simple as in the supermarkets but much more colourful.

Most Malaysians are fond of eating the young leaves of many plants. The sweet potato plant produces edible leaves. They like the purple heart of banana, and the soft creamy pulp from the green coconut. Bamboo shoots are popular and so is breadfruit, baked in hot embers and sometimes served with duck or turtle eggs. Pineapples, large and sweet, sweet juicy sugar cane, papaws, wild fruits, all form part of the Malaysian diet. Bananas are bought by the 'hand'. A banana hand is a bunch of bananas as it is cut from the stalk and is composed of a number of 'fingers' or individual bananas. Milk is not popular at all and when it is available it is usually tinned or powdered and an imported product.

Jaggery sugar, a product of the palm tree, is taken in large quantities. It is very sweet and rich with a sweet, sugary odour and there is no real substitute for it in the West. Use either molasses or the darkest, sweetest, softest and most moist sugar when making a Malaysian pudding calling for *jaggery*.

Traditionally Malaysians do not drink alcoholic beverages, although the modern generation is breaking away from this tradition. Tea is the drink of the Chinese, always without milk and sugar. The Malaysians prefer coffee, especially in the morning. During a meal plain water is considered the best drink. There are a number of bottled soft drinks made from local fruits, such as passion fruit or pineapple. Sugar cane water, which is simply the juice of the cane squeezed through a mangle, fresh pineapple juice or green coconut water are prepared by the street vendors. The only alcoholic drink which can be called indigenous is *toddy*, a palm juice containing albuminous matter which readily ferments. From the *toddy* the Malaysians make *arrak* or so-called palm wine, but it bears no likeness to wine (*see* page 65).

FRIED RICE (*Nasi Goreng*)

There are several recipes for a *nasi goreng*; this is a basic one.

6 servings:

2 cups (2½) long grain cooked rice
3 tablespoons (3¾) peanut or vegetable oil
2–3 red chillies, thinly sliced or chilli powder
3 small red onions or 1 white onion, sliced
1 spring (green) onion, sliced
thinly sliced meat, i.e. pork, chicken or beef
shelled fresh prawns

salt, pepper
1 teaspoon (1¼) dark soy sauce
1 teaspoon (1¼) light soy sauce
Garnish:
1 egg, made into a thin omelette, shredded
a little cucumber, pared and finely sliced
a bunch of coriander or parsley, finely chopped
1 red chilli

Heat the oil and fry the first quantity of chillies and all the onion until a light brown. Add the meat and prawns (if using cooked prawns stir these in later). When the meat and prawns are cooked, add the rice, mix well, add salt, pepper and soy sauces, again mix and fry, stirring frequently until thoroughly cooked. (If using cooked prawns, add them at this point and watch that they are not overcooked or they will toughen.) Serve on a large hot platter with the garnish.

PILAU (*Nasi Minyak*)

4–6 servings:

1 cup (1¼) long grain rice
2 oz. (¼ cup) butter
1 small piece finely chopped fresh ginger or 1 teaspoon (1¼) ground
1 in. stick cinnamon or ½ teaspoon (⅔) ground
4 cardamon seeds
4 cloves

2 small chopped onions
1–2 cloves garlic, chopped
3 cups (3¾) hot chicken stock or water
salt
Garnish:
2 tablespoons (2½) seedless raisins
1 tablespoon (1¼) almonds, blanched and slivered

Heat the butter and fry the spices, add the chopped ingredients and fry gently to a golden-brown. Add the hot stock and salt, cover the pan and bring the whole to a boil. Add the rice, cover tightly and continue cooking over a fairly low heat until all the liquid has been absorbed. Stir a little, lower the heat even more and continue cooking until the rice is dry and well cooked. Take the pan from the heat, leave for a while in a warm place to complete the drying (if the rice is not dry enough), remove the whole cinnamon and cloves and serve the pilau garnished with raisins and almonds. Serve with a curry and *sambal*.

CHICKEN SOUP (*Soto Ayam*)

6–8 servings:

1 dressed chicken
1 medium-sized onion, chopped
2 cloves garlic, chopped
salt, pepper
whole chillies or chilli powder, to taste
a little fresh ginger, chopped
1 tablespoon (1¼) soy sauce

Garnish:
1–2 hard-boiled eggs, sliced
potato crisps
carrot, leeks or spring (green) onions, shredded
rice cakes (optional outside of the East)
chillies, finely chopped or cayenne pepper

Put the chicken into a large pan with cold water, between 6 and 8 cupfuls (7½–10). Add the onion, garlic, salt, pepper, chillies and ginger and cook over a moderate heat until the chicken is tender. Take the chicken from the pan, strip the flesh from the bones and cut it into thin strips, almost shredding it. Strain the stock, return it to the pan, add the soy sauce and reheat.

When serving the soup, put some shredded chicken into each bowl, add the garnishes, except the crisps, a little in each plate. Pour the boiling soup over the top, add the crisps and serve at once. It is curious how good potato crisps can taste as a soup garnish. (A crisp is known in the United States as a potato chip.)

COCONUT SOUP (*Sothi*) (Tamil)

3–4 servings:

2 cups (2½) each thick and thin coconut milk (see page 238)
3 small red onions
a few small prawns or shrimps or pieces of white fish
1 tablespoon (1¼) vegetable oil

2 dry red chillies, seeded and chopped
2 fresh green chillies, seeded and chopped
a little star anise (see page 246)
a little powdered turmeric
juice of small lemon

Peel the onions and thinly slice them into rings and cut the rings in half. Wash and shell the prawns and slice, removing the black vein. Heat the oil in a saucepan, add the onion, cook for a few minutes, add the chillies and star anise. Stir all the time with a wooden spoon (the Malaysians use half a coconut shell), and cook until these ingredients are a light brown.

Add the thin coconut milk and the turmeric and bring to a slow boil, stirring all the time for 10 minutes. Add the chopped prawns or alternative ingredients (or a little of all of them) and cook very gently for a further 10 minutes. Add the remaining coconut milk and bring again to boiling point, stirring all the time, until the mixture thickens. Take the soup from the heat, add the juice and serve immediately.

Instead of the two fresh chillies, 1 teaspoonful ($1\frac{1}{4}$) chilli powder may be used.

MEAT COOKED IN A SOY SAUCE (*Nasak Daging*)

3–4 servings:

1 lb. beef or lamb
1 teaspoon ($1\frac{1}{4}$) aniseed
1 teaspoon ($1\frac{1}{4}$) cumin seeds
4 tablespoons (5) oil
2 tomatoes, peeled and quartered
2 red chillies, seeded and split or chilli powder

1 large onion, thinly sliced
2 small red onions (optional)
2 cloves garlic, crushed or chopped
3 tablespoons ($3\frac{3}{4}$) soy sauce
a pinch salt
$\frac{1}{4}$ pint ($\frac{2}{3}$ cup) water

Wash the meat and slice it thinly. Pound the aniseed and cumin seeds to a powder and rub this into the meat. (Or use powdered spices.) Heat the oil and, as it begins to smoke, add the meat and fry until it browns. Add the remaining ingredients and cook gently until it is tender. Serve the meat in the sauce with rice.

FISH WRAPPED IN BANANA LEAVES (*Otak-Otak*)

This is an important Malaysian dish. Instead of banana leaves, which are not usually available in the West, use aluminium foil.

4–6 servings:

$1\frac{1}{2}$ lb. firm white fish, without bones
24 shelled prawns or large shrimps
3 banana leaves or foil
Sauce:
1 cup ($1\frac{1}{4}$) grated or desiccated coconut
2 cloves garlic

4 dried chilli peppers or $\frac{1}{2}$ teaspoon ($\frac{2}{3}$) chilli powder
a good pinch ground turmeric
salt, pepper
$\frac{1}{4}$ cup ($\frac{1}{3}$) thick coconut milk (see page 238) or fresh cream

Lightly roast the coconut in a thick, dry pan until a golden brown. Pound the garlic, chillies, turmeric and the browned coconut to a paste. Add salt and pepper and mix with the coconut milk. Pour this mixture into the top of a double boiler and cook slowly until it thickens. Leave to cool. This makes the sauce.

Clean, skin and cut the fish into strips. Spread out the banana leaves or foil on a table. Have toothpicks ready if using leaves. Mix the prawns into the coconut sauce and spread some of this mixture on each piece of leaf and arrange the fish on top. Fold the leaves into neat packages, carefully tucking in the sides. Secure the leaves with toothpicks; foil, of course, secures itself.

Steam between 20 to 30 minutes. Serve the *otak-otak* hot, in the leaves or foil in which they are cooked. About 4–6 bundles will be made, but much depends on the size of the pieces of leaf or foil.

PRAWNS COOKED IN COCONUT MILK (*Udang Masak Lemak*)

3–4 servings:

12 prawns scampi size (U.S.A. butterfly   cooking oil
  size)   a good pinch turmeric powder
1 onion   1 cup (1¼) thick coconut milk (see page 238)

Shell and wash the prawns and remove the black veins. Peel and slice the onion finely and cut the slices into half. Heat a little oil and fry the onion and the turmeric. Add the coconut milk and the prawns and cook over a moderate heat until these are pink and the liquid thickens without curdling.

    This dish is served with plain boiled rice. If fresh prawns are not available, cook the onion and coconut milk for 10 minutes, add the cooked prawns and let them simply become hot. Shrimps can be cooked in the same manner. White fish, cut into cubes, can be used instead or to make more of the dish added to the prawns.

CURRIED PRAWNS (*Kari Udang*)

At first sight this recipe looks as though it could not be attempted outside of Malaysia; but substitutes are possible if the eastern products are not available. Instead of *blachan*, any strongly flavoured fish paste can be used; for candle nuts, any kind of oily nut, such as peanut or Brazil, or this item can be omitted. Tamarind, although not impossible by any means to buy, can be replaced by lemon juice or a mild vinegar; good quality grated coconut can take the place of fresh, and lemon balm or lemon rind instead of lemon grass.

2 servings:

1 lb. shelled prawns or large shrimps
½ cup (⅔) tamarind juice or 1 tablespoon (1¼) lemon juice
1 cup (1¼) thick coconut milk (see page 238)
1 cup (1¼) thin coconut milk (see page 238)
salt, sugar
oil for frying
Paste:
6 red chillies, seeded and finely chopped

1 piece lemon grass or substitute, finely chopped
1 small piece fresh ginger
3 cloves garlic
4 candle nuts (see page 237) or substitute
1 square toasted blachan or 1 tablespoon (1¼) shrimp paste mixed with anchovy essence

Pound all the paste ingredients together until smooth. If using a blender, add a little water.

    Heat a little oil in a saucepan and fry the paste for 2 minutes. Add the prawns and stir the paste and prawns together. Simmer for 5 minutes, then gradually add the thin coconut milk, stirring all the time. Simmer for 20 minutes, then add salt and sugar. Finally stir in the tamarind juice and the thick coconut milk. Continue simmering until the prawns are completely impregnated with the flavour of the curry; do not let the mixture boil, otherwise the prawns will toughen and the coconut milk curdle.

    Serve with rice and prawn *krupauks* or crackers available in the Oriental provision stores.

    In many parts of the Far East prawns are plentiful and reasonably cheap. They are always sold fresh and never ready cooked.

VEGETABLE CURRY (*Masak Lemak*)

2 servings:

1½ lb. cabbage or carrots, turnips, etc.
2 small red onions or 1 white
2 fresh red chillies or chilli powder to taste
1 cup (1¼) each thick and thin coconut milk (see page 238)

1 small potato
a little anchovy essence
salt
1 teaspoon (1¼) ground turmeric

Slice the onions and chillies, discarding the seeds. Wash and cut the cabbage into 1-inch pieces. Put the thin coconut milk, potato, anchovy essence, onion, chillies, salt and turmeric into a pan and cook until the potato is half-cooked. Add the cabbage, cook for 5 to 7 minutes, then add the remaining thick coconut milk, bring to a slow boil, stir and remove from the heat. Serve hot with rice.

CABBAGE ROLLS (*Masar Gobeh*)

4–6 servings:

12 whole cabbage leaves, large and un-broken
½ lb. minced (ground) chicken
¼ lb. minced (ground) prawns or shrimps
¼ lb. cooked white fish
2 tablespoons (2½) soy sauce

a dash both pepper and monosodium glutamate
oil for frying
1 cup (1¼) water or stock
1 teaspoon (1¼) cornflour (cornstarch)

Drop the leaves into boiling water and simmer for 5 minutes, take from the pan, lay each leaf separately on a table and cool. Mix the chicken, prawns, white fish, 1 tablespoonful (1¼) soy sauce, pepper and monosodium glutamate. Blend thoroughly. Put a small portion of the filling on to each leaf, roll carefully, tucking in the sides; secure with a toothpick or thread by simply wrapping this round and round the leaf, leaving the ends loose.

Heat a little oil and fry the rolls until brown. Add the water, the remaining soy sauce and simmer for 30 minutes. Take the rolls from the pan and put aside but keep hot.

Mix the cornflour with water to a thin paste, add this to the gravy, bring to the boil and cook, stirring all the while, for a few minutes until the gravy is thick. Pour this over the cabbage rolls.

If using thread, remove this before serving.

FRIED MEAT WITH PEANUT SAUCE (*Goreng Daging Kuah Kachung*)

3 servings:

1 lb. lamb
1 tablespoon (1¼) soy sauce
salt
1 teaspoon (1¼) sugar
1 small piece fresh ginger, chopped

Peanut sauce:
2 tablespoons (2½) peanuts
4–5 chilli peppers, seeded and chopped
oil for frying
¼ pint (⅔ cup) water
salt, sugar

Clean the meat and cut it into small pieces, beating each piece with a back of a knife. Mix together (or put in a blender) soy sauce, salt, sugar and ginger and marinate the meat in this mixture for 30 minutes, longer if time permits.

To make the sauce, roast the peanuts in a dry pan, remove the loose brown skins and finely grind the nuts. Pound the chillies. Heat a very little oil, fry the pounded chillies for a minute, add the peanuts, water, salt and sugar and cook for a few minutes. Keep this hot.

In another pan heat a little more oil and lightly fry the meat on both sides. Add the marinade plus a little water, if necessary. Simmer the meat until it is tender, add the sauce and serve hot.

Ready roasted and salted peanuts do very well in this recipe and save time. Cayenne pepper may be used instead of pounded chillies, but make the sauce sufficiently pepper-hot to be piquant.

FRIED EGGS WITH SOY SAUCE (*Goreng Telor*)

2–4 servings:

4 eggs
1–2 large onions
2 cloves garlic
1 chilli pepper, seeded or chilli powder to
   taste

½-in. piece fresh ginger or a little ground
1 tablespoon (1¼) oil
1 tablespoon (1¼) lemon juice or vinegar
½ pint (1¼ cup) hot water
1 tablespoon (1¼) soy sauce

Finely chop the onions, garlic, chilli pepper and ginger. Pound to a paste, a blender will do this. Heat the oil in a pan, break in the eggs, one by one, and fry. Take the eggs carefully from the pan and put aside. Fry the paste, add the lemon juice, water and soy sauce. Stir this to a thick sauce, add the fried eggs and heat for 1 minute only.

POACHED EGGS (*Tumis Telor*)

2–4 servings:

4 eggs
2 red onions or 1 white
a little blachan (see page 237) or anchovy
   essence
2 cloves garlic

salt
1–2 red chillies or chilli powder
1 tablespoon (1¼) oil
2 cups (2½) strained stock
a little vermicelli, cut into small pieces

Peel the onions and chop them finely. Pound together with the *blachan*, garlic and salt. Chop the chillies and remove the seeds. Heat the oil in a saucepan and fry the chillies and paste for a few minutes, gradually add the stock, bring to the boil. Add the vermicelli and cook for 10 minutes. Break the eggs, each separately, and carefully drop into the hot liquid. Cook gently until the eggs set. Serve in a deep dish, or in the pan in which the eggs were cooked.

BEEF SIDE DISH (*Sambal Daging Lembu*)

¼ lb. minced (ground) beef
1 tablespoon (1¼) cooking oil
4 fresh chillies, seeded and pounded

1 large onion, diced
salt to taste

Heat the oil and fry the chillies and onion. Add salt and meat, stir and cook until the meat is brown.

This rather simple *sambal* is served with rice but can also be used as a sandwich spread.

If fresh chillies are not available, use chilli powder or cayenne pepper.

SALAD DRESSING (*Kuah Lada*)

2–3 red chillies, seeded, chopped and pounded
1 clove garlic, pounded
½ teaspoon (⅔) salt

1 tablespoon (1¼) vinegar
2 tablespoons (2½) water
pinch sugar

Pound the chillies and garlic together to a paste adding the salt as you pound. Add the remaining ingredients. Or put it all in a blender.

CUCUMBER SALAD (*Achar Timun*)

2 servings:

1 small or ½ a large cucumber
¾ tablespoon (1) dried prawns or shrimps
1 small onion, peeled and thinly sliced
1 red chilli, seeded and sliced or chilli powder to taste

salt
½ cup (⅔) thick coconut milk (see page 238)

Wash and thinly peel the cucumber and cut into 2-inch lengths. With a small knife cut thinly round and round the circumference towards the centre. Roll up the strip and thinly slice. Repeat with all the cucumber pieces. Wash and pound the prawns. Put the cucumber, onion, chilli, prawns and salt into a glass dish, add the coconut milk, chill and serve.

If dried prawns or shrimps are not possible, use potted or cooked shrimps, plus a little anchovy essence.

SWEET SAMBAL (*Sambal Manis*)

A sweet *sambal* that can be served with almost any curry.

2 tablespoons (2½) roasted peanuts
a little blachan (see page 237) or a highly flavoured shrimp paste
4 chillies, seeded and dried

6 red onions or 1 large white
oil for frying
1 slice pineapple, chopped
salt, sugar

Pound the peanuts, discarding the skins. Toast the *blachan*—ignore this advice if using shrimp paste. Pound the chillies and onion, fry in a little oil for a few moments, add the pineapple, *blachan* or shrimp paste and peanuts. Mix thoroughly and fry for a few minutes; add salt and sugar, stir and serve in a small glass dish.

If using tinned pineapple, drain it well and do not use any sugar. The chillies and onion can be pounded in a blender. Failing *blachan*, or even a strong shrimp paste, mix some anchovy essence into a mild shrimp paste or into soy sauce.

COCONUT CUSTARD (*Sarikauji*)

4–6 servings:

8 egg yolks or **4 whole eggs**   **2 cups (2½) thick coconut milk** (see **page**
3 oz. (⅓ cup) sugar   **238**)

Whisk the egg yolks with the sugar until thick and creamy. Gradually add the coconut milk and pour this mixture into a lightly greased bowl or mould and cover with wax paper or aluminium foil. Put the bowl into the top of a double-boiler and steam gently until the custard thickens. Leave to cool, then set in a refrigerator.

This custard can also be baked in a very low oven in the same manner as ordinary custard. There are several recipes for *sarikauji*; similar custards are prepared in Indonesia, the Philippines and Thailand.

SAGO PUDDING (*Gula Malacca*)

Gula malacca is a sugar obtained from the coconut palm. It is sweet but has an odd, almost burnt flavour. In this recipe I suggest dark soft brown sugar as a substitute.

4 servings:

½ lb. (1¼ cups) dark, soft brown sugar   **½ lb. (1½ cups) sago**
1 whole coconut or 1 lb. grated coconut   **2 pints (5 cups) water**

If using a whole coconut, break it and scoop out the flesh and grate this finely. Make a very thick milk with the coconut (*see* page 238).

Dissolve the sugar in ½ cup (⅔) of water, put into a saucepan and cook to a thick dark syrup.

Put the sago into a pan, add the remaining water, bring to the boil and cook until the sago is soft and transparent. Put the sago into a fine strainer and hold it under running water, rinsing it until the water runs clear. Pour the sago into a rinsed mould and leave to set.

Turn it out to serve with the *gula malacca* syrup and coconut milk.

Singapore

It is in Singapore that East and West meet on a culinary spree, a truly polyglot city of Chinese, Malays, Indians, Indonesians and Europeans of all nationalities. Each community goes its own culinary way, yet each contributes something to the general fascinating melée of cuisines. The Straits Chinese have evolved their own version of Chinese cooking, which is basically Chinese but with varied extraneous influences which are very robust.

Shopping in Singapore is a joy to one and all, and not in the least to the gastronomically minded. Many Europeans prefer the supermarkets and the cold storage stores, but for those whose culinary tastes lie in the East, the Eastern markets are a haven. Here mingle rich and poor all intent on but one thing, the buying of good food.

The food in the Eastern markets is less elegant, less splendid, certainly less uniform than in the West and no one could call the markets splendid examples of hygiene, but they do offer exciting possibilities to the culinarily adventurous.

On a recent visit to Singapore I spent a happy last hour in the market. I watched the curry man with his curry blends for all occasions. One shopper bought 20 cents' worth of beef curry spices and the curry man scooped up from his stock a bit here, a pinch and a spoonful there with great expertise and handed her a paper package with exactly enough curry spices for one beef curry. Shades, I thought, of India where the cook grinds away on his curry stone. And beef? Never. The next customer wanted fish curry and the curry man handled this request with the same aplomb, choosing different spices. I followed the two women down the alley; both repaired to the coconut-grating man, buying the required quantity of freshly grated coconut.

From spices to fish, not such fun as in Hong Kong but of good quality and absolutely fresh. And then to meat, most of this seemingly from Australia and New Zealand, all neatly labelled and firmly priced—no bargaining here.

I found the pickle section and one stall held my attention for such a long time that the dwarf-size vendor talked to me. She had a veritable cornucopia of ingredients for a witches' brew: dried fish and

miserable-looking dried octopus, withered duck skins and strange esoteric pieces of meat. Dark interesting and potent. Fascinated, I studied it all but nevertheless resisted all blandishments to buy from the tiny saleswoman, a minute witch herself, I guessed. Who knows, thought I suspiciously if I sampled her concoctions I might find myself flying through the air on her besom.

What a pleasure it is to eat in Singapore. First the weather is perfect and one can eat anywhere, from the plush hotel restaurants, where they serve *sole Véronique* or Australian carpet bag steak, a good Sunday curry or an Indonesian *rijsttafel*, to the hundreds, maybe thousands, of Chinese street stalls which line the pavements, clutter the roadway and fill the beaches. These are the haunts of the office and other workers and those who feel that the real way in which to discover Chinese food is to do as the Chinese do. Some streets, such as Albert or Bugis Street, are especially popular for their street-side cooking. Amidst a riot of colour from surrounding markets with an atmosphere of cooking, of noise, this is the district where late diners foregather after the cinema, concerts etc. One may linger at the stall which specializes (and these stalls do specialize) in fish ball soup or perhaps take a bowl of wet noodles with bits of pork, shrimps, vegetables and liver, or maybe nibble at 'thousand-year-old-eggs' (*see* page 175), an oyster omelette, or a bowl of sharks' fin soup.

Amidst the cooked food stalls are the fruit stalls, the vendors prepared to sell fruit by the pound or by the bite-sized piece. As always in the East, the fruit is exotic in appearance and usually in flavour. There are bananas from bright yellow to the deepest red; oranges and mandarins; lichees and a similar fruit called dragons' eye; waxy yellow-green star fruit, not strictly a fruit, a sort of pod with vertical ribs but cool and juicy and flesh which cuts into star-shaped slices; papaws, golden, sweet and deliciously tender; orange persimmons which are so good if eaten at exactly the right time; passion fruit, which always look so ancient; and red *rambuttans* with their curious spiky hedgehog-looking outer skin which is really soft and pliable, the fruit inside being white and sweet with a lichee-like flavour and consistency.

I was also taken to the Great World—there is also a Happy World and a New World, very much alike—an amusement park with, naturally, restaurants to suit all pockets and a mass of eating stalls. If one decides on fish one chooses it from a tank, for no Chinese thinks of settling for a fish he has not personally seen swimming. While this is being cooked one asks the fish vendor to tell the Cantonese duck man that one fancies a leg or so of duck or goose. With a sort of bookmaker's tick-tack signal he sends the message. I have eaten some of the most delicious roast poultry at these Canton duck roasting stalls. The birds are roasted in huge oil drums lined with clay. At the bottom of the drum is a small wood fire with plenty of flame and red hot. The top of the drum is firmly covered and the poultry is hung around the side of the drum, attached to long iron hooks.

We had been invited by a Chinese friend to dine and our dinner was meticulously ordered well in advance. The restaurant was large and its décor of the utmost simplicity, as usual with Chinese restaurants, the emphasis being on food. We sat at a round table, Chinese style and with Chinese etiquette (*see* page 148). Immediately young girls came to offer us steaming hot towels to wipe our hands and faces.

The meal began with chicken stuffed with birds' nest soup and garnished with thin strips of vegetables. It was subtly seasoned. This was followed by sucking pig, the skin roasted, crisp and tender and cut into squares for easy eating with chopsticks.

As soon as we had finished with the skin, the piglet was rushed away for reheating and the next course arrived, ducks' skin, crisp and hot, placed on a pile of vegetables, cooked as only Chinese vegetables can be cooked, *al dente*, surrounded by those thousand-year-old eggs.

(1) *White sea bass*; (2) *pomfret*; (3) *black grouper or garoupa* (4) *milk fish*

All this demolished, steamed pomfret appeared—a favourite in these waters. All through the meal we drank tiny cups of Chinese tea, the cups being refilled as soon as the slightest evidence was shown of the tea having been sipped. The fish was followed by roast chicken and, by this time, I began to wonder how much we could continue to eat. However, there was not much left of the chicken and then the pig was brought back, all his tender succulent flesh cut into minute pieces. It did not seem to me that any of us could take another bite of food but somehow the pig too disappeared and the rice came. In between we had also been served soup, just to keep our taste buds working. Finally, we were brought more hot towels. Thus we knew the end had come. It had all been delicious and, although it seemed we had eaten a lot, we rose from the table pleasantly full but not stuffed.

TA PIN LO (Steamboat, Mongolian *or* Chinese Chafing Dish)

There are many schools of thought on this unusual and entertaining style of cooking. Some recipes are more complicated than others. The one I give is pretty simple and can be adapted easily enough to Western-style utensils. But first I must describe the Chinese chafing dish, called 'Fire Kettle' in Peking and 'Steamboat' elsewhere.

Steamboats vary slightly but the most general pattern, which is found through Mongolia to Tibet, is round with a funnel or chimney in the centre surrounded by a deep 'moat'. This rests on an open-sided container into which charcoal is placed. When the charcoal burns brightly the heat rises up the chimney, the sides of which heat the moat, which contains the liquid for cooking. The charcoal from time to time has to be fanned to keep it red hot. A lid for the moat has a hole in the centre to allow the chimney to stick up above it. (*See* colour plate, page 52.) Usually these steamboats are made of brass or copper, but tin-lined. Tibetan chafing dishes are very elegant with engraved patterns in silver on the brass.

The steamboat is placed in the centre of the table at arms'-length for the guests sitting around. It is important to insulate the table from the charcoal furnace.

If a Chinese-style chafing dish is not available, an electric hot plate, on top of which is placed a large deep pan, can be used instead. But a Peking Fire Kettle is not only decorative, it is a talking point.

Whatever type of chafing dish is used, the serving and eating procedure can be the same.

There are two ways of preparing food for the chafing dish. One is to cook everything in the kitchen and transfer it to the chafing dish on the table. This relegates the steamboat from being a useful utensil to merely a showpiece.

The authentic manner of preparing a chafing dish meal is to arrange all the raw foods on the table in small dishes or trays. Each guest then takes what she or he wants, holds it firmly with chopsticks and dips it into the boiling soup. It thus cooks while one waits. This procedure is sensible as guests select only what they want from the several dishes. The raw food is, of course, cut into small pieces so it can be popped into the mouth with the chopsticks. Being small the pieces cook immediately.

Now chopsticks. Most people can quickly acquire the knack of dealing with them. But I did experiment with fondue forks and chop forks and found these did equally well—and less falls back into the soup. It doesn't matter, however, how much falls back into the soup, as the lost pieces are retrieved later with a soup spoon.

Obviously this form of cooking and eating at the table can be messy. But the Chinese, I am told, measure the success of the dish by the state of the tablecloth afterwards—the messier the more successful. However, they do cautiously use a paper cloth, or one could use a plastic spongeable tablecloth.

It is nicer to use Chinese bowls and dishes in which to put the food. But again, provided dishes are pretty, this is not an essential. The small bits of food are arranged in shallow dishes. Each guest should have a shallow bowl or deep plate, as well as a small bowl for soup, and a soup spoon, Chinese style too if possible. The Chinese versions of these items are so cheap to buy in the West, it seems to me if one is going to the trouble of giving a steamboat party one might as well buy a few Chinese items to make the meal as authentic as possible.

10–12 servings:

1. Enough chicken stock, made from the bones, skin etc. of the chicken, to fill the moat and some over to replenish, if necessary, for the final assault on the soup.
2. Chicken meat which has been stripped from the bones and cut into very thin strips, about $1\frac{1}{2}$ in. in length.
3. About $\frac{1}{4}$ lb. of Chinese noodles. These must be soaked for 30 minutes before being placed on the table on a large plate.
4. About 1 lb. of fresh fish. The Chinese prefer to use fresh prawns but, although these are delicious, it is not essential, any good fresh fish can be used, also cut into thin strips for easy serving.
5. 1 lb. of spinach, thoroughly washed and only the leaves used. Other vegetables which cook rapidly may be used, but always cut into strips or thin rounds. Lotus root is popular but I doubt if it is easily obtainable in the West. It is crisp and cooks easily in the boiling stock.
6. About 1 lb. of liver. This must be cut into fine strips of $1\frac{1}{2}$-in. length.
7. 1 to 2 pairs of kidney, sliced, washed, all the skin and gristle removed, and cut into thin strips.
8. 6 large dried mushrooms, Chinese type. These must be soaked for 30 minutes in warm water, the stems removed and the caps cut into medium-thick slices.
9. A handful of spring (green) onions, split into halves lengthwise.
10. 1 lb. loin of pork, cut into $1\frac{1}{2}$-in. thin strips.
11. 10–12 eggs (in other words, one for each guest), raw and in the shells.
12. About $\frac{1}{2}$–1 lb. fillet of beef, cut into $1\frac{1}{2}$-in. long pieces.

Some people add shredded lettuce and white cabbage.

When arranging the dishes of raw foods, colour schemes are important. For example, the bright red of the beef should be alongside the green of the spinach; onion next to the kidney or liver etc.

Perched proudly in the centre of the table is the steamboat filled with absolutely boiling strained chicken stock. Using chopsticks, guests drop into the stock pieces of the raw ingredients. Then the lid is put on the steamboat but only for a matter of minutes. The lid is then removed and the battle begins. Guests take out from the stock the food they put in, dipping their choice into a sauce (see page 114) before eating. And so continue taking from the bowls of food surrounding the steamboat.

Now the eggs. Sometimes these are beaten by each guest in a small bowl and used as a dip before cooking the raw food in the stock. Others prefer to break their egg into their soup bowl when the time for soup arrives, the hot stock being poured over it, a method I favour. At one steamboat party I attended the eggs were poured into the boiling stock after all the ingredients had been eaten and before the stock was served as soup. These are small items of choice, nothing is rigid.

Should the fire lose its strength, the lid of the steamboat is put on and the charcoal fanned. The interval allows guests time to breathe and talk. A really good steamboat meal can last for two or three hours but usually it is a happy occasion, the challenge of chopsticks making for friendly competition among foreigners.

Small bowls with sauces are put in front of each guest. One has soy sauce, another vinegar and often there is a chilli sauce mixed with hot sesame oil. Other garnishes include sesame oil, Chinese wine, sesame paste, Chinese parsley cut into small pieces, chopped spring onion and shrimp sauce.

Now what to drink with this? Correctly one serves small porcelain cups filled with warm Chinese wine. The cups roughly are the size of coffee cups.

It is also usual at such a meal to offer real Chinese tea, the recipe for making this is in the China section (*see* page 179).

CHICKEN AND CORN SOUP (*Sook Muy Tong*) (Straits Chinese)

4 servings:

1 chicken
1 large tin sweet corn
a dash of pepper
1 teaspoon (1¼) salt
½ tablespoon (⅔) monosodium glutamate

1 tablespoon (1¼) Chinese wine or dry sherry
3 tablespoons (3¾) cornflour (cornstarch)
2 eggs, well beaten

Strip the white meat off the chicken and cut it into very thin strips. Put the remaining chicken into 4 cupfuls (5) water to make a stock. Cook until reduced to 3 cupfuls. Strain. Put the corn into a pan with the chicken stock and bring to the boil. Sprinkle the pepper, salt, monosodium glutamate, wine and cornflour over the meat, then rub it together so that the mixture is absolutely blended. Mix in the beaten eggs. By this time the stock is boiling; let it boil 1 minute more as the heat of the stock alone must cook the chicken meat. Add the chicken meat and at the same time turn off the heat under the pan and stir the mixture well. Serve at once.

LETTUCE AND FISH BALL SOUP (Chinese)

4–6 servings:

12 small fish balls
4 cups (5) fish stock, strained
2 lettuces, washed and finely shredded

1 teaspoon (1¼) salt
pepper

Bring the stock to the boil, add the fish balls, salt and pepper. Then add the lettuce, cook for a few minutes longer and serve hot.

Fish balls:
Mix 1 lb. of mashed, cooked white fish with salt and pepper, a little finely chopped shallot, or onion, enough flour to stiffen and 1 egg to bind the mixture. Break off pieces and shape these into small balls.

Drop these into the boiling soup. As soon as they float they are done.

If hurried, tinned fish such as salmon or shellfish may be used to make the fish balls.

NOODLES (*Mah Mi*)

Chinese or Singapore *mi*, or noodles, are similar to Italian spaghetti, but somewhat fatter, butter-yellow and sold already cooked in the Singapore markets. Italian spaghetti may be used as a substitute.

4 servings:

Garnish:
1 cup (1¼) crabmeat lightly fried
red and green sweet peppers, sliced
celery, finely chopped
1 thin firm omelette, cut into narrow strips
3 spring (green) onions, finely sliced
cucumber, peeled and grated, to taste

¼ lb. noodles
½ lb. boiled pork
1 lb. prawns, preferably fresh
4 tablespoons (5) peanut oil
4 cloves garlic, crushed
salt
3 cups (3¾) fish stock
¼ lb. bean sprouts, tails removed

First prepare the garnish. Mix the first six ingredients.

Cut the pork into shreds and shell the prawns. Heat the oil in a deep pan, fry the garlic until a light brown, add the pork, prawns, salt and stock. Bring to the boil and add the bean sprouts. On top of this add the noodles and quickly cook for 5 minutes. Turn everything on to a hot platter, separate lightly with a fork, or chopsticks, add garnish and serve immediately.

If using Italian spaghetti, it should be pre-cooked a little before adding it to the rest of the ingredients. Instead of raw sliced onions, fried ones may be used. Pre-cooked prawns should be added immediately before the noodles.

FRIED RICE (*Nasi Goreng*) (Straits Chinese)

6–8 servings:

8 cups (10) cold cooked rice
¼ lb. dried Chinese mushrooms
3 red or green chillies or chilli powder to taste
2–3 spring (green) onions
¼ lb. lean pork
¼ lb. cooked ham
¼ lb. cooked white chicken meat

4 tablespoons (5) peanut or vegetable oil
1 large onion, chopped
small shelled prawns to taste
6 chicken livers, chopped
salt to taste
2 eggs
2 sprigs parsley, finely chopped

Soak the mushrooms in water for 30 minutes. Seed and pound the chillies. Peel and chop the spring onions. Cut the mushrooms into thin strips, discarding the stems. Cut the pork, ham and chicken into thin strips.

Heat the oil until sizzling hot. Reduce the heat and fry the chillies and chopped onion until they are cooked but not brown. Add the prawns (unless using pre-cooked prawns, which can be added

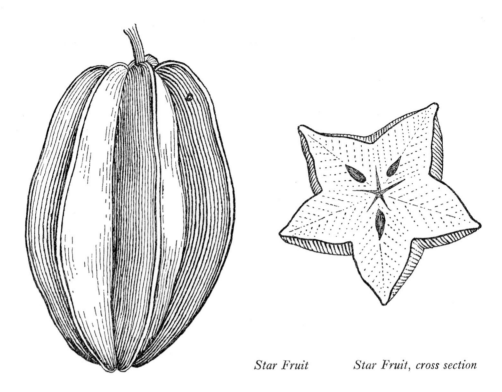

Star Fruit   *Star Fruit, cross section*

later), pork, chicken, ham, mushrooms and livers. Simmer until these are cooked, add the rice and stir gently to mix the ingredients. Season with salt but not pepper if using red chillies or chilli powder.

Beat the eggs lightly and pour them over the rice. Stir continuously until the eggs are cooked and the rice is dry. Add the chopped parsley, mix this into the rice and garnish with the spring onion. Serve immediately on a hot platter.

DRY CHICKEN CURRY (Straits Indian)

4–6 servings:

2 chickens, about 2 lb. each, cut into pieces
a little oil for frying
6 cloves garlic, chopped
$\frac{1}{2}$ lb. onions, thinly sliced
1-in. piece cinnamon
1 teaspoon ($1\frac{1}{4}$) chilli powder

4 cloves, ground
4 cardamon seeds
1 teaspoon ($1\frac{1}{4}$) powdered turmeric
$\frac{1}{2}$ lb. tomatoes, peeled and chopped
1 large piece fresh ginger, thinly sliced
salt to taste

Heat the oil, add the garlic and onions and fry until these change colour; add cinnamon, chilli, cloves, cardamom and turmeric, stir well, add the tomatoes and ginger and fry until lightly browned. Add the chicken pieces and salt, brown these; cover the pan and cook until the chicken is tender. Serve with rice and *sambals*. This is a very dry curry and fairly hot but the quantity of chilli can be lessened according to taste. Any of the *sambal* recipes in this book can be used with this curry.

CHICKEN SATAY (*Satay Gai*) (Straits Chinese)

4 servings:

1 boiled chicken
1 tablespoon (1¼) cumin seeds
2 tablespoons (2½) coriander seeds
¼ lb. (½ cup) sugar
salt

Sauce:
2–3 red chillies, seeded and sliced
½ lb. roasted peanuts
soy sauce and vinegar to taste
coconut or vegetable oil, flavoured with lemon balm

Pound the cumin and coriander together in a mortar or a blender. Add the sugar and salt. Cut up the chicken into small pieces, put these on to a large plate and mix with the pounded ingredients. Thread the pieces on to small skewers (in Singapore they use the spines of the palm leaf). Grill these over charcoal, if possible; alternatively, the pieces can be dry-fried in a thick pan, each piece being first moistened with a little coconut or vegetable oil.

To make the sauce, pound the chillies and peanuts together and put into a saucepan, add soy sauce, vinegar, ½ cupful (⅔) water, the remaining pounded ingredients and 1 tablespoonful (1¼) of coconut oil or enough to make a medium-thick sauce. Stir and bring all this to the boil; cool before serving.

SWEET-SOUR PORK SPARERIBS (*Pai Kwat*)

4–6 servings:

2 lb. pork spareribs
2 each red and green sweet peppers
peanut, vegetable or sesame oil
2–3 cloves garlic, finely chopped
2–3 slices fresh pineapple, cut into cubes

Sauce:
2 tablespoons (2½) mild vinegar
1 tablespoon (1¼) cornflour (cornstarch)
1½ tablespoons (2¼) soy sauce
2–3 tablespoons (2½–3¾) water

Mix the sauce ingredients together in a bowl. Chop the spareribs into inch-sized pieces. Cut each pepper into 6 pieces, discarding the seeds. Heat a little oil and fry the spareribs pieces until browned and cooked through. Put these aside. Reheat the oil, add the garlic, stir 1 minute, add the peppers, fry for a few minutes, then add the pineapple cubes. Fry until they change colour. Add the spareribs, mix gently, but thoroughly, then add the sauce. Continue cooking, stirring all the while, until the sauce has thickened. Serve hot with rice, either plain or fried.

Winged Bean

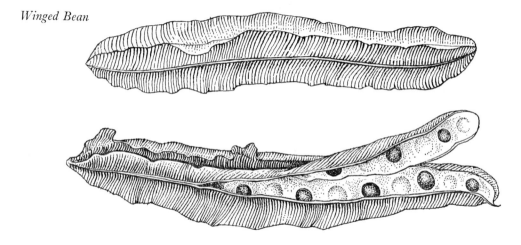

SWEET-SOUR PORK (*Tim Suen-Goo Lo Yuk*) (Straits Chinese)

2–3 servings:

1½ lb. loin of pork
1 tablespoon (1¼) Chinese wine
2 tablespoons (2½) soy sauce
2 tablespoons (2½) flour
1 tablespoon (1¼) cornflour (cornstarch)
oil for deep frying
3 green sweet peppers, seeded and cut into
  quarters
1 medium onion, peeled and quartered
1 large carrot, cut into small wedges and
  cooked for 8 minutes'

1 bamboo shoot (about 4 oz.), cut into
  small wedges
2 slices fresh or tinned pineapple, each
  cut into 4 pieces
4 tablespoons (5) sugar
3 tablespoons (3¾) soy sauce
1 tablespoon (1¼) Chinese wine
2 tablespoons (2½) mild vinegar
4 tablespoons (5) tomato sauce
1 tablespoon (1¼) cornflour mixed with
  water to a thin paste

Cut the pork into 1½-inch cubes and mix with the next 4 ingredients. Heat the oil and fry the pork cubes until they are crisp and golden-brown. Turn on to a hot-plate. Pour away all but 5 tablespoonfuls (6¼) of the oil, reheat and sauté the next 5 ingredients.

In the meantime put the remaining ingredients, except the cornflour, into a bowl, stir well together and add to the sautéed items in the pan. Let this mixture come to the boil, add the cornflour paste and stir constantly until the sauce thickens. Add the pork, mix well and serve hot.

Chicken is cooked in the same fashion.

FRIED GAROUPA WITH A DARK SAUCE

4–6 servings: depending on size of fish

1 garoupa
6 dried Chinese mushrooms
salt
lime or lemon juice
4 tablespoons (5) peanut oil
a few spring (green) onions
1-in. piece fresh ginger or 1 teaspoon (1¼)
  ground

1 tablespoon (1¼) soy sauce
1 tablespoon (1¼) Chinese wine
1 teaspoon (1¼) sugar
1 cup (1¼) warm water
1 tablespoon (1¼) cornflour (cornstarch)
2 tablespoons (2½) dark vinegar
1 sprig parsley

Soak the mushrooms for 30 minutes in water and then cut into thin strips, discarding the stems. Thoroughly clean the fish, lightly score and rub with salt and lime juice. Heat the oil, add onions and ginger, then the fish. Brown on both sides, then lower the heat and fry the fish until it is cooked through. Take it from the pan but keep hot.

Fry the mushrooms in the same pan, add the soy sauce, wine, sugar and 1 cup (1¼) warm water. Cook this for 5 minutes. Mix the cornflour with water to a thin paste. Stir this into the pan, add the vinegar and simmer for 20 minutes. Take out the onions and ginger and discard. Arrange the fish on a hot platter, pour over it the sauce to cover completely and serve at once, garnished with parsley.

The *garoupa*, pronounced grouper, is a large meaty fish, roughly the size of a turbot, heavily scaled and grey in colour. Any meaty fish may be used in its place.

Indonesia

So much has been written of the *rijsttafel* (*see* page 120) that many of us forget there is any other Indonesian cooking at all. This is a great mistake. Indonesia has, in fact, an interesting cuisine, the combination of several. To have some idea of Indonesian cooking it is necessary to know something of the country.

Indonesia is an island country in all truth, a nation of thousands of islands. Many of the islands are large, Java alone accounting for 57,000,000 inhabitants. Some islands, however, are specks in the ocean, many no larger than a peasant's holding.

Java is mainly Muslim. The Javanese attitude to food is sober, drinking no wine and eating no pork. Although their dishes are fairly highly seasoned, never as much as the dishes of the out-going, open-hearted Sumatrans. The latter eat a lot of meat, in particular buffalo, plenty of chillies and turmeric, making their food rather more like that of India. Also Javanese food is much sweeter than that of the Sumatrans, while in Bali the food can be hot.

Other influences on Indonesian cooking are interesting. Both Hinduism and Buddhism have given it vegetarianism. Islam came along with its own cooking and its few taboos, then the Portuguese and later the Dutch who stayed for 350 years and not only influenced Indonesian cooking but also allowed it to influence their own. *Rijsttafel* is one dish which has become almost more Dutch than Indonesian —certainly one can buy all its ingredients and spices in Holland. Many wealthy and sophisticated Indonesians have adopted the Dutch breakfast of coffee, eggs and bread, although the more traditional and those with less money still remain faithful to the typical Indonesian breakfast of *cassava*, rice or steamed bananas.

Probably the most important culinary influence, however, is Chinese and this has penetrated the cooking of the country to such an extent that often even the expert finds it hard to decide whether a dish is traditional or of Chinese influence. Soy sauce is used in many Indonesian dishes as a matter of course.

Rice is the basic food of the islands and its growing is the heart of daily life. After a good rice harvest an air of contentment settles upon the country. There is rice, we will eat, is the feeling. Other staple crops are *cassava*, bananas and, of course, coconuts. Coconuts grow everywhere and there are always plenty of small boys around, knife between their teeth, ready to shin up the palms like agile monkeys to bring down a fresh green fruit, immediately slash off its top and hand you the coconut, like a large cup to drink its liquid contents.

Fruit is abundant, although not necessarily cheap. Bananas, as usual in the Far East, are of all sizes and colours. There are oranges albeit rather woody, sweet tangerines, limes, lemons, avocados and durians. Papaws are plentiful and relatively cheap, mangoes abundant, pineapple available all the year round. *Rambuttans* are so cheap that people seem always to be carrying around a bunch of these thirst-quenching red fruit. Breadfruit is important, as is the jackfruit, which is similar but much larger.

In the markets thousands of pigeons flutter; they make good eating and, like chickens, are sold alive. There is plenty of coffee, cocoa, tea, sugar as well as all the ingredients required for Chinese cooking.

As far as Jakarta is concerned, there is a woeful lack of good restaurants. There are small portable or ambulant kitchens where whole meals may be eaten. Some of these are sheds, keeping off the sun, others are simply long tables without any pretension. Many workmen and children go off in the morning without breakfast but buy it instead from the travelling kitchens. Some of these consist simply of a basket on the back of the vendor. However, the basket will usually contain well-cooked rice and a side dish to go with it. Then there is the man with the bamboo pole perched across his bent shoulders like a yoke with two cans on either end, which look like milk cans but contain crisp cakes made from rice flour and shrimp paste. Another type of kitchen is a tiered glass case which carries, of course, rice but also jars of spices and *sambals*, cooked noodles, cabbage, spoons and plates. Finally there are the dried-fish vendors who serve their specialities on plates made from squares of banana leaf. In general Indonesian women are good cooks, but Indonesian cooking in general, like so much Oriental cooking, requires more preparation than actual cooking.

Finally there is fish—for not only the land but the water supplies food, and fish is one of the main sources of protein in the Indonesian diet. There is fish in plenty, tuna fish, mackerel, milk fish, sardines, anchovies etc., but curiously enough Indonesia has the lowest average fish consumption of any maritime nation in the world.

THE RICE TABLE (*Rijsttafel*)

The Rice Table as the Indonesians know it is a simple manner of eating and can be served either at luncheon or dinner. From this has developed the *rijsttafel*, which is the old Dutch colonial extravagant interpretation of the simple Indonesian form. It has become something fantastic, a meal in its own right, like the once-famed Sunday curry tiffins of the old British colonials in India and in Singapore.

In the days between the two most recent world wars travellers in the East took the trouble to spend a day or so at the Hotel des Indes in Jakarta simply to try its *rijsttafel*. Unhappily I was not travelling in the East in those days, although judging from what I have since seen and heard, I missed a lot. My first experience was in Singapore. That this ritual must at times have palled is certain for on record is this description of it from a disgusted contributor to a local paper: '*Rijsttafel* is not a meal but a buffalo wallow . . . a swinish repast, an invention of the Prodigal Son when he was no longer able to endure total divorcement from the swill tubs which had become second nature to him.'

Nowadays people in Europe do not need to travel to Jakarta or Singapore. They can go to Amsterdam where restaurants serve a good *rijsttafel*.

And yet, I ask myself, is the *rijsttafel* any heartier than a full *smörgåsbord*? I have blanched at the sight of a full-blast Scandinavian assault on a genuine *smörgåsbord*.

Anyway, let us not be put off. Eaten and served with discretion, this dish is worth trying and is, I think, one of the hostess's answers to the servantless meal which is not a buffet. It does mean that the host and hostess are not forever dashing back and forth to the kitchen to fetch the next course; all the dishes can be put on the table at the same time and with enough table warmers they remain hot.

First let me look back on that first *rijsttafel*. We went into the dining-room just as the major-domo swept in, proudly holding aloft a huge platter of steaming hot rice. Behind followed a seemingly endless procession of 'boys' in single file, each carrying one or two dishes. In front of each of us at table was a soup plate with a fairly wide brim, the correct *rijsttafel* dish. Into this we piled the rice and then we began to pick and choose from the myriads of side dishes.

First there are soups, usually two, either of chicken or vegetables, and generally one is curried. These are poured over the rice, then one takes from any of the forty-odd dishes. The following gives an idea of what one can expect from a well-developed Rice Table.

Fresh vegetables and fruit cut into fine strips and served in several dishes. These are to combat the effect of some of the very hot curries. Then several kinds of hot sauces and chillies; these should be taken with caution, they can even make an Indian quiver. There are various ketchups—not the sort we buy in the grocers—thinly sliced cucumbers and pickled gherkins, peeled, cored and sliced tomatoes, thin rings of raw and crisply fried onions, garlic grated and mixed with lime or lemon juice and served in a small china bowl, aubergine and other *sambals* (recipes are given for several of these side dishes). Sweet peppers thinly peeled and roasted until they crackle; small pickled mushrooms, grated orange rind, candied orange and lemon peels, and slices of raw banana, or long fried banana slices, roasted and grated coconut, roasted almonds, peanuts, cashew nuts and a tamarind chutney (this is very good but difficult to get in the West). Dates, raisins, hard-boiled eggs whole or chopped, grapes, mangoes, croquettes, shrimp balls, bits of fried fish, chicken cooked in different ways, and prawns galore, there is positively no end.

But it also means that for the amateur preparing a *rijsttafel* it is simple. First cook the rice, a gleaming white, steaming hot mound of it, and serve it in a large bowl or platter; put this on a table heater to keep hot and serve as many as possible of the dishes mentioned. And presto, invite guests to a 'serve yourself' meal with a difference. The food is served at the table and *rijsttafel* is eaten with a fork and spoon. If one is having a *rijsttafel* in a restaurant, an extra table is brought alongside, on which is set out the tremendous array of dishes, and the diners help themselves as they please.

In the choice of dishes, remember certain rules. Combine bland with sharp, spicy with mild, hot with cold, sweet with sour. Have fish, meat and vegetables and remember the cardinal rule is that flavours must not be repeated. There can be a dozen side dishes or forty, and many of these one can buy already prepared at the better delicatessens or supermarkets. If one prepares a meal for eight people and suddenly decides to have twelve, then only a couple more dishes need to be added.

Many of the dishes can be made well in advance, kept overnight and gently reheated.

As one would imagine it is not usual to eat much after such a feast. Dessert is the order of the day. But what a choice there is in the East. I suggest go expansive and buy as fine a variety of fruit as you can and as exotic as possible.

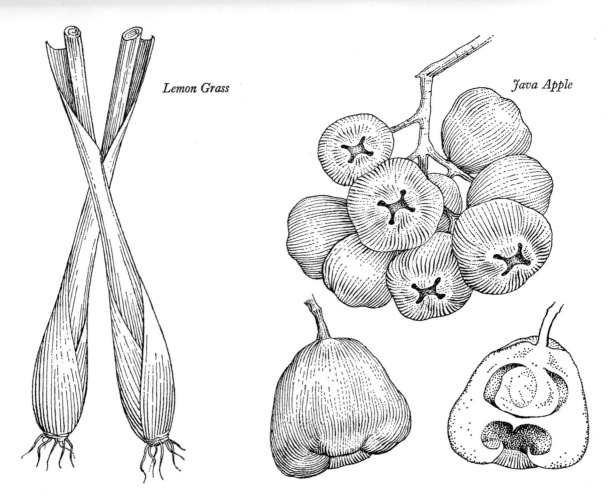

Lemon Grass

Java Apple

RICE (*Nasi*)

If the cooking of rice varies in all rice-eating countries, it varies even more in Indonesia. Each island has its own theory on cooking rice so that, although I am giving two Indonesian methods in this chapter, obviously it is not the complete picture.

Indonesians have their own theories about the amount of rice a man or woman can, or maybe should, consume. For example 1 cupful of raw rice when cooked should be sufficient for 3 men and for 6 women. One cupful of rice usually makes 2, when cooked. This rule is not infallible, for rice varies so much.

SOFT COOKED RICE

3–6 servings:

1 cup (1¼) raw rice, preferably long grain   **2 cups (2½) water**
salt

Put the rice, salt and the water into a pan and bring to the boil. Lower the heat, cover tightly and cook for 20 minutes. Do not stir. The rice will be cooked through and flaky. If you cook more rice than 1 cupful at a time, it might well take longer to cook. To tell whether the rice is cooked, squeeze a grain; if it mashes it is done.

HARD COOKED RICE

This is used more for pilaus, also for rice which is later to be fried.

3–6 servings:

1 cup (1¼) rice, preferably long grain	salt
1½ cups (2) water	

Cook in the same manner as for soft cooked rice.

Rice cooked in the fashion described is based on rice of good quality. It should be neither soft nor mushy, fluffy and entirely dry when cooked.

FRIED RICE (*Nasi Goreng Djawa*) (Java)

6–8 servings:

6 cups (7½) cooked, cold rice, long grain	1 teaspoon (1¼) blachan (see **page 237**)
3 tablespoons (3¾) peanut or vegetable oil	4 cloves garlic, finely chopped
½ lb. shelled prawns	1 tablespoon (1¼) fresh coriander, finely chopped
½ lb. cooked shredded meat, beef, pork or chicken or all mixed	
	2 tablespoons (2½) soy sauce
2 tablespoons (2½) clear stock	1 teaspoon (1¼) brown sugar
salt, pepper	Garnish:
1½ oz. (3 tablespoons) butter	2 or 3 thin omelettes, cut into shreds
Seasonings for pounding:	1 small cucumber, diced
4 fresh red chillies, seeded and crushed or chilli powder	10 small onions, sliced and fried until crisp
6 small onions, finely chopped	salt and crisply fried prawn crackers

Pound the seasonings (this can be done in a blender). Heat the oil and fry this mixture, then add the prawns, meat and the stock. Stir and cook until the meat and prawns are hot. Add the rice, salt, pepper and butter and simmer for 10 minutes, stirring often. Pile the rice on a hot platter and garnish with the remaining ingredients.

Dried or tinned fried onions may be used in the garnish as long as they are made hot.

GRATED COCONUT AND PEANUTS (*Serundeng*)

To be served with *rijsttafel*.

1 cup (1¼) desiccated or grated coconut	1 tablespoon (1¼) coriander seeds, ground
2 cups (2½) fried peanuts	1 teaspoon (1¼) caraway seeds, ground
1 tablespoon (1¼) cooking oil	salt
1 small onion, finely chopped	3 tablespoons (3¾) soft brown sugar
3–4 cloves garlic, finely chopped	1 tablespoon (1¼) tamarind juice or mild vinegar
1 teaspoon (1¼) shrimp paste (see **page 246**)	

This recipe produces enough for 1 saucer or shallow bowl as a side dish.

Heat the oil and fry the onion, garlic, and shrimp paste for 2 minutes. Add the coriander, caraway, salt, sugar and tamarind and stir all this well. Add the coconut, mix this into the spices and cook over a low heat, stirring all the time, for 20 minutes, or until the mixture is a good brown. Add the peanuts and mix all the ingredients thoroughly together.

The mixture can be served at once or put into a jar, tightly covered, to preserve the crispness.

The shrimp paste is available in Oriental departments of larger stores and supermarkets of the West.

PRAWN CRACKERS (*Krupuk Udang*)

Uncooked prawn crackers can be bought at Chinese or Oriental shops. They should be fried in very hot oil and if the oil is boiling hot, will puff up immediately. The crackers should be removed and drained before they change colour.

Served with rice dishes and *rijsttafel*.

FRIED BANANAS (*Pisang Goreng*)

To be served with *rijsttafel*.

Peel as many firm bananas as required and cut them into slices lengthwise, approximately each slice about ¼-inch thick. Heat enough butter to sauté the banana slices until a light brown on both sides. Serve very hot.

SHREDDED OMELETTE (*Dadar Irish*)

3 eggs	**butter**
salt, pepper	

Beat the eggs, rather more than is usual for an omelette, add salt and pepper. Heat a little butter in a pan, pour in the beaten egg, spread well over the pan and cook until set. Roll and cut into thin strips.

Side dish for *rijsttafel* or garnish to a pilau.

FRIED GARLIC SAUCE (*Sambal Djelantah*)

3–4 cloves garlic, finely chopped	**½ teaspoon (⅔) salt**
1 tablespoon (1¼) peanut oil	**1 teaspoon (1¼) shrimp paste** (see **page 246**)
1 teaspoon (1¼) chilli powder	**½ tablespoon (⅔) soft brown sugar**

Heat the oil, add the garlic and stir well. Then add the remaining ingredients and cook to a sauce.

HOT SAUCE (*Sambal Badjak*)

1 tablespoon (1¼) butter or **oil**	**1 teaspoon (1¼) peanut butter**
1 onion, finely chopped	**½ cup (⅔) milk** or **coconut milk**
1 teaspoon (1¼) sambal ulek	

Heat the butter and fry the onion until it is beginning to change colour. Add the *sambal ulek* and stir thoroughly. Stir the peanut butter into this mixture and, stirring all the while, gradually add the milk and bring this to the boil. This *sambal* is served with bamboo shoots, carrot, string beans and chicken or liver dishes as well as with *rijsttafel*. *Sambal ulek* is a bottled product prepared from fiery hot peppers. It is not only used as in the above recipe, but also as a *sambal* alone, served in a small porcelain bowl. *Ulek* simply means ground.

HOT SOY SAUCE (*Sambal Ketjap*)

½ cup (⅔) soy sauce

¾ tablespoon (1) chilli peppers, seeded and crushed or chilli powder

1–2 cloves garlic, crushed

1 teaspoon (1¼) molasses or soft brown sugar

Combine all these ingredients and serve in a small dish with the *rijstafel*. Sometimes very tiny chillies or 'bird peppers' are used whole, not crushed or broken at all.

HOT TOMATO SAUCE (*Sambal Tomat*)

4 tomatoes, peeled and chopped

2 red chilli peppers, seeded and crushed or chilli powder

1 teaspoon (1¼) prawn sauce (below)

salt

Soak the chilli peppers in a little water for 15 minutes. Mix well and mash with the remaining ingredients.

This sauce is especially popular in the Celebes but there the prawn sauce is not used; instead a few drops of used frying oil are added. Then this *sambal* is called *Dabu Dabu Lilang*.

PRAWN SAUCE (*Sambal Udang*)

3–4 servings:

10–12 prawns, peeled

1 tablespoon (1¼) peanut or vegetable oil

2 chilli peppers, seeded and chopped or chilli powder

1 small onion, chopped

1 tablespoon (1¼) peanut butter

salt

1 teaspoon (1¼) sugar

2–4 tablespoons (2½–5) water

Heat the oil and fry the chillies, onion, peanut butter, salt and sugar. Stir until this is blended and the onion begins to soften. Add the prawns, stir, add the water and cook over a moderate heat for 10 minutes or until the prawns are pink and firm. Serve cold.

Can be prepared with tinned or frozen prawns.

EGGS IN COCONUT SAUCE (*Sambal Goreng Telor*)

6 servings:

6 hard-boiled eggs, shelled and halved

1 tablespoon (1¼) peanut or vegetable oil

1 onion, sliced

1 clove garlic, chopped

1 tomato, peeled and sliced

2 chilli peppers, seeded and chopped or chilli powder

salt

1 teaspoon (1¼) sugar

½ cup (⅔) coconut milk (see page 238)

Put the eggs into a deep dish and keep them hot. Heat the oil and fry the onion and garlic. As these brown, add the tomato and chillies, salt and sugar. When this begins to thicken add the coconut milk. Cook to a thick sauce and pour this mixture over the eggs.

To be served as a side dish.

EGGS IN A YELLOW CHILLI SAUCE (*Telor Pindang*)

3–4 servings:

6 hard-boiled eggs
oil
1 onion, finely chopped
1 clove garlic, chopped
1 tomato, peeled and chopped

2 cups (2½) coconut milk (see page 238)
1 tablespoon (1¼) chilli powder or to taste
1 teaspoon (1¼) powdered turmeric
salt

Shell the eggs, peel and cut into halves. Heat a little oil and sauté the onion and garlic and when brown add the tomato and simmer until this softens; gradually add the coconut milk, stirring all the time, then the remaining ingredients, except the eggs. Bring this to the boil, stir and rub through a sieve. Return the sauce to the pan, add the eggs and cook over a low heat for 3 minutes.

SPINACH AND CORN SOUP (*Sajur Bajam*)

6–7 servings:

½ lb. spinach, after cleaning
2 corn cobs, fresh or frozen or 1 tin whole
   kernels
6 cups (7½) meat stock
1 bay leaf

1 onion, chopped
1 clove garlic, crushed
1 teaspoon (1¼) salt
1 small sweet potato, diced

If using corn cobs, the corn must be scraped off before it is added to the soup. Cut the spinach into strips. Heat the stock, add the bay leaf, onion and garlic, salt, sweet potato and corn and cook for 5 minutes, add the spinach and continue cooking until the spinach is soft. In this recipe frozen spinach is acceptable. An ordinary potato may be used if sweet potato is not available, plus sugar.

MIXED VEGETABLE SOUP (*Sajur Tjampur*)

6 servings:

2 tablespoons (2½) butter or cooking oil
2 cloves garlic, crushed
1 small onion, thinly sliced
½ cup (⅔) chicken meat, diced
a little fresh ginger, finely chopped or
   pinch of ground
8 cups (10) clear stock
½ cup (⅔) white cabbage

½ cup (⅔) string or french beans
1 tablespoon (1¼) celery, diced
a good handful bean sprouts
1 tomato, peeled and chopped
1 bay leaf
salt, pepper
½ cup (⅔) fine noodles, cooked

Heat the butter, add the garlic and onion and lightly brown, then add the chicken and the ginger. Stir, cover and cook for a few minutes, add the stock, bring to the boil, add the remaining ingredients and continue cooking until the vegetables are tender. Remove the bay leaf. Serve very hot.

Nothing must be overcooked, barely cooked is almost better. Some recipes also add either fresh chopped coriander or a teaspoonful of coriander seeds. The latter are fried with the garlic; fresh coriander is added at the last moment.

A sort of Eastern minestrone and very substantial, served with *rijsttafel*. To the Indonesians a soup is not a very liquid dish, so this *sajur* with rice and a *sambal* is a main course.

STRING BEAN SAMBAL (*Sambal Goreng Buntjies*)

4 servings:

1 lb. (3 cups) string, french or runner beans, sliced
1 tablespoon (1¼) vegetable oil
1 onion, sliced
3 cloves garlic, sliced
2–4 chilli peppers, sliced, seeds discarded or chilli powder

1 teaspoon (1¼) shrimp paste (see page 246)
1 cup (1¼) coconut milk (see page 238)
1 tablespoon (1¼) brown sugar
1–2 bay leaves
salt
1 tablespoon (1¼) tamarind or lemon juice

Heat the oil and fry the onion, garlic, chilli peppers and shrimp paste for a few minutes, stirring all the time. Add the coconut milk, sugar, bay leaf, salt and tamarind. Bring to a gentle boil, reduce the heat and simmer for 5 minutes. Add the beans and cook these until they are tender. Just before serving, add the juice. Remove the bay leaf.

CHICKEN LIVER SAMBAL (*Sambal Goreng Hati*)

6 servings:

1 lb. chicken livers, chopped
6 hard-boiled eggs, shelled
2 tablespoons (2½) butter or oil
1 small onion, finely chopped
3 cloves garlic, chopped
2 chilli peppers, seeded and finely chopped or chilli powder
1 teaspoon (1¼) shrimp paste (see page 246)

1½ cups (2) thick coconut milk (see page 238)
salt
1–2 bay leaves
¾ tablespoon (1) sugar
2 tablespoons (2½) tamarind or lemon juice

Wash the livers and drain. Make a deep cross on top of each egg. Heat the butter and fry the onion, garlic and peppers. Stir well and add the shrimp paste. Cook a further 2 minutes and add the coconut milk, salt, bay leaves and sugar. Bring to the boil, lower the heat and simmer for 10 minutes. Add the livers and continue simmering for another 15 minutes. Five minutes before serving, add the eggs and the tamarind, stir thoroughly but gently.

A side dish. Failing coconut milk, use cows' milk or a stock. The flavour will be different but the *sambal* still good.

SAUTEED SHRIMPS WITH GINGER (*Udang Tumis Djahe*)

3–4 servings:

1 lb. fresh shrimps or prawns, shelled
1 tablespoon (1¼) peanut or other oil
2 tablespoons (2½) light soy sauce
1 scant tablespoon (1¼) brown sugar

1 tablespoon (1¼) mild vinegar
salt, pepper to taste
1 tablespoon (1¼) finely chopped ginger
2 tablespoons (2½) dry sherry

Heat the oil in a frying pan, add the soy sauce, sugar, vinegar, a little salt, pepper and the ginger. Stir and cook gently for a few minutes. Add the prawns, stir them into the mixture and cook over a high heat for just 5 minutes. Add the sherry just before serving. Serve hot.

BAKED SPICED FISH (*Ikan Bandeng Panggang*)

4–6 servings:

1 2½–3 lb. fish
salt, pepper
2 cloves garlic, minced
½ cup (⅔) melted butter

2 tablespoons (2½) lemon juice
¼ cup (⅓) soy sauce
2–3 chilli peppers, seeded and ground or chilli powder

Clean the fish, slit it open to remove the centre bone. Mix salt, pepper and garlic and rub this mixture inside the fish. Reshape the fish and put it into a large baking pan. Mix the butter, juice, soy sauce and chillies and pour this over the fish. Bake in a hot oven for 30 minutes or until the fish is tender, basting frequently.

Serve the fish garnished with wedges of lemon, chopped fresh coriander or parsley.

Almost any large firm fish will react favourably to this treatment.

Bandeng is an estuary fish, a square sort of sole.

MARINATED GRILLED FISH (*Ikan Ritja-Ritja*)

3–4 servings:

1 2½ lb. fish
3 red chillies, seeded and chopped or chilli powder
ginger to taste, finely chopped
5 cloves garlic

2 onions, finely chopped
1½ tablespoons (2) lemon juice
1 cup (1¼) fish stock
salt

Make a paste or marinade of the chillies, ginger, garlic, onions, lemon juice, salt and fish stock. Clean the fish and remove its head and tail. Make some deep gashes in the body to let the marinade soak in. Marinate the fish for 30 minutes. Grill the fish, preferably over charcoal, basting from time to time with the marinade.

Serve with spicy pickles.

BRAISED CHICKEN IN MINAHASSA STYLE (*Ajam Isi Di Bulu*)

Minahassa is part of Celebes Island.

3–4 servings:

1 dressed chicken
salt, pepper
6 tomatoes, peeled and coarsely chopped
6 onions, coarsely chopped
1 tablespoon (1¼) red pepper, ground
1 tablespoon (1¼) green chilli pepper, pounded

½ cup (⅔) scallions or spring (green) onions, finely chopped
1 cup (1¼) water
1 small piece lemon grass (see page 241)
1 lemon leaf or lemon verbena leaf

The quantity of chilli peppers can be considerably reduced. Wash the chicken and cut it into serving pieces. Rub each piece with salt and pepper. Put into a saucepan and add the remaining ingredients. Bring to the boil, lower the heat and simmer until the chicken is tender.

This dish is one of those which improves by being made the day before it is required. Originally it was cooked in a bamboo container (*bulu* means bamboo) and roasted over a charcoal fire, the container being turned round several times. But this is almost an impossibility today.

FRIED CHICKEN (*Ajam Goreng*)

2 servings:

1 frying chicken
2 cups (2½) water
salt, pepper

1 teaspoon (1¼) garlic salt
½ cup (⅔) tamarind juice or mild vinegar
oil for deep frying

Halve the chicken. Bring the water to the boil, add the chicken and simmer for 10 minutes. Strain off the stock. Add the salt, pepper, garlic salt and tamarind to the chicken and cook for 5 minutes. Heat the oil, enough to deep fry the chicken, and fry until a light brown.

GRILLED CHICKEN (*Sate Ajam*)

4 servings:

1 chicken or 4 chicken fillets
¼ teaspoon (⅓) black pepper
½ teaspoon (⅔) salt
2 tablespoons (2½) ketchup or a mixture of light and dark soy sauce
Sauce:
chilli powder to taste

2–4 cloves garlic, chopped and fried
1 teaspoon (1¼) dark soy sauce
¼ cup (⅓) chicken stock
4 tablespoons (5) peanut butter
lime or lemon juice to taste

Cut the chicken flesh into small pieces and thread these on to skewers. (Indonesians prefer to use thin bamboo sticks which are sometimes available in Oriental shops.) Mix the pepper, salt and ketchup and pour this over the chicken pieces. Cook these gently in a frying pan for 20 minutes. Take from the pan and grill until brown. Serve on the skewers accompanied by the sauce. If the chicken is very tender it can simply be dipped in the ketchup, salt and pepper and grilled raw. It then takes about 15 minutes to be perfectly cooked.

To make the sauce, pound together the chilli powder, garlic, soy sauce and stock. You can use a blender. Add the peanut butter and about 1 tablespoonful (1¼) of lime or lemon juice.

SWEET SATE (*Sate Manis*)

3–4 servings:

1½ lb. beef or pork fillet	2 red chillies, seeded and crushed or chilli
salt	powder
1 teaspoon (1¼) pepper	4 tablespoons (5) peanut butter
1 tablespoon (1¼) honey	1 tablespoon (1¼) soft brown sugar
butter or oil	1 tablespoon (1¼) tamarind juice or lemon
1 onion, finely chopped	1 tablespoon (1¼) soy sauce
4 cloves garlic	crisply fried onion rings as a garnish

Cut the meat into ¾-inch cubes, flatten these and put into a bowl with salt, pepper and honey. Leave for several hours or overnight. Thread on skewers, 2 or 3 pieces on each, preferably bamboo sticks, but small metal skewers are as good.

Heat just enough butter to grease the pan, add the chopped onion, garlic and chillies and fry. Add salt. When these are cooked, add the peanut butter, sugar and enough water to make a thick sauce. Stir well, add the tamarind juice and soy sauce, stir and cook until it is again thick.

Grill the cubes of meat, brushing each piece first with a little melted butter or oil and soy sauce. When the meat is brown on both sides arrange it on a hot plate and serve piping hot with a little of the sauce on top of the meat. The remaining sauce is served separately garnished with the fried onion.

There are small charcoal grills for making *sate*. The kebabs can be cooked under a gas grill as well. The sticks must be turned 2 or 3 times to make sure the meat is browned all round. Chicken and lamb *sate* is also made in Indonesia.

BASIC RECIPE FOR MOST VEGETABLES (*Sajur*)

Usually vegetables in Indonesian cooking are 'stir-fried', in a similar manner to the Chinese method of cooking them. In this way they retain their crispness, colour and flavour. A very hot pan is absolutely essential and usually the vegetables take only a matter of between 5 and 10 minutes to cook.

As almost always in the East, the vegetables are cut up into bite-sized pieces, washed and drained completely dry before being cooked.

Heat enough oil in a deep frying pan to fry the quantity of vegetables you are preparing to cook. Add a little onion or garlic and cook these for a couple of minutes, this is to add extra flavour to the vegetables but both can be omitted. When the pan and the oil is very hot, add the chopped vegetables. Cook over a high heat, stirring all the while.

Those vegetables which do not have sufficient liquid of their own need a little water added to the pan. Cover and steam the vegetables for 5 minutes. Such vegetables as broccoli, string beans and cauliflower need a little longer cooking but not as much as we in the West usually prescribe.

MIXED VEGETABLE SALAD WITH A PEANUT SAUCE (*Gado-Gado*)

6 servings:

The following quantities are approximate.

½ lb. white cabbage, chopped
½ lb. string, or french beans, cut into 1-in.
   lengths
½ lb. spinach, cleaned and chopped
a handful bean sprouts
2 potatoes, boiled and sliced
1–2 hard-boiled eggs, sliced
onion, sliced and crisply fried
prawn crackers (see page 124)

Peanut sauce:
oil
1 onion, minced
4 cloves garlic, minced
2 red chillies, chopped or chilli powder
salt
½ cup (⅔) peanut butter
1 cup (1¼) coconut milk (see page 238)
1 tablespoon (1¼) lemon juice
sugar

Peanut sauce: heat a little oil and fry the onion, garlic and chillies, add salt, peanut butter and coconut milk. Bring this to the boil, add the tamarind and enough sugar to give the sauce a sweet-sour flavour.

Cook the cabbage, string beans, spinach and bean sprouts separately until tender and crisp.

In the same order as given put a layer each of the cooked vegetables into a salad bowl, then add the potatoes and the egg. Pour the peanut sauce over the top and serve with fried onions and prawn crackers.

To this salad is often added shredded coconut as a garnish.

Gado-gado should not be served with other dishes; if necessary rice may be served with it, but *gado-gado* is sufficient unto itself. If preferred, the vegetables can be served separately on a large plate as a vegetable platter with the peanut sauce poured over the top. This is a great favourite with connoisseurs of Indonesian food.

CABBAGE AND EGGS (*Orak Arik*) (Java)

2 servings:

½ lb. cabbage, shredded
2–3 eggs
1 tablespoon (1¼) butter or oil
1 large onion, chopped

salt, pepper
3 tomatoes, peeled and chopped
¼ lb. bean sprouts (optional)

Heat the fat and fry the onion until soft, add the cabbage and stir this until it begins to look wilted. Add salt and pepper and cover the pan. Let the cabbage steam and when it is almost cooked (this is a matter of a few minutes) stir it well, add the tomatoes and bean sprouts. When the tomatoes are cooked, add the eggs and stir constantly until the eggs are set.

The most important point in this dish is to keep the cabbage from becoming soggy. If using tinned bean sprouts they must be well drained.

SWEET BANANA FRITTERS (*Pisang Goreng*)

4 servings:

4 ripe bananas, mashed
2 eggs, well beaten
sugar to taste
2 tablespoons (2½) flour

oil
Garnish:
soft brown sugar mixed with powdered cinnamon

Combine the eggs, sugar and bananas and beat until the mixture is well blended. Add flour, enough only to make the mixture somewhat firm but not heavy. Heat a little oil, take a tablespoonful of the mixture and drop it into the oil and fry on both sides until a light brown. Serve hot sprinkled with the garnish.

Also very good as a garnish is a mixture of roasted ground sesame seeds and sugar and, of course, a sprinkling of lime or lemon juice.

Another version of the *pisang goreng* is to cut peeled bananas in 3 or 4 diagonal pieces, roll these in flour and then in a coating batter, finally frying in deep fat.

TAPIOCA PUDDING (*Bubur Dalima*)

The British have done great culinary injustice to tapioca, sago and rice. For so many of us, these three ingredients have meant tears and tantrums. In the East they mean staple foods and not milky messes.

4–6 servings:

¼ lb. (½ cup) tapioca or sago
¾ cup (1) soft brown sugar or to taste
3 cups (3¾) water

a little red colouring or pomegranate juice
pinch of salt

Soak the tapioca overnight. Cook it with the remaining ingredients until it is thick and set. Pour it into a dish and let it get quite cold. Serve with cold milk or cream. Or try using thick coconut cream which is nicer.

Dalima means pomegranate. In Indonesia palm sugar is used in this pudding which is a teatime speciality.

Cambodia

Cambodian cooking is one of detail, but many of their ingredients are quite impossible to find in the West, although in Paris some of the Cambodian spices are obtainable and also several Cambodian specialities, such as their *nguoc-nam* sauce. Equally impossible is it to translate many of the ingredients of this country since they do not have a Western equivalent. Although much of the cooking is influenced by the Chinese, Cambodians are justly proud of their French cooking which can be found in the capital, Phnom Penh.

The basis of their diet is rice and there are many varieties. Rich and poor alike eat rice but here the similarity in diet finishes. Next to rice the most prized dietary essential is the national sauce, *nguoc-nam*, which has a basis of soy sauce, fish paste and brine. There are many such pungent sauces, all with their own particular odour which usually repels non-Asians but which they first learn to live with and then to like. There is one typical sauce made from salt cod and tamarind juice, another of tinned anchovies, lemon balm, fennel and hot chillies, another which is a mixture of fresh sardines, green mango, coconut milk and *nguoc-nam*.

Mutton is not eaten in Cambodia at all; pork and beef are highly prized. Poultry, especially chicken and duck, is eaten a lot, so is the humble pigeon and sparrow. Much of the pork is from pigs who are descendants of the wild black pig and there are some interesting pork recipes, including one for stuffing pigs' feet. Chicken, pork and shellfish are often used together in one recipe.

Astonishing is the word for the quantity of fish to be found in Cambodia, both river and sea fish. Prawns, crayfish, cuttlefish, sea-urchins and carp; the Cambodians have their own version of a highly spiced bouillabaisse. Considerable quantities of fish are salted and dried, and extremely good is their wood-smoked fish, for smoking fish and meat is a Cambodian speciality. Rightly considered delicacies are dishes prepared with fish roe and the milt. There are some tempting little prawn balls, as well as a large variety of excellent fish soups.

Vegetables are in profusion, everything which appears on the European market plus yams, taro, sweet potato, bamboo, of course, a type of turnip or kohlrabi, various pumpkins or squash cucumbers, marrows, water chestnuts, capsicum (sweet peppers) and a great many edible leaves for which there is no useful European name. They have herbs, including chives, not usually found in the Orient and one suspects the French influence; mint is an important ingredient in many dishes, including salads; lemon grass or lemon balm is greatly used, so is lotus and lotus seed, bindweed etc. Like the Thais, the Cambodians use flowers in their cooking.

Fruits are those usual in the East, pineapples, *rambuttans*, guavas, lichees, custard apples, star apples, mountain apples and mangosteens. There is the star gooseberry and the fruit of the strawberry tree. Here the *pomelo* is decorative rather than tasty and is trained to grow with five curled, finger-like appendages at the top and is thus called, rather nicely, 'The Hand of the Buddha'.

A true Cambodian breakfast is a Chinese-style soup with vermicelli, or perhaps a rice soup. Coffee is usually taken with milk, Chinese tea is appreciated but the Cambodians generally are not great tea drinkers. 'Old people and monks drink tea', I was solemnly informed.

PORK SOUP WITH GINGER (*Samla Chaphek*)

6 servings:

½ lb. lean pork
½ lb. liver
1 kidney
1 small piece fat bacon
1 tablespoon (1¼) fat
several cloves garlic
6 cups (7½) meat stock

a little nguoc-nam (see page 133)
1 tablespoon (1¼) vinegar
1 tablespoon (1¼) brown sugar
1-in. piece ginger, finely chopped
salt, pepper
chives, fennel, coriander to taste, finely chopped

Cut the pork, liver, kidney and bacon into small pieces. Score the kidney pieces. Heat the fat in a saucepan and brown the garlic, add the stock, *nguoc-nam*, vinegar and sugar. Bring the stock to the boil, add the pork, kidney, bacon and ginger and continue to boil. When the meats are half-cooked add the liver, lower the heat and cook for a further 5 minutes. Add salt, pepper, chives, fennel and coriander.

THREE PRINCES SOUP (*Samla Bei Krasat*)

8 servings:

1 small chicken
1 lean pork chop
8 cups (10) water
salt, pepper
fat for frying
1 tablespoon (1¼) garlic, thinly sliced
2 eggs, well beaten

3 large prawns
2 fillets mackerel
1 tablespoon (1¼) chives, finely chopped
2 tablespoons (2½) coriander
¼ head of firm white cabbage, finely shredded

Strip the chicken meat from the bones keeping the pieces as large as possible. Put the bones, giblets and the pork chop in a pan and add the water, salt and pepper. Bring to the boil, lower the heat and simmer for about 1½ hours. Strain. Heat a little fat and fry the garlic until brown. Put this aside.

Pour 1 cupful (1¼) of the stock into the beaten eggs, stirring all the while. Return the remaining stock to the pan and bring again to the boil. Thinly slice the chicken meat, prawns and mackerel. Drop first the chicken into the stock, then add the prawns and mackerel. Add the chives, coriander and cabbage. Cook for 10 minutes then add the egg and stock mixture, stir the soup well, add the garlic and serve at once.

CURRIED SHRIMPS WITH CUCUMBERS (*Kari Bangkang Khong Lasak*)

4–6 servings:

2 lb. raw shrimps, shelled
3–4 tablespoons (3¾–5) fat
1 pint (2½ cups) coconut milk (see page 238)
1–2 cucumbers, thickly sliced
Flavouring:
1 tablespoon (1¼) garlic, crushed
1 tablespoon (1¼) spring (green) onions, chopped
1 tablespoon (1¼) fennel root or seeds to taste

1 tablespoon (1¼) coriander seeds
pepper to taste
3 large dried chillies or chilli powder to taste
a pinch saffron, soaked in water
Seasoning:
salt, sugar
tamarind or lemon juice
nguoc-nam (see page 133) to taste

Pound all the flavouring ingredients to a paste, or put them in a blender with a little liquid—the saffron water might well be sufficient but if not, add a little water or extra coconut milk. Heat the fat, add the shrimps and fry these in the hot fat until they change colour, then add the pounded flavourings, stir these for a few minutes and cook gently. Gradually stir in the coconut milk, let it come slowly to the boil, then simmer and add the cucumber slices and seasonings. Cook until the cucumber is soft.

If fresh shrimps are not available, cooked ones may be substituted and should be added after the cucumber is tender. Cows' milk may be used instead of coconut milk.

PRAWN BALLS (*Pranet Bangkang*)

2 servings:

3 large prawns
salt, pepper, garlic and fennel root to taste

1 tablespoon (1¼) fat bacon, chopped
oil or fat for frying
1 tablespoon (1¼) parsley, finely chopped

Shell the prawns, drop them into a pan of salted boiling water and cook until they are a light pink. Take from the pan at once. Pound the condiments (be generous in these flavourings) to a paste, add the bacon and continue pounding, add the prawns and pound the whole to a homogeneous mass. Break off small pieces, shape into balls and fry these in hot fat until a golden brown. Garnish with the parsley.

FRIED CHICKEN WITH GINGER AND MUSHROOMS
(*Mean Chhar Khnhei Nu'ug Phset Kream*)
This is a dish in which all ingredients are 'to taste'.

4 servings: approximate.

1 chicken
lean pork
dried mushrooms, soaked until soft
garlic
fat bacon for frying
sugar, nguoc-nam (see **page 133**) and
  vinegar

ginger, preferably fresh, finely chopped
chives, finely chopped
1 scant tablespoon (1¼) flour
1 cup (1¼) stock or water
salt, pepper
fennel leaves, finely chopped

Cut the chicken into as small pieces as possible. Cut the pork into cubes. In this recipe the gizzard. liver and heart of the chicken are included, but do as you please. Cut the mushrooms into strips. Crush or finely chop the garlic—and the Cambodians use a lot. Fry the bacon until the fat runs, add the garlic and let this brown. Add the pork, stir and cook until this changes colour, add the chicken, sugar, *nguoc-nam*, and vinegar to taste. At this point taste the dish; it should be slightly sweet-sour. Add the mushrooms, ginger and chives and stir well but gently. Simmer. Mix the flour with the stock to a paste. Stir this into the pan, add salt and pepper to taste, cook a further 5 minutes, and serve garnished with fennel leaves.

The amount of flour to say 1 chicken and 1 lb. of cubed pork should not be more than 1 table-spoonful (1¼) with about 1 cupful (1¼) of water.

This dish is very simple and can be made quickly, and with all pork or even prawns or shrimps mixed with pork.

HUNTER'S CHICKEN (*Mean Kau Lau*)

4–6 servings:

1 large chicken
a little fat
1 lb. lean pork, chopped
fennel leaves, finely chopped
1 oz. (3–4 tablespoons) dried mushrooms,
  soaked in water and coarsely chopped

salt, pepper
brown sugar
nguoc-nam (see **page 133**)
6 potatoes

Heat the fat and brown the chicken and take it from the pan. Mix the pork, fennel, mushrooms, salt and pepper. Stuff this mixture into the chicken. Place the chicken in a steamer. Mix about 1 table-spoonful (1¼) of sugar with the *nguoc-nam* and baste the chicken. Cover the pan and cook the chicken until tender, then baste the chicken 3 times at 5-minute intervals, re-covering the chicken each time. Take from the heat. Boil the potatoes and when they are tender drain off the liquid and add 2 table-spoonfuls (2½) *nguoc-nam* mixed with a little sugar. Cut the chicken into serving pieces and serve with the potatoes and the stuffing as a garnish.

The quantity of fennel used depends on taste and this can be changed to another herb if fennel is not available.

MOULDED RICE (*Bay Poum*)

6 servings:

4 cups (5) cooked rice
lean pork or ham in the same quantity as
   the chicken meat
1 chicken leg

¾ lb. fat pork or bacon
garlic and mild onion, coarsely chopped
nguoc-nam (see page 133)
salt, pepper

Cut the lean pork and the chicken meat from the leg into small pieces. Heat the fat pork in a saucepan and when the fat runs add the garlic (as much as the taste buds will allow) and the onion. Add the chicken and the pork and when this is cooked add a little *nguoc-nam* and finally the rice. Remove the fat pork. Stir all the ingredients together adding salt and pepper to taste. Pour this into a mould, press it down and leave awhile but keep it hot. Then carefully turn the rice out on to a hot plate and garnish with sliced gherkins or pickled vegetables or thin rounds of lemon.

GRAPE SALAD (*Nheam Phler Tumpeang Chou*)

3–4 servings:

a large bunch of sweet green grapes
½ lb. each cooked chicken, pork and lobster
   meat
lemon juice

sugar
nguoc-nam (see page 133)
garlic and spring (green) onion rings,
   lightly fried

Cut the grapes into halves (they should be large, fleshy ones) and take out the seeds. Cut the meats and lobster into small pieces, about the size of the grape halves. Mix all these ingredients together, add lemon juice, sugar and *nguoc-nam*, and finally garnish with the garlic and onion rings.

GRAPEFRUIT SALAD (*Nheam Krauch Thlong*)

2–3 servings:

1 large grapefruit, or some tinned sections
3 tablespoons (3¾) grated and toasted
   coconut
3 tablespoons (3¾) cooked and chopped
   prawns or shrimps

3 tablespoons (3¾) cooked and thinly
   sliced tripe (optional)
4 tablespoons (5) fat bacon, crisply fried
1 tablespoon (1¼) kapik phat

Although quantities are given for this salad, they are rather to taste. If *kapik phat* paste is not available use some dried, crumbled prawns or shrimps or forget about it. *Kapik phat* is a paste of ground fresh shrimps or prawns. Peel the grapefruit and cut the flesh into sections. Mix all the ingredients and garnish with lemon-flavoured leaves.

BAKED BANANAS (*Chek Dot Muoy Bap Phseng*)

Somewhat flatten and peel as many bananas as required and arrange them in a flat baking dish. Sprinkle generously with brown sugar and grated lemon rind. Add water to come halfway up the bananas, and bake in a moderate oven until the water is absorbed and the bananas are soft. Take from the pan, cover with cooked orange slices or with orange marmalade and return to the oven and cook for a further 10 minutes. Serve immediately. Whipped cream can be added as a garnish.

Vietnam

Although the Vietnamese cuisine has taken much from Chinese cooking, it has always remained a separate entity, preserving its own flavour and distinct from other Oriental cooking.

Four underlying principles govern the art of Vietnamese cooking: usefulness, beauty, medicinal qualities and ceremonial requirements.

The thriftiness of the Vietnamese is reflected in the first principle. They do not and will not waste any edible material, using many ingredients not normally used in neighbouring countries. Roots, the bark of trees, the internal organs of animals, and almost any herb or non-poisonous vegetable.

As with the Japanese, the Vietnamese like to give pleasure to the eye at the same time giving delight to the palate and attach considerable importance to the medicinal value of their food. So, besides boasting of taste and appearance, they hail the therapeutic value of their dishes.

Finally, the ceremonial aspect expresses itself when meals are offered as a gesture of symbolical piety to their departed. For such dishes there is stress laid on purity in their cooking.

The diet of the Vietnamese is not sophisticated, being based on local products. But this does not mean that the Vietnamese are hidebound in their tastes. On the contrary, from what I understand of the Vietnamese character, they will try anything they can afford and anything that can be imported, which is both cheap and regular, will soon be incorporated in their day-to-day diet. The most surprising things will be eaten and adapted to Vietnamese taste.

What makes Vietnamese cooking distinctive is the use of herbs and local vegetables—some not obtainable elsewhere. For example, mint is used extensively but it is not the mint of the West, being milder and with a somewhat smaller leaf. But the difference is such that the Vietnamese when abroad prefer to omit this important ingredient from their dishes rather than use the stronger flavoured mint which, to their taste, is overwhelming.

A typical Vietnamese meal starts with a soup usually prepared from chopped meat and fish, seasoned with a fish sauce, and vegetables. Then a meat or fish dish, or perhaps both. The meat dishes mainly of pork, chicken and duck, seldom beef and almost never mutton.

The Vietnamese have hardly any use for milk and none for milk products. What puddings they have are often made from ground lentils crushed and flavoured with sugar to which various flavours are added. Arrowroot is also used in the making of puddings as is sticky rice. Many of these pudding preparations are wrapped in banana leaves and steamed.

On the table there are always pickles of which there is considerable variety, either in vinegar, or in a fish sauce. These are not chutneys but are served as side dishes. Chillies and fish sauce—*nguoc-nam*—accompany every meal. Hot ingredients, such as pepper, is added to the food at table. For seasoning soups the Vietnamese prefer to use coconut water which gives a slightly sweet flavour to their fish and sauces or dried prawns. A favourite Vietnamese soup is made from spinach and generously flavoured with dried prawns or shrimps.

The Vietnamese eat with chopsticks. In days gone by the rich used ivory chopsticks or red ones decorated with gold. Red was considered auspicious. For the poor there was bamboo and wood. Crockery is similar to that used by the Chinese. Small bowls for rice, larger ones for soup and a porcelain soup spoon. All dishes are placed on the table at the same time.

Today tables and chairs are usual but typical of the country was a large, square divan table. On this one sat crossed-legged (Vietnamese women also wear trousers). The food would be arranged in the centre of the divan and it was usual to eat in groups of four. There was one common dish for each type of dish offered. These divans are still found in the villages but seldom in the sophisticated home.

There is but slight difference in the cooking of North or South Vietnam, it is similar to the difference between Scotland and England or New York and New Orleans. There are some dishes which the Vietnamese would consider as a northern dish just as we the British consider haggis belongs to Scotland or Americans gumbo to the Creoles.

Fruit is good and plentiful, the usual types of the East. There are oranges but on the whole these are not good. Mostly they are green and thin-skinned, oval rather than round in shape and seldom if ever squeezed to make juice.

Both fish and meat are popular for there are no taboos in Vietnam. Beef is popular or would be if the price were low; mutton or lamb does not have many adherents but the hump of the buffalo has. However, pork is by far the most popular of all the meats and this is used in a number of ways as well as being the main ingredient of some splendid sausages and a pâté.

The Vietnamese pâté is a speciality and it is not one which we can readily reproduce at home. For this the meat must be absolutely fresh, so fresh that it is 'hot' from the slaughter house. Even one-day-old meat is not good enough. The meat, it is insisted 'must be sticky to the fingers'. It is possible to obtain this pâté in Paris where there are a number of excellent Vietnamese restaurants.

The basis of all alimentation is rice. The country belongs to the paddy fields. There is also mountain rice. The wealthy and the poor eat rice and drink tea but here their similarity in diet finishes. The poor eat a lot of fish, sea fish as well as river fish, but the latter is preferred. When one thinks of Vietnam with nostalgia it is of a country criss-crossed with rivers and of the curious light in the damp air.

Next to rice comes *nguoc-nam*, the fish sauce of Vietnam. It is traditional and the essential daily food of everyone, rich and poor alike. The Vietnamese believe that it is highly nutritious, bracing and filled with vitamins. It is given to the sick and lying-in women. Like all these fish sauces, its odour is repellent but again those foreigners who can surmount this obstacle, and obstacle it is, become passionate *nguoc-nam* adherents.

Nguoc-nam sauce is produced through a slow process of fermentation in which the fish is protected by the use of salt. If one wishes to have a rare quality of *nguoc-nam* the fish should marinate for ten years, but the usual time is six months or so. It is sold in bottles and jars and some 50 million litres of it is produced in a year, which gives some indication of its popularity.

Vietnamese cooking is not simple, to do things simply goes against the grain. Nor will they willingly give away their recipes; my struggle was therefore long and arduous. It is said that this is due to the old custom of giving a meal to a prospective bridegroom when the bride-to-be had to cook as many rare dishes as she could manage. No one gave away a recipe.

Among the more famous dishes of Vietnam is *chajo*, a kind of rolled pancake usually stuffed with bean sprouts, hard-boiled eggs and thinly sliced meat. An infinite number of omelettes heavily flavoured with herbs is eaten. One favourite is stuffed with crab meat, Chinese mushrooms and smothered with thinly sliced spring (green) onions. A great delicacy is the rock oyster. These are prised from the rocks in great chunks and taken to the markets. If you buy rock oysters you get them rock and all. They are not cheap. The Chinese so-called 'lacquered duck' has become naturalized but it is not considered a Vietnamese dish, any more than Birds' Nest Soup is.

As everywhere in the East, the markets are always crowded and one is continually bumping into preambulating 'eating shops' carrying hot bowls of soup or *pho* which is the local pot-au-feu. These bowls are carried on the ends of bamboo rods which are balanced across the vendors' shoulders. Vendors also serve rice, dried fish, bananas and tea.

Basically there are two main meals daily but the Vietnamese are inveterate nibblers, always ready to eat between meals. It was the custom and still is in parts of the remoter country for the women to eat after the men. But today things are moving fast and I wonder how many people also believe that the four indispensable virtues to make a good wife still apply. They are a competence in all the arts of the house, especially cooking; a natural beauty which is not aided by artifice; a beauty of language conforming to all its forms, and absolute faithfulness.

Apart from the general introduction to Vietnamese food in this section, I think an additional note should be added. Except in homes Vietnamese food is not easy to find. This is because Vietnamese cooking is time consuming and even restaurateurs are reluctant to give up much of their time. Another reason, I am told, for this reluctance to serve Vietnamese food is that the Vietnamese themselves are such good cooks of their own dishes that when they go out they prefer to eat either Chinese or French food.

The Vietnamese claim considerable variety in their dishes and claim to have not one national dish, but a dozen. Many are dishes prepared with extreme care and patience, the work of women who do not mind spending all day on getting one meal ready. The shopping list for a really good Vietnamese meal may run up to a hundred or more items.

The most distinguishing thing about a Vietnamese meal is the use of the famous *nguoc-nam*, a kind of fish sauce which appears again and again. The dishes are not especially 'hot' in flavour, rather more piquant. Even so some are too piquant for the average European, but usually seasonings are added by the individual to suit his or her own taste. However, for the foreigner an important point about a Vietnamese meal is the freedom of choice, for all the dishes are placed on the table at the same time and one moves from one dish to the other, taking as much of each and in whatever order one fancies.

BO BAY MON

Literally translated this means 'seven beef dishes' and this is just what it is. Each dish is prepared in a different manner. Some have beef diced, others minced or made into a pâté. Each dish has its own traditional sauce.

COM TAY CAM

This is considered a special treat and consists of rice cooked in a covered earthenware pot with a mixture of mushrooms, chicken and pork, sliced very thinly. It is served with a ginger sauce.

CHAO TOM

This dish comprises individual sticks of sugar cane around which is rolled a spiced shrimp paste and is then boiled. It is eaten as a 'do-it-yourself' rolled sandwich. Rice dough is spread on a large leaf, the shrimp paste is stripped off the cane and a few marinated vegetables are put on top. The whole thing is then wrapped up and dipped into *nguoc-nam*. It is eaten with chopsticks.

BEEF SOUP (*Pho*)

This is a traditional Vietnamese soup, substantial with an infinite variety of ingredients, depending on the traditions of the cook. It resembles a consommé and is always carefully prepared. The order in which the ingredients are added is important to ensure that the delicate flavour of each is retained. The ingredients can all be obtained in this country, with the exception of the Vietnamese mint. Apple mint is the best substitute.

12 servings:

Stock:
2 lb. shin of beef
1 beef stock cube
1 large marrow bone
2 large onions, halved
fresh ginger
star anise to taste (see **page 246**)
Soup:
2 lb. dried rice noodles

rump steak, about ½ lb., uncooked and
finely shredded
6–8 spring (green) onions, finely chopped
Vietnamese mint or **apple mint**
monosodium glutamate to taste
nguoc-nam (see **page 133**)
lemon juice

To prepare the stock, dissolve the beef cube in warm water, add the shin of beef, the marrow bone, the halved onions, ginger, and star anise to as much water as your largest pot will hold. Bring to the boil and cook gently for 2–3 hours, the longer the better. Strain. Chop the beef into very small pieces. Put aside.

To make the *pho*, drop the rice noodles in boiling water and boil for 5 minutes. Drain and put into large soup bowls. Add a layer of the finely shredded uncooked rump steak, the chopped cooked beef and the spring onions. Add a few leaves of mint.

Bring the stock which was put aside to the boil, add a little monosodium glutamate and 2–3 table-spoonfuls ($2\frac{1}{2}$–$3\frac{3}{4}$) fish sauce. Pour the stock over the *pho* (soup), squeeze in a few drops of lemon juice and the soup is then ready to serve.

BEEF VERMICELLI (*Bun Bo*)

6 servings:

2 lb. frying steak
1 lb. (2¼ cups) rice vermicelli
2 onions, finely chopped
salt, pepper
1 ridge or ½ large cucumber, peeled and
   chopped

4 oz. (¼ cup) peanuts, roasted and crushed
Sauce:
4 tablespoons (5) fish sauce
2 tablespoons (2½) water
1 teaspoon (1¼) vinegar
pinch of sugar and cayenne pepper

Bring plenty of water to the boil in a saucepan, add the vermicelli and cook it for 5 minutes. Place it under cold running water for 1 minute to keep the vermicelli firm and then drain. Divide into 6 warmed bowls or soup plates. Cut the meat into slices and fry it with the onions, salt and pepper for a few minutes. Arrange the cucumber on top of the vermicelli. Add the meat and onions and top with peanuts. Serve the sauce separately. One mixes the sauce into one's own portion, rather as a dressing into a green salad.

Rice vermicelli and fish sauce are sold in most Chinese and Oriental stores. If rice vermicelli is not available, use folded medium cut vermicelli. When steak is expensive, use half the quantity.

CHICKEN SALAD (*Nôm Gà*)

3–4 servings:

2 chicken breasts
1 thick piece belly pork
6 prawns
1 cucumber

2–3 small carrots
wine vinegar
sugar and salt
peanuts to taste, roasted and ground

Boil the chicken breasts and belly pork until tender. Take from the pan and leave both until cold. Shred the chicken into fairly large pieces; cut the pork into thin strips (cutting across the meat) and slice the prawns. Peel and slice the cucumber, rub salt into it then rinse. Grate the carrots. Mix these ingredients with a dressing of wine vinegar, sugar and salt. Sprinkle generously with ground roasted peanuts.

The type of cucumber used in this recipe is small and sweet, a ridge cucumber would be the nearest equivalent. The quantity of dressing is 'to taste'.

STUFFED RICE PANCAKES or ROLLS (*Cha Gio*)

These are small 2-inch rolls, depending on the manner in which they are prepared. They resemble the Chinese spring roll but made with a crisp crust of fine rice flour or rice leaves. They usually contain shrimp or crabmeat, pork and noodles as well as chopped vegetables, and all the ingredients for the stuffings are finely chopped. They are then rolled in thin rice flour wrappings or 'leaves', and deep fried. They are very popular with the Vietnamese.

6 servings:

1 lb. minced pork	1 egg
3 black mushroom caps, finely chopped	salt, pepper
1 small, finely chopped onion	rice flour wrappings
¼ lb. carrots, grated	oil for deep frying

Mix the mushrooms, onion, carrots and egg with the meat and add salt and pepper. Separate the rice leaves, sprinkle lightly with water to soften and place on each 2–3 tablespoonfuls (2½–3¾) of the mixture and roll into sausage shapes. Make sure the edges are tightly sealed. Deep fry them in boiling oil.

If rice flour wrappings are not available, use Chinese spring-roll leaves or squares of fine *strudel* pastry.

Serve with a green salad.

STEAMED EGG (*Trling Hâp*)

The Vietnamese are great egg eaters and prepare them in every possible way. The following recipe is one of the most common ways of preparing egg.

3 servings:

4 eggs	½ onion, finely chopped
2 large dried Chinese mushrooms	¼ lb. crabmeat or 12 peeled shrimps
small quantity Chinese vermicelli	salt, pepper
¼ lb. lean pork, minced	

Beat the eggs with salt and pepper to taste. Soak the mushrooms for 20 minutes and the vermicelli for 5 minutes. Thinly slice the mushrooms and cut the vermicelli in short bits of about 1 inch long. Chop the crabmeat or shrimps into small pieces. Mix this with the vermicelli, pork, mushrooms, and the onion, add the beaten egg and mix well. Put the whole mixture into a deep soup plate or Pyrex bowl and steam for about 20 minutes or until firm.

Alternatively the preparation can be fried by pouring it into hot fat, lowering the heat and slowly frying for 5 minutes. It then becomes an omelette.

China

Not the least of China's ancient arts is the art of cooking. It is a very old nation, the oldest living nation on earth, so it is not surprising to find that it is the cradle of all cooking east of India.

Throughout China's long history, through its periods of bright achievement and of darkest stagnation, the people have continued to cook and to eat. Often the sheer necessity for survival has taught the Chinese never to despise anything which might possibly be edible. Curiously they have taken immense risks, but experimenting with new items of food and combinations of flavourings and seasonings has made their cooking one of the most interesting, even fascinating, in the world.

They have taken the culinary art seriously, as they do music. There are books written on the art and pleasures of cooking, not only on how to cook but how to eat, and the result has been a cuisine which many knowledgeable people feel is unsurpassed. There runs a charming Vietnamese proverb: 'Eat in the Chinese fashion, live in a French house, marry a Japanese wife . . . and with this you have the secret of happiness.'

There are also three words in the Chinese language which perhaps sum up their epicurism. *Ten*, *yen*, *hen*. Or wait, avoid, attack. Wait when one is offered a plate which does not please, avoid those where the quantity exceeds the quality, and attack when one is offered a plate of perfection.

'The art of Chinese cooking depends on the art of mixing,' wrote the philosopher Lin Yutang. I would say that the art of Chinese cooking lies in the art of cutting. To watch a Chinese cook at his cutting board working with his sharp knives is to watch a fierce knife-dance, each movement perfection, up-down, up-down. He knows that this cutting will decide the ultimate quality of his cooking, cutting with the grain, each piece exactly the right size for perfect mingling, cooking and eating with chopsticks.

Another point in Chinese cooking is that in all the markets and shops small portions are sold. No one minds if all one wants is a chicken's wing, an ounce of pork, or a thin sliver of liver. The average Chinese cook prefers variety rather than quantity—quality he takes for granted.

China is a vast country and it would be a rash person indeed who would attempt to describe Chinese food collectively. It is as if one were asked to describe European food where there is a wealth of difference between Sicily in the south and Sweden in the north. In a country the size of China regional differences are marked. What is eaten in the Mongolian and Muslim restaurants is vastly different from the wine-cooked delicacies of Nanking. Any Chinese gourmet can tell immediately from which area or which school of Chinese cooking a dish originates.

Basically there are five main schools of Chinese cooking with several minor or lesser schools interwoven. The 'Big Five' are: Canton, Szechuan, Honan, Fukien and Shantung.

(1) CANTONESE COOKING:

This is the form of Chinese cooking best known to the foreigner, simply because 95 per cent of all restaurants outside of China are Cantonese. The Cantonese are a coastal people, footloose and wandering. Where they wandered they took their cooking with them, which was one of the finest in the land. There are several reasons for this. Their long stretch of coastline gives them a tremendous variety in sea food which they always use to advantage. Canton is the rice bowl of the country. It was the early Cantonese traders who became rich when their ports were opened to the West. Always interested in food, these newly rich traders would vie with one another in inventing dishes or in finding the perfect cook who could prepare one dish superbly and better than anyone else.

Cantonese cooking today is considered by many learned Chinese gourmets the finest of the Chinese schools of cooking, broader in base, more international with a great deftness of touch and delicacy in flavouring, and more variety. It contains oddities, not only from a Western point of view but from fellow Chinese. I do not mean oddities of the 'puppy dog tails' variety but dishes like turtle skirts, sea slugs, octopus, frogs' legs and game. Their use of herbs is so marked that there is a Chinese jibe that they use 'medicines' in their cooking. It is the school of the quick-fry-stir cooking, sophisticated food where the sweet-sour sauces are neither too sweet nor too sour.

To get a job as a Cantonese cook in a home or a first-class restaurant the aspirant must have studied his craft for eight years. When he applies for the job he is given four simple tests. This is called 'knocking on wood' also 'knocking on the brick'. If he passes his test he gets the job.

(2) SZECHUAN COOKING:

A province in the south-west of China with two definite schools of cooking. It is mainly famed for its hot, even fiery, cooking and its sweet dishes. The dishes, however, are more subtly flavoured than those of India. Szechuan cooking also produces the best ham in China and has a large variety of fungi. Its cooking is described as fairly representative and exceedingly inventive.

(3) HONAN COOKING:

Honan was once the capital of China and the seat of the Court so its cooking is rich, as befitting an erstwhile capital. It specializes in sweet and sour dishes. Its variety probably is more limited than in the other schools of cooking but it always maintains a high standard. Among the dishes for which the province is especially noted is a custard in the form of a soufflé omelette, 'One Fish in Four Forms', 'Walnut Kidney' in which the kidneys are cut into the size of a walnut and crisply fried, and dishes which contain the 'Monkey Head' mushrooms which grow exclusively in this province. According to the Chinese, this mushroom is even tastier than the truffle of Europe.

(4) FUKIEN COOKING:

Another province with a fine coastline and, therefore, much emphasis on fish cooking with a special penchant for shrimps and shrimp sauces. It is good all-round cooking, light and full of flavour. Fukien cooks have a fondness for crystal clear soups and soupy dishes in general. It is also the home of paper-wrapped foods and dishes with little adornment, depending on original flavour for its appeal. Fukien produces the best and richest soy sauce.

(5) SHANTUNG COOKING:

Here the cooking depends less on the exotic than on long-tested skills, natural inventiveness and imagination, never at any time forgetting the cardinal sin in Chinese cooking, monotony. They are fond of such delicacies as swan's liver cooked in wine and specialize in a form of cooking they call soft-fry. Scallions, chives, leeks and garlic all figure prominently in Shantung cooking.

These then are the basic schools of Chinese cooking, but the winds of change are blowing even through the traditional schools. Today the Chinese cook depends less on the exotic to make his culinary point. Dishes such as larks' tongues, apes' lips, camels' humps and owls' eggs which, although perhaps not everyday dishes, were not infrequent, have well-nigh disappeared. Bear's paw, a rather glutinous mass of meat belonging to the German pig's trotters school of cooking (it has something of the consistency of fat ham), is still available in Hong Kong, Taiwan and the Mainland. But, once manna to the Chinese—and very expensive—it is no longer considered essential to tempt the jaded appetite. However, whatever these changes, it is most unlikely that the Chinese culinary genius will ever lose his touch.

An interesting aspect of Chinese cooking is its morality. Certain dishes are for certain occasions. For example, take that extremely popular but seasonal dish called *ta pin lo* (steamboat, *see* page 112). Try to persuade a restaurateur to serve one of these out of season. Even if locally he is famed for this dish he will positively refuse to do so.

Where this morality is particularly shown is in the traditional banquet or a dinner where guests are invited. There was a time, in living memory no less, when such a dinner meant forty courses, several hours of steady but delicious eating of a meal which took a team of experts several days to prepare, for Chinese cooking is more preparation than cooking. Now even fourteen courses is considered somewhat ostentatious, twelve is more usual for a grand affair, six or seven for a small effort.

Eating out has become a modern habit, the result of modern living where wives too must work and homes are overcrowded. There was a time when only men went to restaurants; banquets were held at home. These, even for the middle classes, were days of spacious living.

Banquet dishes, whether for small or large dinners, are served in a special order. Both in the type of food served and the method of serving, it is different from the everyday meal. All tradition must be followed. Banquets generally are served at round tables each seating ten or twelve people. If ordering a dinner in a restaurant, which most people do, food is prepared 'per table', and if there is one guest more or less it makes no difference either in the seating or the price.

Beef is not served at banquets (by banquet is meant a dinner at which there are guests, not a meal to which one invites the Lord Mayor). 'Do not eat the cow,' say the Chinese, 'for it is a hard-working and *sympatico* beast. The pig is another matter. His only mission in life is to be eaten. But the chicken, this is poetry in gastronomy.' The banquet must be sumptuous, well thought out, correctly served, each course coming in individually, not all at once as for family meals.

A good banquet will begin with two bowls of nuts and two of fruit. Chinese wine might well be served with this. On the table will be four small dishes of cold food, small eats or hors-d'œuvre. When these are toyed with, four dishes are brought in, hot but still small. After them come the eight big dishes which are served one at a time.

Half way through appears the sharks' fin soup, first because it is liked, second because it is expensive. This is also the sign that the wine cups are to be refilled and also emptied. After the sharks' fin soup has been poured into the small bowls and everyone has commented on its flavour and cleaned his bowl, the next dish arrives. What this is depends on the area, the school of cooking etc. It might well be Peking duck, that lacquered splendid beauty, or roast sucking pig.

Last of all comes the fish and the reason for this is curious. The tone word for fish is exactly the same as the tone word for 'to spare'. The Chinese do not say they have finished a meal, they say they have 'to spare'. An expression which comes from the days when the Chinese peasants had little enough to eat.

After the 'Big Dishes' come the sweet dishes, usually four different kinds, and after these rice with eggs or roasted meat or noodles with soup. There is little guide for the unfortunate foreigner at his first banquet as to when he is going to finish the meal. A whispered conversation at one such meal brought the information that 'usually there is nothing after the fruit'. This follows the tea and cigarettes.

Finally hot towels, which appear at the beginning of the meal, reappear, and when the meal is over the guest of honour leaves first, followed by the remaining guests, the host leaving last.

The first choice of the Chinese cook is chicken—his repertoire includes three hundred ways of cooking it. Then he considers duck, where again the repertoire is fantastic, and finally he thinks of pork and wonders which of the two hundred and one ways he should prepare it, and which of the sixty ways to steam fish.

In days gone by the Chinese preferred a square table seating two at each side. Nowadays the preference is for the round table and ten is the usual number seated. It is usual to sit on stools. The round table, the stools and the communal dishes which are arranged in the centre of the table makes for elasticity as far as the number of people who can be accommodated at one meal. Each person at table has the minimum essentials, chopsticks, a spoon and a rice bowl. Chopsticks may be of ivory, bamboo, silver, wood or even plastic. Bowls usually are of porcelain, except among the very poor when they are of enamel.

Table setting is not difficult to master. Each place setting for a Chinese meal includes the rice bowl, porcelain soup spoon, a somewhat shallow smaller soup bowl, a small shallow dish for sauce, a larger one for the main dishes and a tea cup. These six pieces can be bought as a set in any porcelain store in Chinese areas. A Chinese dinner set, therefore, consists of ten such place sets, plus the serving dishes. These include special bowls for sharks' fin soup, covered soup dishes, long platters for fish, some bowls which are not unlike Western cream bowls and various-sized porcelain spoons, some very small for sauces.

Etiquette is complicated for a banquet, for the seating is determined by the position of the door through which comes the food. Facing this door is the favoured position to see each course as it arrives. The host sits at the lowest end of the table, which is usually south and near to the serving door. The guest of honour is therefore always seated furthest from his host. It is correct for the guest of honour to demur and protest but to be finally persuaded.

Finally, as a mild note of amusement, the 'boarding house reach' so frowned upon in the West,

Indonesian Rijsttafel (see page 120)

is positively correct in Chinese etiquette. Not only is it correct, but the host as a sign of politeness will pick up what he considers to be a choice morsel and stretch right across the table, from south to north, to drop it neatly into a guest's bowl. Chinese children are taught to clean up their rice bowls and not to concentrate only on one favourite dish throughout the meal. And must certainly never touch food with their fingers. Incidentally, the Chinese were not introduced to chopsticks until the seventeenth century.

Chinese eating times appear to be elastic. They eat when they are hungry even though they will eat their three meals daily. In the middle of the night somewhere an eating house will still be serving its clients. A popular form of modern Chinese eating is the *dim-sum*, the collective Cantonese name for a range of small eats, some sweet, some savoury. Literally the name means 'to touch the heart' and there are as many as one hundred varieties. These are served, usually, between meals in large roomy restaurants which give the *dim-sum* girls space to walk around and peddle their wares, trays strapped over their shoulders, like a cigarette girl's tray. On the *dim-sum* tray are titillating morsels, dumplings, chicken livers, meat balls and so on. All are neatly arranged in sets of four in small bamboo baskets.

The good *dim-sum* cook is in great demand and he usually cooks for more than one restaurant, rushing hither and thither.

A blind spot in the Chinese cuisine is their puddings. Peking Dust, toffee apples, and one or two of the milk and egg dishes are probably the best. But for the most part they remain too sweet for most Westerners.

No description of Chinese food would be complete without mention of some of their special dishes. For instance a dish of ham cooked in honey or fried seaweed which melts in the mouth, or spiced roast duck, in which the bird is first rubbed in rice wine and flavoured with star anise (*see* page 246). Chickens' breasts stuffed with mushrooms, boned chickens stuffed with nuts. There is nothing of the pig which does not find itself in the Chinese cook's pan, including a dish of the pig's stomach, stuffed with barley, something which should bring joy to the haggis eater.

Another interesting dish is 'Beggar's Chicken'. This is a whole chicken, killed and cleaned for roasting but not feathered, stuffed with salt cabbage and aromatic herbs, wrapped in a lotus leaf and then encased in a mud packing. It is thrown into the hot embers of an almost dying fire, baked and opened with ceremony with a silver hammer (some beggar) or else dashed dramatically to the floor to crack open its casing. The chicken is tender, some might say too tender, for it tears into shreds rather than cuts.

There are idiosyncrasies in Chinese cooking. The Chinese do not consider shark as a fish, nor a sharks' fin soup as a soup. If looking for sharks' fin, look among the sundries on the menu. There are several methods of cooking this but the glutinous northern method is not usually acceptable to foreigners. It was the Cantonese who devised the famous soup. Sharks' meat is not generally used, except that of the young shark which is purchased from the cooked meat vendors, mixed with shrimp and fat pork and stuffed into peppers. This palatable dish is served to the passing labourers.

Dog, monkey's brains, field mice and snakes. Touchy subjects. The Chinese, however, are not touchy about snake dishes. Snake dishes are winter dishes served usually as main dishes but very much as soups.

Once the Westerner has recovered from the initial shock of having eaten snake, one admits they are palatable. It is possible to order a dinner in a snake restaurant in which all the courses are of snake, all the different edible varieties well disguised. I do not understand why they should be disguised.

Japanese Tempura (*see page* 198)

'The Meeting of the Three' is for example three edible varieties of snake in the same dish garnished with chrysanthemum petals. A similar dish is 'Three-Snake-Wild-Cat' which is shredded filleted snake, three varieties, and bamboo shoots garnished with chrysanthemum petals and lemon leaves.

Many dishes mean something symbolical to the Chinese and they give them fanciful names. I like the title 'The Dragon, the Lion and the Phoenix' although I like less the description. The dragon is represented by the snake, the chicken is the phoenix, and the lion a cat. I do not know if I have eaten cat. I would rather not know.

Lizards also have their place in the Chinese kitchen, and so does a dish of rice worms. Red and yellow, they are served in a bowl over which is poured pure rock salt. This causes their hypersensitive skins to burst and suddenly one is faced with a wriggling mass of red and yellow something. There are dishes of tree beetles, which taste only of the sauces into which they are dipped, and of pig's testicles.

The only alcoholic beverage which really goes with Chinese food is rice wine and this is widely used throughout China and where Chinese cooking predominates. Like the Japanese sake, it is served in small cups and these are frequently filled during the course of an evening. As with eating, there are many traditional rules for drinking. Wine is usually served warm, and wine cups and wine canisters vary in shape and size.

Wine is served at all feasts, whether a wedding or a funeral. It is part and parcel of the meal, without it a meal, however splendid, would lose its dignity. With wine, say the Chinese, as with the French, the level of the meal rises. But the Chinese traditionally drink only with their meals, only those who have acquired Western habits would call for a drink either before or after a meal. To order a drink at a restaurant, one must also order something to eat.

The choice of dishes for a Chinese meal is memorable. There are dishes for every occasion. The Chinese, like the Japanese, like to eat things in season (to a certain extent, for one must remember the vast quantity of dried and preserved foods which are part of the Chinese cuisine), and food must be prepared in such a manner that it brings the season to the eye or the senses, even if they be hot dishes on a hot day they must nevertheless appear cool. A considerable amount of thought goes into the choosing of menus, partly because there is such a great choice but also because all Chinese like to think they are gastronomes, and have felt this way since the days of Confucius who wrote:

> *No one does not eat and drink:*
> *But few can appreciate the nicety of taste.*

However, it must be admitted that the Chinese, man for man, is far more interested in food than his counterpart in the West, even including the French. There is among the Chinese a ritualistic approach to food.

There are two main varieties of Chinese vermicelli, neither of them resembling Italian vermicelli, made from green beans and seaweed respectively. The green bean vermicelli is used in both hot and cold dishes and needs only briefly being dropped into boiling water before being used, while the seaweed type needs soaking for twenty minutes in lukewarm water before being cooked. The shiny type of vermicelli is considered the best.

There is a fair amount of wine used in Chinese cooking, especially in northern cooking. It is also used as a marinade. Both wine and soy sauce are used to eliminate fish smells and the odour of certain meats. Wines are made from fruits, melons, game, herbs and even snakes. Some are similar to brandy or whisky, some to sherry and sauternes. Some are mild, others rather strong or even very fierce.

Dim-sum boxes. Chopsticks correctly held

Wine is not considered as a drink for pleasure but more as a medicament or a food. Snake wine flavoured with herbs is said to cure rheumatism and improve poor blood. There is a tigerbone wine, pear wine, orange wine, rice dew wine and a glutinous rice wine. As with the usual Western wines, these wines require ageing. Some are available in Oriental stores.

BEAN or PEA SPROUTS (*Ngas Choy*)

These are very simple to make at home, almost in the same manner that children grow mustard and cress. Use either a non-rust metal rack or better still a loosely woven basket. Suspend this over a large bowl. Cover it with a double layer of wet cheese cloth, sprinkle a layer of tiny peas or soy beans over this and cover in turn with another layer of wet cheese cloth. See that the water drains off properly after frequently sprinkling generously with water for it can become slightly stagnant and the sprouts will absorb some of this unpleasant odour. The sprouts are ready after 5 to 7 days, depending on the temperature. Soaking them too long also makes them stagnant.

If making them often it is best to prepare them in small batches at different times so that you are always prepared. Although all Chinese cooking experts say remove the small pod adhering to the sprout it really is not a crime if this remains; certainly we have eaten the pods with relish. Bean sprouts take only a matter of minutes to cook.

FRIED BEAN SPROUTS (*Ch'ao Tou Ta'ai*)

4–6 servings:

1 lb. bean sprouts
4 oz. (½ cup) pork fat or lard
4–6 large Chinese mushrooms, soaked and thinly sliced
1 head celery, shredded

salt to taste
1 tablespoon (1¼) soy sauce
¼ cup (⅓) stock
1 teaspoon (1¼) cornflour (cornstarch)

Heat the fat in a frying pan, add the mushrooms and celery and fry for a few minutes. Add the bean sprouts, salt, soy and stock and cook for 3–5 minutes. Mix the cornflour with enough water to make a thin paste. Stir this into the beans and cook until it thickens. Serve hot.

Tinned bean sprouts may be used.

BASIC FRIED RICE (*Chow Fan*)

4–6 servings:

3 cups (3¾) cold cooked rice
2 slices lean bacon, diced
2 tablespoons (2½) oil
3–4 eggs, well beaten

2–4 spring (green) onions, cut into thin strips
monosodium glutamate to taste
1 tablespoon (1¼) light soy sauce

Heat frying pan and fry the bacon until it is crisp. Take out the bacon, add the oil to the pan, heat this add the eggs and quickly, before the eggs set, add the rice. Stir this vigorously and work the rice into the eggs, stirring until all the rice is coated with the eggs. Return the bacon to the pan, add the spring onions, monosodium glutamate and finally the soy sauce. Mix this well and serve at once.

Serve as an accompaniment to other dishes. To it may be added strips of cooked pork, shelled shrimps or prawns.

TEN PRECIOUS RICE or FRIED RICE (*Chow Fan*)

6–8 servings:

4 cups (5) cold cooked rice
½ lb. prawns or shrimps, shelled
½ lb. uncooked chicken breast
½ cup each ham and pork, finely chopped
2–3 spring (green) onions
2–3 dried mushrooms, soaked and thinly sliced

1 small piece bamboo shoot, thinly sliced
3–4 eggs
1 tablespoon (1¼) soy sauce
peanut, sesame or vegetable oil
1 cup (1¼) shelled peas
salt to taste

Dice the prawns, meat, onions, mushrooms and bamboo shoot. Whisk the eggs with soy sauce and put these aside until required. Heat a deep frying pan and rub it with oil, add the vegetables, except the spring onions, and when these are almost cooked add the meat and prawns and finally the spring onions. As soon as these ingredients are properly cooked, add salt.

In another pan heat 2 tablespoonfuls (2½) of oil until it smokes. Add the rice, stirring it evenly and well. When it is thoroughly reheated, stir the fried ingredients into the rice, stir again so that all is thoroughly mixed, then add the beaten eggs, stir again quite rapidly, and continue cooking over a good heat until the eggs are cooked and the whole fairly dry. Serve at once, for the hotter the rice the better it will taste.

FRIED NOODLES (*Jou Szu Ch'ao Mien*)

6 servings:

1 lb. very fine Chinese egg noodles
1 tablespoon (1¼) cornflour (cornstarch)
6 tablespoons (7½) peanut or vegetable oil
1 small onion, shredded
4 large dried mushrooms, soaked for 30 minutes, thinly sliced

½ lb. bamboo shoots, shredded
¼ lb. each raw pork and chicken, shredded
1 tablespoon (1¼) soy sauce
1 cup (1¼) stock
salt
1–2 egg omelette, shredded

Cook the noodles in boiling salted water until they are soft but not sticky. Drain in a sieve and rinse in cold water. Mix the cornflour with water to a thin paste and coat the meat with this. Heat 2 tablespoonfuls (2½) of oil until it is smoking and pour this over the noodles, separating them as much as possible. Return the noodles to the pan and fry, stirring all the time until a golden brown. Turn the noodles out on to a hot dish and keep hot.

Add the remainder of the oil and fry the onion to a light brown, add the mushrooms and cook for a moment or so, then add the remaining ingredients except the omelette. Cook this for 5 minutes to make a sauce. Take out half of this sauce and put aside but keep hot. Add the noodles to the pan and mix everything together, stirring it all very lightly. Pour this all back into the hot noodle dish and over the top pour the remaining sauce. Garnish with the shredded omelette.

Often Chinese wine is added to the sauce.

SAVOURY DUMPLINGS (*Cha Siu Bao*)

Dumplings are so much a part of the Chinese way of cooking, in 'small eats' or *dim-sums*, that at least one recipe must be included. Dumplings come in all sizes and with varied stuffings. These dumplings are for a sweet soup.

4 cups (5) flour
½ cup (⅔) fine sugar
3 teaspoons (3¾) baking powder
¼ cup (⅓) pork fat or lard

1 cup (1¼) cold water
1 lb. cooked pork, cut into small cubes
oyster sauce and white vinegar
oil for deep frying

Mix the flour, sugar, baking powder, fat and water together to form a dough. Knead this well for 8 minutes. When the dough is soft and pliable, cut it into strips; it is a pretty large piece of dough. Roll these strips into 'sausages' 1½ inches in diameter. Break off small pieces of the dough and flatten each piece. Mix the pork with enough oyster sauce and white vinegar to give flavour. Heat the oil and fry the pieces of pork until crisp and tender, then slightly cool. Push into each piece of dough a cube of the meat and then shape the pieces into dumplings, covering up the hole. Get the steamer ready and put a square of wax paper over the top part of the steamer and on this arrange the dumplings, about ½ inch apart. Steam over a bubbling boiling heat for 20 minutes and serve very hot.

The recipe makes a lot of dumplings and can well be halved.

SOUPS

ABALONE SOUP (*Pao Yu Tong*)

6 servings:

½ small tin abalone (see page 235), thinly sliced
4 Chinese mushrooms
1–2 thin slices pork
1 teaspoon (1¼) cornflour (cornstarch)
1 tablespoon (1¼) soy sauce
a little sugar

1–2 tablespoons (1¼–2½) peanut oil
2–3 slices fresh ginger, chopped
½ teaspoon (⅔) salt
pepper to taste
1 spring (green) onion
2 thin slices ham, cut into strips
1 teaspoon (1¼) monosodium glutamate

Soak the mushrooms for 30 minutes, remove the stalks and slice the caps very thinly into strips. Cut the pork into fine strips, mix this with the cornflour, soy sauce, sugar and a very little oil. Heat a small quantity of oil in a saucepan, add the ginger, salt and pepper, and fry for 2–3 minutes, add 6 cupfuls (7½) of hot water and bring this to the boil. Add the mushrooms, onion and the pork. Stir well, bring again to the boil, cover the pan, lower the heat and cook gently for 10 minutes. Add the ham, monosodium glutamate and the abalone, cook gently again for exactly 5 minutes and serve at once.

BIRDS' NEST SOUP (*Yin Wa Tong*)

Birds' nests have been known to the Chinese as a delicacy even longer than they have known their other favourite, sharks' fin. When the Imperial Palace in Peking was taken over from the last of the Manchu monarchs, a large quantity of birds' nests was discovered in the provision room, but no sharks' fins.

These birds' nests, so much enjoyed throughout South East Asia and elsewhere in the world where there is a sizeable Chinese community, are no ordinary nest of twigs and dried leaves. On the contrary, they are the nests of a particular kind of swift or swallow which makes its home around the crags or cliffs of the China coast, in Malaysia and some even in Australia.

The nests vary somewhat. In shape they have one flat side where it was attached to the wall of the caves, while the outside is the shape and size of a tablespoon or serving spoon. Some are made almost entirely from the dried glutinous saliva of the birds, and these are known as white nests and sell for the most money. Other nests are full of feathers and sea debris, and are known as black nests. These are cheaper. But either type is considered by the Chinese to have a high protein value since the birds feed on small fish as well as an assortment of seaweed and other extraneous matter floating in the sea.

The nests are pried from the crevasses, crags and ledges of caves often at great heights (one such cave in Malaysia has been described as cathedral-like in its size and awe-inspiring gloom). The base of the caves and cliffs is thick in guano, giving an almost carpet-like tread plus a decidedly pungent smell.

The nest collecting season is carefully chosen to allow for the building of the white nests in June and July which is made a closed season to ensure future supplies. White nests are collected but once a year, black nests twice a year. March and April are collecting months for both types of nests, September for black nests only.

Men risk their lives to collect the nests so it is no wonder they are so expensive. Nests on the roofs of caves are collected with the aid of long ladders. Some nests are gathered by hand, others with the aid of long-pronged forks. All the white nests are taken first, then comes the assault on the black ones.

The nests are then bundled together and taken to a store shed, for this is a well-organized business, and checked by officers of the Forest Department, at least this is so in Malaysia where most of the finest nests are found. They are then sold with the government taking its cut or percentage.

From this point they are prepared, cleaned and the feathers and other adherents picked off. Then they are ready to provide the tasty morsel which Chinese gourmets all over the world cherish. The best nests are those which have the least feathers but the price is finally decided by the shape and size. But even lesser qualities are still highly prized. Nowadays, as with the sharks' fins, birds' nests are sold ready for the pot in a pre-prepared form which makes it easier for the housewife-cook.

Incidentally, the Chinese believe that the chemical processes which take place in these nests when exposed for a long time to the elements lend them a tonic value, and those who eat them are assured of a long life and good health. In actual fact, birds' nests have little flavour of their own, the real flavour comes from the soup in which they are cooked and their garnishing. Do not overcook the nests or they will disintegrate.

Birds' nests are divided into grades. For example, one ounce of first grade equals 8 oz. after it has been soaked. Second grade equals only 5 oz. after soaking. Fourth grade even less, and so on. But these distinctions apply only to those areas where the birds' nests are a matter of everyday cooking. And methods of cooking vary according to the place and quality of the birds' nests.

Manila Yellow is considered by gourmets as the best; the white nests of Borneo and what was once Indo-China are used for the preparing of savoury dishes, while Thai birds' nests are for sweet dishes, also used as a tonic—half a cupful of birds' nest in stock is considered very strengthening.

8–10 servings:

3 oz. prepared birds' nest or half a box
8–10 cups (10–12½) strained chicken stock
4–6 dried Chinese mushrooms, soaked and sliced
6 water chestnuts, coarsely chopped

2–3 teaspoons (2½–3¾) cooked ham, diced
1 tablespoon (1¼) cornflour (cornstarch), mixed with water to a thin paste
1 teaspoon (1¼) salt

Soak the nest for 30 minutes in tepid water. Clean off any foreign substance (it is doubtful that you will find much). Have the stock quite boiling and cook it for 20 minutes. Add the nest, mushrooms, chestnuts and ham and cook for another 5–10 minutes. Stir in the cornflour paste, add salt and continue cooking for 5 minutes, stirring all the time.

Instead of mushrooms and water chestnuts, which are a garnish, hard-boiled plovers' or pigeons' eggs may be used, quails' eggs are even nicer and much used in the East. Another garnish is shredded chicken breasts. Chinese cooks also like to completely de-bone a chicken, return it to its former shape, the body stuffed with birds' nests. This is sometimes served in deep dishes with chicken stock as a soup, i.e. you take the chicken out first with chopsticks and then ladle out the soup with the small Chinese-style soup spoons.

Birds' nests are usually sold in cellophane packages or tins, and they will keep for years.

There is, by the way, a sweet dish made from birds' nests. The nest is simply cooked for 30 minutes and then sugar is added.

MUSHROOM SOUP (*Ch'ing Tun Hua Ku Tong*)

4 servings:

¼ lb. Chinese dried mushrooms, soaked for 30 minutes and chopped
½ chicken
salt
1 slice fresh ginger, chopped

1 spring (green) onion, chopped
1 tablespoon (1¼) Chinese wine or substitute
6 cups (7½) water

Chop the chicken into pieces, the size is not important. Put the pieces into water and cook gently for 3 hours together with the remaining ingredients. Strain, but use the mushrooms in the soup as a garnish and, if liked, the chicken flesh stripped from the bones and shredded.

This soup will not have the same flavour as a mushroom soup made with fresh mushrooms.

SHARKS' FIN SOUP (*Yu Chi Tong*)

Sharks' fins come from India, Korea, Japan, Mexico, the Philippines and Norway. The best comes from the Philippines and is by far the most tender and contains the most edible meat. Sharks' fins have no taste when they are fresh, only after they have been sun-dried or cured do they become tasty.

The cooking of sharks' fins used to be laborious and many recipes for this popular soup give instructions for long preparations, soaking it in cold water for 3 days, then long simmering until its sandy skin is easily removed etc. Nowadays sharks' fins are usually sold in pre-prepared form, an almost instant sharks' fin, which requires only soaking for a matter of hours.

Sharks' fins are expensive anywhere. They are in fairly short supply and however sold their preparation somewhere along the line is time consuming. Even so, among the Chinese it is traditional to serve sharks' fin soup at important dinners, and a Chinese cook is prepared to stake his reputation on the quality of his soup.

4–6 servings:

½ lb. sharks' fin
1 tablespoon (1¼) sesame, peanut or vegetable oil
1-in. piece fresh ginger, thinly sliced
1 spring (green) onion, sliced
2 tablespoons (2½) Chinese wine (see page 153)
8 cups (10) chicken stock
½ lb. chicken breast, shredded

8 shrimps, shredded
2 teaspoons (2½) soy sauce
1 tablespoon (1¼) cornflour (cornstarch)
Seasoning:
1 tablespoon (1¼) Chinese wine
1 teaspoon (1¼) sesame or peanut oil
1 teaspoon (1¼) light soy sauce
pinch of salt

Soak the fin for 12 hours or overnight or until the salt has completely disappeared. Put the fin into a pan with plenty of water and boil steadily for 3 hours, or if still salty, change the water and reboil until the fin is completely free of salt. Drain and dry.

Heat the first quantity of oil and fry the ginger and onion and add the first quantity of wine. Let this simmer for a few minutes, add the fin and fry for a few minutes, add half the stock, much of which will be absorbed by the fin. Mix the chicken and the shrimps with the soy sauce. Heat a little more oil in a frying pan and lightly fry the chicken and shrimps. Add to the fin, stir thoroughly then add the remaining stock and the seasoning ingredients. Simmer. Mix the cornflour with enough water to make a thin paste, stir this into the soup and cook for 5 minutes.

Serve the soup hot. Put one bowl of cooked or tinned bamboo shoots cut into fine strips on the table and another with vinegar. Each person adds a little of the vinegar to the soup to bring out its flavour and the bamboo shoots are added as a garnish.

If buying sharks' fin in a package, study the instructions carefully. Nowadays much of it is sold pre-cooked and ready for the pot.

SHREDDED PORK WITH CABBAGE SOUP (*Suet Choy Yoke See Tong*)

6–8 servings:

½ lb. lean pork, cut into shreds
½ lb. white cabbage, shredded
1 tablespoon (1¼) peanut or vegetable oil
small piece fresh ginger, chopped

8 cups (10) chicken stock
salt, pepper
spring (green) onion, finely chopped

Heat the oil in a saucepan, add the ginger and the stock, then the salt and pepper and bring to a boil. Add the cabbage and pork and cook gently between 7 and 10 minutes. Serve very hot sprinkled with spring onion.

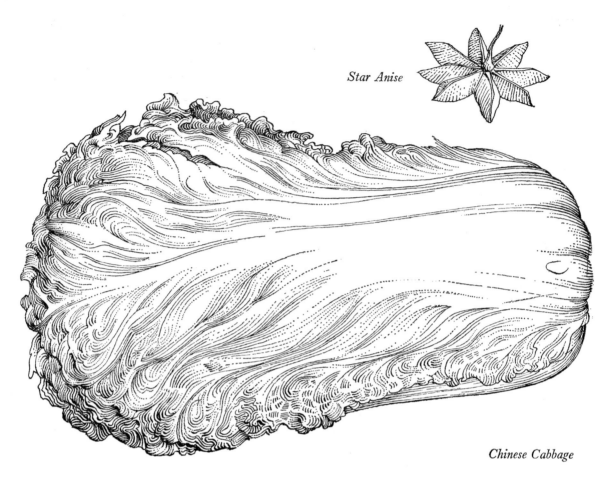

Star Anise

Chinese Cabbage

SHRIMP AND EGG SOUP (*Har Yun Darn Far Tong*)

4–6 servings:

½ lb. shrimps
2 eggs, beaten with 2 tablespoons (2½)
   water
1 tablespoon (1¼) peanut or vegetable oil

6 strips fresh ginger
6 cups (7½) chicken stock
salt, pepper

In this recipe, preferably raw, shelled shrimps should be used but pre-cooked will do.

   Heat the oil, add the ginger, stir and fry for a minute or so, add the stock and seasoning to taste. Bring to the boil, add the shrimps and cook until these are pink, if using raw, otherwise only a minute to heat. Pour in the beaten eggs, stirring as you pour, simmer for 2 or 3 minutes and serve hot.

WINTER MELON SOUP or POND (*Doon Gwah Joog*)

This soup belongs to the class of Chinese banquet soups but it is sometimes served for a special family meal. It is a conversation piece, for the soup is served in the large, silvery-green winter melon in which it is also cooked. The winter melon is grown in the United States; Holland is now beginning to grow it for use with Indonesian cooking. It is or can be truly enormous and is a soft frosty silver-brushed green colour with a white flesh. However, where there is no winter melon, I think a solid pumpkin would do almost as well, although there is no doubt that a pumpkin would give the soup some of its slightly sweet flavour.

Cut off the top of the melon, scoop out the seeds and a good deal of its white spongy flesh; the scooped out flesh can also be made into a soup. The melon is now like a large bowl.

Chop (and the following measurements are approximate) ¼ lb. each of raw duck, chicken and pork meat, dried oysters, Chinese (or Westphalia or Parma) smoked ham into thin strips. Put all this into the melon and fill it up with chicken stock. Salt, pepper and Chinese wine may be added.

Steam the melon with its contents in a large pot for about 2 hours. While it is cooking dice 2 or 3 dried mushrooms (previously soaked) with about the same quantity of shrimps or crab or lobster. These should be added at the end of the cooking as they require only the minimum of cooking, although the mushrooms can be added earlier. Abalone is also often added or lotus seeds, bamboo shoots etc.

When lifting the melon from the saucepan, do this carefully, although it is hard to do it otherwise. The soup is served in the melon and this half inside another container. It is all much easier than it sounds. But some help is required in handling the melon when it is hot. Do not overcook, otherwise the outside will become too soft and the whole thing will collapse. Incidentally I wrap the melon in a cloth so that two of us can pull it out easily. Also I have a saucepan large enough to take a grid as a base; this I put into the pan, add plenty of water and rest my melon on top.

'Soup-in-a-Melon' usually is served as the last dish at gala dinners, 'because your guests may need some different-looking dish to cheer them up', I was told, and the taste of this soup is quite different from the usual run of soups. The melon or pumpkin which is used as a vessel to hold the soup adds much to its flavour.

ABALONE SALAD (*Bow Yee*)

4–6 servings:

1 small tin abalone (see **page 235**)
1 head celery, fresh or **tinned**
sugar, salt

1–2 teaspoons (1¼–2½) peanut, vegetable or or sesame oil
1 tablespoon (1¼) light soy sauce

Drain the abalone. Cut into very thin slices. Wash the celery and cut into diagonal slices. Mix both these ingredients with salt and sugar and add the oil and soy sauce, enough to lightly coat the abalone and celery. Chill and serve.

Do not use more celery than abalone.

Abalone is sold pre-cooked and ready to eat.

CHINESE SALAD DRESSING (*Leng P'en*)

2 tablespoons (2½) mild vinegar or **lemon juice**
2 tablespoons (2½) light soy sauce

1 tablespoon (1¼) sugar
1 tablespoon (1¼) peanut or **vegetable oil**

Mix the first three ingredients together, then gradually stir in the oil. Serve with thinly sliced cucumber, lettuce, tomatoes etc., and with sliced cold meat. A little finely chopped fresh ginger is a good addition.

PRAWNS IN CHILLI SAUCE

2 servings:

1 lb. fresh prawns
peanut or vegetable oil for frying
6 spring (green) onions, cut into strips
2–3 cloves garlic, crushed
1 tablespoon (1¼) fresh ginger, sliced
1 tablespoon (1¼) Chinese wine

1 tablespoon (1¼) soy sauce
1 teaspoon (1¼) sugar
black pepper and salt
1 tablespoon (1¼) each tomato and chilli
  sauce

Shell the prawns and devein them. Heat the oil until it is very hot, drop in the prawns (if they are very large, cut them into halves) and fry for 2 minutes. Drain on absorbent paper.

Pour off all but about 2 tablespoonfuls (2½) of the oil and reheat what remains in the pan over a high flame. Add the spring onion, garlic and ginger and stir until the onion changes colour. Discard the garlic. Add the wine, soy sauce, sugar, pepper and salt. Stir for a few minutes, add the prawns, again stir and finally add the tomato and chilli sauces, still stirring. Serve immediately.

SHRIMPS AND GREEN PEAS (*Ching Dao Ha Yan*)

4–6 servings:

1 lb. shrimps or small prawns
2 teaspoons (2½) cornflour (cornstarch)
sesame or vegetable oil
1 teaspoon (1¼) salt
1 teaspoon (1¼) monosodium glutamate
1 teaspoon (1¼) light soy sauce

1 teaspoon (1¼) sugar
1 small piece ginger, finely chopped
2–3 spring (green) onions
1–2 cloves garlic, finely chopped
1 lb. packet frozen peas

If using raw shrimps, these must be shelled and washed and dried. Make a sauce. Mix the cornflour with enough water and a little oil to a thin paste, put into a small pan, add salt, monosodium glutamate, soy sauce and sugar, bring this to a gentle boil and cook for 3 minutes. In another pan heat 1 tablespoonful (1¼) of oil, add the shrimps and cook until they change colour, then add the ginger, spring onions, garlic, green peas and sauce. Cook until the peas are tender and serve hot.

This is a side dish to be eaten with other small dishes and for this reason serves between 4–6 people. If using cooked shrimps or prawns, add these after the peas as they require only heating.

PRAWNS IN SOY SAUCE (*Hung Shao Tui Hsia*)

2–4 servings:

1 lb. prawns, preferably fresh
3 tablespoons (3¾) peanut or vegetable oil
3 thin slices fresh ginger
1 spring (green) onion, sliced
Sauce:
3 tablespoons (3¾) soy sauce

2 tablespoons (2½) Chinese wine
½ teaspoon (⅔) each salt and sugar
1 teaspoon (1¼) cornflour (cornstarch)
  mixed to a paste with water

If using fresh prawns, wash them thoroughly but do not remove their shells, simply clip off the whiskers and feet and pull out the black vein. (If using prepared prawns, read but ignore this advice and go on to make the sauce.) Mix the sauce ingredients and put aside for a moment. Heat the oil and when it smokes add the fresh prawns, ginger and onion. Stir to coat the prawns with the oil, add the sauce, stir it well into the oil and cook the prawns until they are done, i.e. when they are a bright pink. If using pre-cooked prawns, stir the sauce into the oil and cook until this thickens, then quickly add the prawns and continue cooking until they are hot, taking care not to cook them too long or they will toughen. Serve the prawns in the sauce. Frankly for Westerners this recipe is simpler if prepared with pre-cooked shelled prawns.

WHITE FISH IN CRAB SAUCE (*Paak Jup Yu Kai*)

2–3 servings:

2 lb. white fish, boned and cut into cubes
1 egg white, lightly beaten
½ teaspoon (⅔) monosodium glutamate
1 teaspoon (1¼) cornflour (cornstarch)
oil for deep frying
Sauce:
meat of 1 crab or 1 tin, shredded

½ cup (⅔) milk or water
1 teaspoon (1¼) cornflour (cornstarch)
2 teaspoons (2½) melted pork fat or lard
1 teaspoon (1¼) salt

First make the sauce, stir the milk into the cornflour to a thin paste, mix this with the fat and salt and bring to a slow boil. Cook for 3 minutes, add the crab, stir and gently reheat. Put aside and keep hot.

Mix the fish cubes with the egg white, monosodium glutamate and cornflour and fry in deep very hot oil. When the fish is a golden brown, drain and place on a hot dish. Cover with the sauce and serve at once.

FISH IN A HOT SAUCE (*Kan Shao Yu*) (Szechuan)

4 servings:

2 lb. sea bass or similar fish
½ tablespoon (⅔) finely chopped ginger
½ tablespoon (⅔) finely chopped garlic
1½ tablespoons (2¼) soy sauce
3 tablespoons (3¾) Chinese wine or sherry
2 teaspoons (2½) sugar

½ teaspoon (⅔) salt
a few drops of vinegar
oil for deep frying
2 tablespoons (2½) hot sauce (lah yew jeong)

Scale and clean the fish but keep on the head and tail. Slash the sides at intervals diagonally to the bone. Mix the ginger, garlic, soy sauce, wine, sugar, salt and vinegar.

Heat enough oil for deep frying until it smokes, fry the fish for 10 minutes or until it is almost cooked. Take it from the pan. Pour off all but 1 tablespoonful (1¼) of the oil and again heat this until it smokes, stir in the hot sauce and add the remaining ingredients. Stir, return the fish to the pan, lower and heat and simmer for 5 minutes. Serve hot.

FISH COOKED IN OIL

4-6 servings:

1 fish weighing 2–3 lb.   **a dash of cayenne pepper**
4–6 spring (green) onions   **4 tablespoons (5) soy sauce**
peanut or **vegetable oil**

Clean the fish but keep its head and tail intact. Thinly slice the onions into rings, using as much of the green as possible.

Heat the oil in a large, deep pan; it must be very hot indeed. When absolutely boiling, take the pan off the heat and immerse the fish, head first, into the boiling oil. Leave it in the oil for 10 to 12 minutes, still without heat. Take out the fish, arrange it on a plate garnished with the sliced onions, pepper and soy sauce.

In this dish the fish is barely cooked. The pan must not be returned to the heat, otherwise you will get fried fish which is not what we are looking for. Only very fresh fish can be cooked in this way. The fish is cooked not fried in oil.

I tried out this recipe with some fresh grey mullet, using 4 small ones instead of 1 large fish. The fat was boiling hot and, as the fish were immersed in it they sizzled alarmingly. So a large, deep pan must be used to avoid a mess. The fish was perfectly cooked in exactly 10 minutes and delicious.

SMALL BIRDS

Many small birds are considered delicacies by Chinese gourmets. Early spring brings quail and with it such dishes as chopped quail served with lettuce leaf. In the autumn appear the tiny rice birds. As these fly across the rice fields they are driven into and caught in a type of seine net set by the villagers. They are then quickly slaughtered and de-feathered but the head, beak, bones and entrails are left intact. Rubbed with soy sauce, fried in deep oil, they are eaten in one mouthful. These dishes are not usually prepared at home, for there are eating houses specializing in such dishes and the birds are not confined to rice birds.

'CRYSTAL' CHICKEN (Cantonese)

The Chinese name for this dish is a Chinese pun meaning 'cooked through by being soaked in boiling water'. The chicken must be tender otherwise it is not possible to cook it in this way.

3–4 servings:

1 chicken	**1–2 slices fresh ginger**
water	**1–2 spring (green) onions or sliced onion**

Bring to a fast boil enough water to cover the chicken. Insert into the chicken 2 or 3 metal spoons to act as heat conductors. Put the chicken (and its spoons) into the boiling water, add the ginger and onion and bring the water once again to the boil. Let it bubble for 30 seconds, turn off the heat and leave the chicken in the boiling water until it gets cold. The chicken will be cooked.

At this stage the chicken is ready for slicing and eating but, instead, it can be put into a large jar, covered completely with Chinese wine or substitute, the jar sealed tightly and put into a refrigerator. Keep it there for 1 week. The chicken is cut into small pieces to serve.

The chicken is now 'drunken' chicken for it has become thoroughly impregnated with the wine and has a splendid flavour. It is usually served as a party dish with wine and should be eaten slowly to relish all its flavour.

CHICKEN WITH WALNUTS (*Hop To Gai Ding*)

3–4 servings:

1 2–3 lb. chicken	**largish piece fresh ginger, finely chopped**
1 cup (1¼) shelled walnuts (1 lb.) unshelled	**¼ lb. bamboo shoots, sliced**
1 teaspoon (1¼) each salt and sugar	**1 tablespoon (1¼) Chinese wine**
2 teaspoons (2½) Chinese wine	Sauce:
1 teaspoon (1¼) soy sauce	**1½ cups (2) water**
1 tablespoon (1¼) cornflour (cornstarch)	**1 teaspoon (1¼) cornflour (cornstarch)**
peanut or vegetable oil for deep frying	**1 teaspoon (1¼) each monosodium gluta-**
1 egg, well beaten	**mate, light soy sauce, sugar**
2–3 cloves garlic, finely chopped	

Put the walnuts into a pan, cover with cold water, bring to the boil and boil for 3 minutes. Let them cool in the liquid, drain and peel off the skins. Dry thoroughly. Strip the flesh from the chicken as neatly as possible and cut the pieces into strips. Sprinkle salt, sugar, wine and soy sauce over it and mix well. Add the cornflour and mix again. Heat the oil and fry the walnuts to a light brown. Take from the pan as soon as they change colour; nuts burn very quickly. Drain off most of the oil. Coat the pieces of chicken with egg and fry in the hot oil. Add the garlic and ginger, stir well, add a little water and simmer until the chicken is tender. Separately cook the bamboo shoots in water until tender. Drain and add these to the chicken, stir gently, add the wine and continue to simmer while you make the sauce.

Mix the water and cornflour to a thin paste. Add the remaining ingredients and cook in a small pan until it becomes thick and semi-transparent. Stir this into the chicken pieces, add the walnuts, reheat and serve the chicken hot.

Instead of walnuts, almonds may be used. Chicken or goose livers or duck can be cooked in the same manner.

Fresh bamboo shoots take quite a time to become tender and even this timing varies according to the age of the shoots. Tinned bamboo shoots are pre-cooked and require almost no cooking.

FROGS' LEGS AND CHICKEN (*Chow Gai Kau Tin Gai*)

The name of this dish, Double Phoenix Facing the Sun, is a Chinese play on words. In Chinese both the chicken and the frog are called *gai*. The frog is a field chicken and the hen is a 'home chicken'. According to the Chinese, the phoenix also is of the chicken family.

3–4 servings:

½ lb. white chicken meat
½ lb. frogs' legs, meat only
2 teaspoons (2½) Chinese wine
1 teaspoon (1¼) salt
2 tablespoons (2½) cornflour (cornstarch)
1 teaspoon (1¼) monosodium glutamate

2 tablespoons (2½) pork fat or lard
1 piece fresh ginger, thinly sliced
2–3 spring (green) onions, thinly sliced
3–4 fresh mushrooms peeled and sliced
½ cup (⅔) stock
1 teaspoon (1¼) each sugar and soy sauce

Cut the chicken and frog legs' meat into strips and mix with the wine, salt, cornflour and monosodium glutamate and coat thoroughly. Heat a deep frying pan, add the fat, and when very hot add the ginger and spring onions, stir, add the meat and mushrooms. Stir well and when the meat changes colour add the stock, sugar and soy sauce, stir again and cook for about 15 minutes.

If frogs' legs are not obtainable, use all white chicken meat.

CHICKEN LIVERS (*Gai Gen*)

This is one of the dishes served as 'small chow' or *dim-sum*.

3–4 servings: depending on how many side dishes are being served and shared.

1 lb. chicken livers
2 tablespoons (2½) soy sauce
1 tablespoon (1¼) Chinese wine
½ cup (⅔) plain flour

pinch of baking powder
5 tablespoons (6¼) water
oil for deep frying
salt, pepper

Marinate the livers in soy sauce and wine for 15 minutes. Mix the flour, baking powder and water to a thin batter, add the chicken livers and stir well to coat. Heat the oil until it is very hot and drop in the livers. Fry until the batter is a golden brown, take from the pan, drain and serve sprinkled with salt and pepper.

Chopped calves' livers may be cooked in the same manner.

CHICKEN WITH PINEAPPLE (*Po Lo Chih*)

2–4 servings:

1 lb. chicken meat, cut into 1-in. cubes
4 large slices pineapple
1 tablespoon (1¼) cornflour (cornstarch)
1 teaspoon (1¼) salt
2 teaspoons (2½) water
1 tablespoon (1¼) soy sauce

peanut or other vegetable oil
2 onions, sliced lengthwise
2–3 stalks celery, chopped
10 water chestnuts, sliced
4 tablespoons (5) pineapple juice

Philippine Roast Sucking Pig (see page 232)

Put the chicken meat into a bowl, add cornflour, salt, water and soy sauce. Leave until required. Evenly chop the pineapple.

Heat 1 tablespoonful ($1\frac{1}{4}$) oil in a pan and lightly fry the onions. Take these from the pan. Add a little more oil and fry the celery and the water chestnuts for 2 or 3 minutes; take these also from the pan. Check the oil, you need 2 tablespoonfuls ($2\frac{1}{4}$), and lightly fry the chicken until a golden brown.

Add the fried ingredients and the pineapple and stir well. Finally stir in the juice and simmer until all this is reheated. Serve hot with rice.

Pork or even beef may be substituted for chicken in this dish. Tinned pineapple, if thoroughly drained, may be used instead of fresh.

DUCK (*Aap*)

China is said to have more duck than any other country in the world. Many of them live in marshes and are somewhat gamier than the duck we usually serve. But the Chinese turn duck into wonderful dishes. An example is the world-famous Peking Duck, the skin of which is as much, if not more, glorified than the flesh. Less well known but equally delicious is the Szechuan duck.

In Chinese markets whole roasting duck, gleaming and almost bright red, are a common sight hanging alongside hams, roast pork and sausages. These are ready for serving and need simply cutting into chopstick-size pieces to be eaten with rice. Then there are dishes of flat, dried and salted duck which come around the Chinese New Year. They look extremely odd but are much appreciated. Dried salted duck is never eaten with vegetables but usually a piece of it is chopped off and popped into a pan of rice when it is at the bubbling stage and about to be simmered.

Ducks' feet, tongues, livers and gizzards (I have a recipe which starts '2 dozen ducks' tongues') are all appreciated. Ducks' feet boned and very glutinous are a speciality.

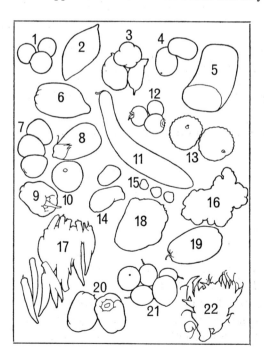

Far Eastern Fruit and Vegetables (1): *limes;* (2 & 3) *sweet potatoes;* (4) *mangoes;* (5) *yam;* (6) *papaw;* (7) *guavas;* (8) *aubergine (eggplant);* (9) *red peppers;* (10) *pomegranate;* (11) *Indian gourd;* (12) *persimmons;* (13) *custard apples;* (14) *cassava or taro;* (15) *areca nut;* (16) *ginger root;* (17) *okra;* (18) *cassava or taro;* (19) *chayote or squash;* (20) *green peppers;* (21) *passion fruit;* (22) *green chilli peppers*

Far Eastern Fruit and Vegetables

DUCK WITH GINGER AND PINEAPPLE (*Po Lo Chiang*)

4–5 servings:

1 4–5 lb. duck
1 teaspoon (1¼) salt
pepper
1 small tin pineapple, well drained
6 pieces preserved ginger

Sauce:
1 cup (1¼) pineapple juice
½ cup (⅔) ginger juice or use finely chopped
  fresh ginger
2 teaspoons (2½) cornflour (cornstarch)

Wash and clean the duck and rub with salt and pepper. Steam the duck whole, until tender. When the duck is tender, take it from the pan, cool and then cut the flesh into small neat pieces. Arrange these in the centre of a dish. Surround the duck with chopped pineapple and ginger arranged alternately, and cover with the following sauce.

Heat the pineapple and ginger juice in a small pan. Mix the cornflour to a thin paste with water add this to the pan, stirring all the while. Bring to the boil and cook until the sauce thickens. To this may be added Chinese wine or soy sauce.

PEKING DUCK (*Kwa Lo Aap*)

This is a recipe for experts, but it is nice to know how it is done. It is a North China dish of crispy roast duck surrounded by stacks of thin steamed bread, frilly green onion tips and dishes of its own special sauce. It is usually served in two stages. The crisp fried skin cut into convenient bite-sized bits and eaten first. These are placed on a large plate in the centre of the table and surrounded by a small dish of a heavy dark sauce, piles of leeks or spring (green) onions, and steamed bread. You pick up a piece of bread with your chopsticks, place it on your plate, then pick up a piece of skin, dip it into the sauce and place it on the bread, add a piece of the leek, fold it all over sandwich-style and eat it, preferably using your chopsticks. The meat of the duck appears as another course.

The duck should be large and fat and after killing should be hung for 3 hours. Then air is blown through a slit in the gullet, which separates the skin from the flesh. Every Chinese gourmet prefers the skin to the flesh, which sometimes appears with the bones in the form of a thick soup.

DUCK WITH CHESTNUTS (*Lut Tze Aap*)

4 servings:

1 3–4 lb. duck
1 lb. chestnuts
2 Chinese dried mushrooms
1 teaspoon (1¼) light soy sauce
1 teaspoon (1¼) sugar

1 teaspoon (1¼) cornflour (cornstarch)
1 teaspoon (1¼) salt
peanut or vegetable oil for deep frying
6 spring (green) onions, finely chopped
1-inch piece ginger, finely chopped

Soak the mushrooms in water for 30 minutes and thinly slice.

Cut a gash on the flat side of the chestnuts, drop them into water and cook for a 15–20 minutes or until their skins show signs of bursting. Or fry them in a little butter over a low fire, shaking them from time to time. When the chestnuts are cool they can be easily peeled.

Chop (or have chopped) the duck, bones and all, into bite-sized pieces or cubes for easy eating with chopsticks. Mix the soy sauce, sugar, cornflour and salt and rub this mixture into the pieces of duck. Heat the oil and fry the pieces of duck for 3 minutes. Take these from the pan, add the onions, ginger, mushrooms and peeled chestnuts and fry for a few minutes. Drain off any excess oil, return the duck to the pan, add hot water to cover and continue cooking until the duck is tender.

FRIED PIGEONS

This recipe comes from a Chinese gourmet who lives in Hong Kong. I think his advice is very kindly, although I have not followed it as I am not able to kill my own pigeons.

'Intoxicate the pigeon with a little bit of spirit before you slaughter it. Any kind of spirit will do. Intoxication is very important in poultry slaughtering. The flesh of a pigeon, or a chicken, when slaughtered in tipsy will be more tender. Besides, it is a traditional Chinese belief that it is a matter of humanity or kindness. Animals or birds, it is believed, suffer less agony when killed during tipsy.' I can well believe this.

2–3 servings:

2–3 pigeons
1 large onion
**½ lb. green vegetable, i.e. cabbage, spinach
  or broccoli**
½ cup (⅔) peanut, sesame or vegetable oil
little fresh ginger, finely chopped
1 teaspoon (1¼) cumin

¼ cup (⅓) Chinese wine
**4–6 dried mushrooms, soaked and thinly
  sliced**
1 tablespoon (1¼) soy sauce
salt to taste
½ tablespoon (⅔) sugar

Singe, wash and bone the pigeons and cut the flesh into strips. Thinly slice the onion and the green vegetable and mix together. Heat the oil in a fairly shallow saucepan and as it begins to smoke add the pigeon flesh, stir, add the ginger, cumin and vegetables. Stir the meat and vegetables continuously with a wooden spoon until lightly browned. Add the wine. Cover the pan and simmer for 5 minutes. Add the mushrooms, soy sauce, salt and sugar. Again stir and continue cooking until the mushrooms are cooked. Serve hot.

The pigeon is considered by the Chinese to be a symbol of faithfulness and marital bliss, although its intelligence is lowly rated. However, neither its symbolic qualities, nor its lack of intelligence stop the Chinese from thinking up numerous succulent dishes for unsuspecting and obviously drunken pigeons.

GARLIC SPARERIBS (*Kao Pai Ku*)

4–6 servings:

2 lb. pork spareribs or small chops
4–6 cloves garlic
1-in. piece ginger
1½ tablespoons (2) rose-water or brandy

1 teaspoon (1¼) 'Five Spice Powder' (see page 240)
6 tablespoons (7½) soy sauce
1 teaspoon each (1¼) salt and sugar

Peel, chop and crush the garlic and the ginger. Mix with the remaining ingredients, except the meat, to a paste. Spread this over the spareribs and leave for 1 hour. Heat the oven. Into this put a pan (a grill pan is the best), fill with hot water. Put the spareribs on a rack over the water and bake for 25 minutes or until they are tender. Separate the ribs—if for chopsticks cut into 3-inch pieces, but if using European utensils, into pieces according to taste.

FRAGRANT PORK (*Chiang Jou*)

6–8 servings:

2–3 lb. boned pork
½ cup (⅔) sugar
1 cup (1¼) Chinese wine or sherry
1–2 spring (green) onions
1-inch piece ginger

4 star anise (see page 246)
3 pieces cinnamon
1 piece dried tangerine peel (optional)
8 cloves
salt to taste

If star anise is not available, use 1 teaspoonful (1¼) of aniseed.

Cut the pork into chunks and put it with the remaining ingredients into a pan. Bring it to a rolling boil and let it continue boiling until the pork is tender, adding enough water only to prevent it from burning. (The idea of the high heat is to prevent the meat juices from seeping out.) When the meat is tender, take it from the pan and cut into 1½-inch cubes. The pork is served plain.

BEEF FLAVOURED WITH OYSTER SAUCE (*Hao Yiu Nui Jou*)

1–2 servings:

½ lb. tender lean beef
½ teaspoon (⅔) each salt, sugar
1 egg white
½ tablespoon (⅔) Chinese wine or sherry
1 teaspoon (1¼) cornflour (cornstarch)
oil

pepper
2–3 thin slices ginger
1–2 spring (green) onions, thinly sliced
2½ tablespoons (3¼) oyster sauce (see page 242)

Finely slice the beef. Mix the salt, sugar, egg white, wine, cornflour and ½ a teaspoonful (⅔) each of oil and pepper and rub this mixture into the meat. Leave for 1 hour. Heat enough oil for deep-frying until it smokes. Fry the meat until it changes colour. Take it at once from the pan and drain. Put aside. Pour off all but 1 tablespoonful (1¼) of the oil from the pan, add the ginger and onion to this, stir-fry, return the meat, add the oyster sauce, stir gently and continue to cook until the meat is reheated.

LAMB WITH ONIONS (*Tsung Pao Yang Jou*)

1–2 servings:

½ lb lean and tender lamb
6 large spring (green) onions
1 teaspoon (1¼) cornflouer (cornstarch),
   mixed to a thin paste with water
3 tablespoons (3¾) soy sauce

1 tablespoon (1¼) Chinese wine or sherry
1 teaspoon (1¼) each salt and mild vinegar
oil for frying
2 teaspoons (2½) minced garlic
1 teaspoon (1¼) minced ginger

Thinly slice the meat and rub the cornflour paste into it. Mix the soy with the wine, salt and vinegar. Heat plenty of oil until it smokes and add the meat. Cook this until tender—a few minutes only. Take out the meat and let it drain. Pour off all but 2 tablespoonfuls (2½) of the oil and reheat this again until it smokes. Add the onions and fry these until they are soft, add the meat, garlic, ginger and the soy and vinegar sauce. Fry for 1 minute—no longer.

SWEET-SOUR DISHES

Sweet-sour dishes are widely known by people who eat Chinese food. Fish is especially good when prepared with a sweet and sour sauce, so is meat (pork seems to have become the best known among foreigners); also vegetables are prepared sweet and sour. The sauce compares or can be equated with the French oil and vinegar dressing, and there are a number of variations of sweet and sour sauces. Some cooks prefer a rather sour sauce, others slightly more sweet.

   The following recipe is a fairly general one—but vinegars differ tremendously in flavour so check for taste.

Sweet-sour sauce:
2 tablespoons (2½) cornflour (cornstarch)
2 tablespoons (2½) vinegar

1 tablespoon (1¼) soy sauce
2 tablespoons (2½) sugar

Mix the cornflour to a thin paste with 2 cupfuls (2½) of water, add the vinegar, soy sauce and sugar. Put this into a pan, cook and stir over a low fire until the mixture boils and is thick. This is a basic sweet and sour sauce which can be used in most sweet and sour dishes, if they are prepared separately.

SWEET-SOUR CARROTS

4–6 servings:

2 lb. carrots, preferably small
2 tablespoons (2½) vegetable oil or pork fat
salt
1 tablespoon (1¼) sharp vinegar

1½ tablespoons (2) brown sugar
1 tablespoon (1¼) dark soy sauce
1 tablespoon (1¼) cornflour (cornstarch)

Scrub the carrots; unless they are coarse, do not peel but cut them into small pieces. Heat the oil and fry the carrots for a few minutes, add salt and half a cupful of water and cook until the carrots are tender. Mix the vinegar, sugar, soy sauce, cornflour and 1 cupful (1¼) of water. Add this to the carrots, stir carefully and cook until the sauce is translucent.

SWEET-SOUR PORK (*Tim Suen Goo Lo Yuk*)

This is one of the most popular Chinese dishes with foreigners; connoisseurs of Chinese cooking are apt to scorn it for its very popularity. However, for many people it dates their first interest in Chinese food.

4–5 servings:

1½–2 lb. lean boned pork, cut into cubes
1 teaspoon (1¼) each sugar, salt, soy sauce
1 egg, lightly beaten
cornflour (cornstarch) for coating
oil for deep frying
1 small onion, quartered
1-in. piece ginger, thinly sliced
1–2 cloves garlic, chopped

2–4 green and red sweet peppers, quartered and seeded
sauce:
1 tablespoon (1¼) cornflour (cornstarch)
½ cup (⅔) mild vinegar
½ cup (⅔) brown sugar
1 tablespoon (1¼) Chinese wine
4 tablespoons (5) soy sauce

Mix the pork with the seasoning (sugar, salt, soy) and leave it until it is absorbed. Add the egg and mix this thoroughly into the pork. Roll each piece of meat into cornflour, put it aside and leave until the cornflour is absolutely wet. The meat must not be dry when fried. Heat the oil until it is very hot and fry the pieces until a light brown. Take the pieces from the pan, drain and quickly fry again, the pork must be well done and crisp around the edges. Take from the oil, drain again and put on to a hot platter, cover with absorbent paper and put into a hot oven to keep warm while you make the sauce. Put the pan with the oil aside.

Mix the sauce cornflour with enough water to make a thin paste, put this into a saucepan, add the remaining sauce ingredients, cook and stir to a thickish, slightly translucent sauce. Keep hot.

Pour off most of the oil from the frying pan, add the onion, ginger, garlic and peppers and cook these over a high heat for a couple of minutes. Add these with the pieces of pork to the sauce and cook quickly. Stir and serve at once.

Sweet-sour pork must be arranged so that the pieces of pork and peppers are more or less of equal size and with plenty of colour. The onion will fall into quarter slices when cooked.

Fish is cooked in the same manner.

EGGS (*Gai Tan*)

Eggs are possibly used to greater advantage in Chinese cooking than in Western cooking, certainly there is more variety in the kinds of eggs used. Chickens' eggs, of course, but also those of the duck, pigeon, quail and plover. They have some interesting combinations of eggs with fish, especially shellfish, with meat and poultry, as well as with vegetables. Cooked as omelettes and thinly sliced they appear as a soup garnish. Quails' and pigeons' eggs are much esteemed, and salted eggs are in considerable demand.

1,000-YEAR-OLD EGGS (*Pee Tan*)

Almost everyone has heard of the '1,000-year-old eggs'—just as most people know that the Japanese eat raw fish. Eggs and raw fish share the biased dislike of those who have never tried either. These eggs, usually duck eggs, are at the most several months old; some Chinese say the best are a mere hundred days old. They are deliciously flavoured and encased in what does undoubtedly look like a very unsavoury casing of mud but is, in fact, a mixture of ashes, tea, lime and salt and rolled in dried rice husks, and buried for the required time. I suppose this description does not make them sound any more inviting, but let me battle on, for they are really excellent as appetizers and deserve to be given a fair hearing.

When the eggs are ready to serve or eat, they are shelled, the casing broken off. The yolks by this time have turned an orange-green colour, the whites or albumen solidified like a dark green jelly or piece of semi-precious stone in shades of deep green. They are eaten with vinegar and ginger slices usually on cocktail-type sticks, and do have an individual flavour which is quite exciting. '1,000-year-old eggs' or as they are sometimes called 'Ming Dynasty Eggs', will keep a long time and are sold in Chinese provision shops.

TEA EGGS (*Cha Yeh Tan*)

The actual process of cooking tea eggs takes several hours. They are often served both hot and cold direct from the vessel in which they are cooked and are a popular railway station 'small-eat'. They have a flavour which is different from eggs boiled in water but not of tea. Their main point is the picturesque marbled effect the tea produces on the clear, smooth egg white.

12 eggs
enough strong black tea to cover
1 tablespoon ($1\frac{1}{4}$) each salt and sugar
stalks of 2 spring (green) onions

1 tablespoon ($1\frac{1}{4}$) aniseed or star anise (see page 246)
1 tablespoon ($1\frac{1}{4}$) Chinese wine
1 teaspoon ($1\frac{1}{4}$) monosodium glutamate

Put all these ingredients into a pan and bring to the boil, lower the heat and cook the eggs gently for about 30 minutes. Take them from the pan, gently crack the shells by rolling them on the table, and return the eggs to the pan. Continue simmering for another 15 minutes, then take the pan from the heat and leave for several hours. When the eggs are peeled the marbled effect will show where the tea stain has penetrated the cracked shells.

Tea bags may be used. Chinese cooks wrap the tea in a muslin bag, otherwise the loose leaves stick to the eggs.

QUAILS' EGGS WITH MUSHROOMS (*Yuen Choon Kum Moon*)

Quails' eggs are used quite a lot in Chinese cooking. They are very good although it takes a little time for the uninitiated to manage them with chopsticks. They are often used to embellish a soup.

4–6 servings:

18 quails' eggs	1 cup (1¼) strained chicken stock
4 oz. dried Chinese mushrooms	1 cup (1¼) water
1 tablespoon (1¼) pork fat or lard	1 tablespoon (1¼) cornflour (cornstarch)
chopped onion or fresh ginger to taste	monosodium glutamate to taste

Soak the mushrooms for 30 minutes in water and then slice discarding the stalks. Boil the eggs until hard, about 15 minutes. Heat the fat in a deep frying pan, add the onion or ginger or both, fry for a minute or so, add the mushrooms, stir, add the stock and water. Bring this to a gentle boil. Mix the cornflour with a little water to a thin paste, add this with the monosodium glutamate to the pan, stir until the gravy is thick, add the eggs and when these are reheated serve as a side dish.

Small chicken eggs can be cooked in the same manner.

OMELETTE (*Fu Yong*)

Just as there are many forms of omelette in the West, so in Chinese cooking there are numerous varieties of *fu yong*.

3 servings:

6 eggs	a little bamboo shoot, shredded
½ lb. crabmeat	2 spring (green) onions, shredded
small piece ginger, finely chopped	2 tablespoons (2½) cooked peas
salt	2 tablespoons (2½) soy sauce
1 tablespoon (1¼) Chinese wine	1 cup (1¼) stock
vegetable oil	1 tablespoon (1¼) cornflour (cornstarch)
Sauce:	
2 dried mushrooms, soaked for 30 minutes, finely chopped	

Make a sauce first to have it ready as soon as the omelette is finished. Heat 2 tablespoonfuls (2½) of oil and lightly fry the mushrooms, bamboo shoot and spring onions. Add green peas, soy sauce and the stock to make a sauce. Bring this to boiling point. Mix the cornflour with water to a thin paste, add this to the pan, and stir until it boils and the sauce is thick and translucent. Serve this poured over the omelette.

Stir the crabmeat and the ginger together. Thoroughly beat the eggs, add salt and wine. Add the crabmeat and ginger. Heat a large, thick-bottomed frying pan, add enough oil to thinly cover and when this is hot add the egg mixture, making 1 large omelette. Let the mixture spread and tilt the pan slightly to let uncooked parts spread round the sides. Continue this until the whole omelette is set. Turn and fry on the other side. Or it can be placed under a grill.

Instead of crabmeat, lightly boiled, shredded white cabbage may be used; shredded chicken or pork meat and lightly fried bean sprouts.

SPRING or EGG ROLLS (*Ch'un Chuan*)

These are a kind of stuffed pancakes and very much 'small eats' and can be prepared with chicken, ham, shrimp, prawns, pork etc. They can be served as an hors-d'œuvre or as part of the main meal. The wrappers, or pancakes, are usually made in advance; they can be kept months in a deep freeze or overnight in a refrigerator. Simply sprinkle cornflour (cornstarch) between each wrapper before freezing and then peel them off like sheets of paper when defrosted and required for use. Or the completed roll can be frozen.

There are several methods of making the wrappers. Some are more difficult to the non-Chinese than others.

(1) Wrapper batter with eggs:
2 eggs
2 cups (2½) flour
2 cups (2½) water
oil

(2) Wrapper batter without eggs:
1½ cups (2) water
2 cups (2½) flour
oil

(1) Beat the eggs, add flour then add the water, beating until the mixture is smooth. Grease a frying pan with a little oil, never too much or the rolls will be greasy. Pour a little batter, about 1 tablespoonful (1¼), into the pan, swish it around and pour off any excess oil leaving a very thin layer of batter in the pan. Leave it on the heat just long enough to set, a minute or so. Take this from the pan and repeat until all the batter has been finished. Makes approximately 35 small wrappers.

(2) Mix the water gradually into the flour, making a smooth batter. Lightly oil a small frying pan, heat the pan (yes, first oil then heat) and brush on the batter with a pastry brush. The wrapper should not be too large, 5–6 inches square. If holes appear, patch them by simply brushing on a little of the batter, using crosswise strokes. Leave this on the heat just long enough to set, about 1 minute or less. Take this from the pan and continue until all the batter has been used up.

All this is much easier than it sounds.

Filling:
3 tablespoons (3¾) oil
2 cups (2½) bamboo shoots, cut into thin strips
3 cups (3¾) bean sprouts
3 tablespoons (3¾) soy sauce
1 onion, finely chopped

3 Chinese dried mushrooms, soaked and finely chopped
1 lb. lean pork, chicken or prawns, minced
1 tablespoon (1¼) Chinese wine
1 tablespoon (1¼) cornflour (cornstarch)
salt
1 largish piece ginger, finely chopped

Heat 1 tablespoonful (1¼) of oil in a large pan and sauté the bamboo shoots. Add the bean sprouts and heat these thoroughly. Add 2 tablespoonfuls (2½) soy sauce and continue to cook for a minute or so. Take this from the pan and keep hot.

Reheat the pan, add another tablespoonful of oil and sauté the onion and dried mushrooms. When these are cooked, remove from the pan and keep hot. Mix the pork with the remaining soy sauce, wine and cornflour, adding salt to taste. Again reheat the pan, add the remaining oil and sauté the pork. When this is thoroughly cooked, add the ginger and all the remaining ingredients, i.e. those you have already cooked.

Spread a little, not more than 1½ teaspoonfuls, of the filling on each of the wrappers. Fold in the sides and roll. Moisten the edges of each wrapper with a mixture of water and cornflour mixed to a paste. Heat oil for deep frying and fry the rolls until brown. Slice diagonally to serve, each piece bite-size.

Spring rolls are thus called because they are eaten during the old-style new year, which was nearer to spring than the present new year.

This recipe makes between 30–35 rolls.

PEKING DUST (*Lut Tze Dan Go*)

Unhappily I have not visited Peking. But I am told that Peking dust is no joke at all. Peking lies in a cold, dry area and is known for its dust storms. A dust storm, as I know from other parts of the East, is certainly not amusing. When the dust swirls it is like a thick, dense choking fog. In Peking there is plenty of dust to eat. Exactly why this pudding is so named, I do not know. But it is a cold weather pudding, or rather it is a pudding that can be eaten in a cold climate. It is one of the few Chinese puddings which is simple for the Westerner to prepare and also enjoy and it makes a dramatic finish to a meal.

2 lb. chestnuts, shelled and boiled	½ cup (⅔) whipped cream
2 tablespoons (2½) fine sugar	a pinch of salt

Put the chestnuts through a food chopper or mincer or better still a ricer and then mash until smooth. Mix this with the sugar, cream and salt. Pile on to a large plate and garnish with:

1 cup (1¼) whipped cream	1 cup (1¼) water
glazed orange slices, cherries, whole wal-	¼ teaspoon (⅓) cream of tartar
nuts or preserved kumquats	1 tablespoon (1¼) lemon juice

Spun sugar:
2 cups (2½) sugar

Spun sugar:
Cook the first three ingredients in a saucepan over a good heat until the syrup begins to colour and spins a thread. If using a thermometer, at 290°F. Take from the heat and add the lemon juice, then plunge the saucepan into a bowl of iced water to prevent the syrup from hardening. Spin the syrup into threads and cover the pudding with this. This is the Peking dust.

Any favourite method you have of producing spun sugar will work to produce the Peking Dust, but Chinese cooks take a couple of sticks and twirl the syrup round and round.

Tinned chestnut purée can be used in the above recipe.

ALMONDS AFLOAT (*Hsing Jen Tou Fu*)

Variously called Almonds Afloat, Almond Tea or Curd. There are a number of different recipes for this very palatable Chinese dessert.

6 servings:

1½ cups (2¼) sweet almonds	1 cup (1¼) sugar
½ cup (⅔) uncooked rice	2 envelopes gelatine
4 bitter almonds or ½ teaspoon (⅔) almond essence	6 cups (7½) water

Blanch and peel the almonds. Wash the rice and soak it in boiling water for 30 minutes. Grind the rice and almonds with 1 cupful (1¼) of water (this can be done in an electric blender). Strain this through a cloth, squeezing out as much of the liquid as possible, at least 1 cupful (1¼). The almond and rice residue is discarded.

Mix the gelatine with cold water to dissolve it, then add the sugar and 5 cupfuls (6¼) of water. Cook this until the gelatine has been completely dissolved. Take it from the pan, add the almond liquid and essence, mix it well, pour it into a flat pan and when cool chill until it sets. When completely set cut into diamond shapes.

Sauce:
1 cup (1¼) sugar

2 cups (2½) water
a few cherries, cut into halves

Mix the water and sugar, stir and cook over a low heat until the sugar dissolves then cook rapidly to a syrup. Let this become cold and serve with the cherries as a garnish.

TEA

Emily Hahn wrote in *China From A to Z*:

> *We drink tea with our rice*
> *And we drink it in between.*
> *Water's not for drinking!*
> *It's just for keeping clean.*

Which pretty well sums up the position of tea in Chinese living.

Tea lore is fascinating. Although much of its early history is shrouded in mystery, a Chinese legend has it that the first cup of this beverage, now of world-wide popularity, was produced by an accident. An absent-minded philosopher while boiling water over a fire made from dried branches of what was obviously the tea plant dropped some of the leaves into his cup. Not noticing, or perhaps not even bothering, he drank the boiled liquid and discovered that the addition of the leaves had produced a stimulating brew. He had, in fact, produced the first cup of tea. However, it was hundreds of years later that the rest of the world was permitted to enjoy the taste of tea.

Not all references to tea which occur in Chinese legend and stories refer to the tea plant as we know it. This is because for centuries there was no actual word for tea. Somewhere in the seventh century A.D. the word *Ch'a* came into prominence. Many plants that may or may not have been tea were mentioned in early papers under varying names of *Ch'an* or *Ming*; *Kia*; *K'u t'u* and simply *T'u*. But it was the last name that was mostly used and Orientalists declare that *t'u*, which is the one name recorded in ancient Chinese writings, refers to tea as we know it. But that is by no means the generally accepted opinion.

In A.D. 780 the *Ch'a Ching*, or *Tea Memoir*, was published, the work of a Chinese scholar Lu Yu and this was a compilation of all the then available information, on its cultivation, its harvesting, its preparation and its serving. For this learned thesis the good Lu Yu was honoured by the Chinese and made the patron saint of tea.

An early mention of tea is ascribed to Confucius in the *Book of Odes* which he edited. Confucius, I find, is always cropping up in matters concerning food. But what is recorded as probably the first mention, at least, first authentic mention of tea, is in a letter from a Chinese general of the Chin dynasty, who was tired. He wrote that he was feeling old and depressed and would like some real *t'u*—tea.

But tea is not all Chinese. Both the Japanese and the Chinese claim divine inspiration in the origin of tea. The Chinese claim—apart from their story of the old man of the forest—that Shen Hung, a legendary Emperor, divinely produced tea in the year 2737 B.C.

The Japanese, to whom tea drinking is an ancient ceremony still performed (*see* page 187), give credit to its origin to a Buddhist saint who, after five years of sleepless meditation, suddenly found his eyelids drooping. Furiously he tore the lids from his eyes and flung them scornfully to the ground. Where they landed sprouted a green bush. Realizing this was divine intervention, the saint brewed its leaves, drank of the brew and was at once stimulated. Thus he was able to continue happily his meditations. As we are told this episode took place in the first half of the sixth century B.C., it makes it difficult to refute. So the Buddhist saint, Daruma, for such was his name, brought tea to Japan.

But tea was not for everyone. Early history records it was reserved for princes and priests, the latter using it for its reputed magical powers. Even in China it was not a people's drink. It was not until the Japanese began planting their own bushes, in A.D. 800, that tea became remotely popular. Then, travellers' stories of this stimulating and pleasant brew began to reach Europe, it was described almost with awe, as the panacea of all ills.

It was as late as the middle of the sixteenth century when Europe really heard of this delectable brew. Naturally it aroused the interest of the merchants so that, even in the beginning of the seventeenth century, the dried leaves started to reach Europe.

China, not unnaturally, was not eager to disclose her secrets, jealously guarded, but like many other such secrets they were finally exposed to the eager world. Her seeds, her plants, her expertise were eventually introduced to other parts of the Far East where tea grows well.

India became a serious rival and has remained so. So did Ceylon, Java and Sumatra where the tea plant flourishes. For the next two hundred years the British and the Dutch East India companies had a near monopoly on the tea trade to Europe and to America.

It was the beginning of the end for the Chinese tea trade. For it was discovered that the tea plants native to India plus the secrets which the Chinese had been forced to divulge, made a perfect tea for the European trade. The Indian tea plants and seeds were encouraged, while the Chinese tea gardens were neglected, until finally the Indian tea trade spread its branches like the massive banyan tree, finally overshadowing China's older industry. Also it brought tea down to the level of the working man's daily cuppa.

The three main types of tea are black or fermented, called by the Chinese 'red tea'. Then there is *oolong*, or semi-fermented tea. Green or unfermented tea. All three types of tea start on the same bush. It is the after treatment that determines their latter characteristics.

Black tea usually makes stronger brews than the *oolong*, or green teas. They are red or golden in colour. Broken leaves, preferred by the British, give a darker colour to the tea. Green teas follow much the same processes of manufacture as black teas and when properly made the better grades of green teas become a greenish-golden liquid with a delicate flavour and aroma. *Oolong* teas, although they originated in the Foochow district of China, now come mainly from Formosa. These delicately flavoured Formosan teas are considered among the finest in the world, termed most aptly the champagnes among teas.

Most Chinese teas are a blend of different varieties of tea leaves and other leaves mixed. Jasmine, camellia, rose, lychee, chrysanthemum and many fragrant flowers and leaves are mixed with tea to make the teas of China, and it suits their tastes. The result of these flavourings depends naturally on the grade of tea used in the mixture.

Special teas are rated as highly among Chinese tea drinkers as such teas are in the West. A tea from Hangkow is highly prized, so too is one called Dragon Well, and *Woo Long*, or Iron Goddess. One is tempted to buy Chinese teas as much for their names as their flavours. But these are but three of many. I rather favour a green tea from South China with the delightful name of Water Nymph.

As Emily Hahn rightly says, the Chinese drink tea all the time. In China it is traditional to offer tea to guests at any time of the day. Also it is customary to put the tea leaves into the guest's cup and brew it right in front of him. Each cup has a lid for this purpose and the idea is simply to show proof that the tea is really freshly brewed and not a rehash in the kitchen. Curiously enough, a 12-hour-old tea is nevertheless considered perfectly all right, with a fresh infusion, of course, of boiling water.

A formal Chinese tea set comes in sets of three pieces, saucer, a cup without a handle and cover. Each person's tea is, as I have already said, brewed in his own cup. The cover is then put on and kept on until the tea has steeped. It is then removed to allow the tea to cool and replaced on the tilt when ready for drinking to keep the leaves in check whilst drinking. When more tea is required, boiling fresh water is poured over the same leaves. This is not frowned upon, on the contrary, everyone knows that the second cup of tea is the best, and the third is considered by some as even better.

The Chinese drink their tea weak, without sugar or milk, even lemon. The usual rule is 1 teaspoonful (1¼) of tea to each 6 cupfuls (7½) of boiling water, in striking contrast to the Western approach to tea making. Hot water should always be on hand. A concentrated infusion of tea with fresh boiling water added produces a good cup of tea.

TEA (*Hsiang Pien*)

1 coffeespoon (1¼) green tea leaves	1 cupful (1¼) boiling water

Put the leaves into a Chinese tea cup, then pour on the water which has just boiled and cover with the lid. Allow it to stand for 3 minutes without stirring. It is then ready for serving.

IN SEARCH OF CHINESE FOOD

Where does one find the best Chinese food? This is a question often posed and often disputed. It is not just which restaurant in any particular city, for almost any capital with pretensions towards the finer aspects of variety in food has its Chinese restaurants. It is a question in which country? Is it mainland China?

Well, this is a hard one to answer, for few foreigners are able to taste the pleasures of the Chinese table in its natural setting. So little is known about present-day China it is not certain as to how many Chinese can eat like their forefathers. However, one should be comforted by the belief that it will take quite a lot of political thoughts to kill the centuries-old culinary art of China.

Outside China, there was a time when Hong Kong claimed to produce the best Chinese food. Among the thousands of refugees who fled into the island colony were many cooks. Needing work they plied their trade and received encouragement. There were enough Chinese around to keep them on their toes and produce true Chinese food.

Singapore had a similar story and many Singaporeans claimed that the best Chinese food was to be found there.

Certainly, both places serve excellent Chinese food.

Then there was Rangoon, at one time quite famous for its Chinese food. Their Chinese cooks had a ritualistic background and one was made to feel aware of the importance of tradition in eating. One did not order lightly.

Phnom-Penh, Cambodia's capital, is another city which claims that Chinese food produced there can compete with the best. And there are other cities in the Far East which boast a similar reputation, such as Bangkok and Kuala Lumpur, capitals where it is easier to find a Chinese restaurant serving authentic Chinese food than Thai or Malaysian food.

Finally we come to Formosa (Taiwan) and it is here that we should give the accolade. This island crammed with Chinese migrants has all five schools of Chinese cooking represented. This is important when one remembers that some 90 per cent of all Chinese restaurateurs of the world are Cantonese. Cooks from all parts of China have found their way to Formosa and many of these were cooks famous in China for the splendour of their cooking before being uprooted.

Most of them have started restaurants, cooking as they had been taught to cook and remaining regional. Thus they keep alive the true spirit of Chinese cooking. Today in Formosa it is possible to try dishes which range from the classically regal dishes of old Peking to the fiery spicy dishes of Szechuan, and the ever bland Cantonese cooking which so many of us know so well.

Japan

'Japanese cooking,' wrote Mock Joya in *Things Japanese*, 'is unique in the world because natural environments in Japan are unique and the characteristic nature of the people is also different from that of other peoples.'

As I travelled through the Far East it seemed to me that two main schools of cooking dominated, the Chinese and the Indian, and in Japan the Chinese influence was extremely strong. When and how it all began probably no one knows, except that Buddhist priests back from religious studies in China brought with them ways of eating and cooking as well as religious thinking. As a result, over the centuries Japan has adopted, adapted and naturalized Chinese cooking to suit Japanese tastes and conditions. Declared by some to be a simple case of robbery there are two distinct schools of thinking on it. There are those who feel that Japan simplified Chinese cooking and reduced its ceremonial rituals; others insist it is exactly the opposite.

Much of Japanese cooking is different, even complicated, and many of their typical recipes are almost impossible outside of Japan. But, even so, there is enough for the interested foreigner to experiment with and achieve good results. It is not such an all-embracing cuisine as the Chinese, nor curiously enough as many-sided; at times it even gives the appearance of being cramped.

Those who feel that the Japanese have improved upon Chinese cooking remark that it has given it added beauty. This is certainly true. Not even the French with their elegant garnishes can compete with the Japanese. The latter have developed the beautifying of food to a positive art. A good cook in Japan needs also to be an artist with a sense of beauty. Colour combinations, arrangement of dishes, are all as much part of Japanese cooking as the actual preparation of the food. Each dish is carefully planned and arranged to produce harmony of colour, space and line.

Eating in Japan is considered a pleasure. Exquisite porcelain, the finest of lacquer, all must have aesthetic appeal. Chopsticks are made of many precious kinds of material, for the rich ivory or ebony, for the poor and casual visitor a half-split type called *waribashi*, made from cedarwood and discarded after being used but once. Many chopsticks, like some tableware, are family heirlooms.

Unlike the Western hostess who indulges in a deep-freezer and will serve her guests raspberries when the snow is thick on the ground, the Japanese hostess considers the essence of hospitality lies in the offering of food in season. Each season brings its own food and it is, therefore, important for the Japanese to express the seasons in the presentation of their food. April expresses itself with cherry blossom as a décor and will be shown in the spring dishes. Autumn is shown with hard-boiled quails' eggs skilfully tinted to represent the autumn colourings. Summer cooking calls for cool glass and dishes of bamboo, while winter asks for heavy dishes, some of which are lovely and enviable.

Nowadays both in homes and restaurants the Western-style table is becoming popular but still the short-legged table has its place as well as the lacquer trays in which each person is served individually, the bowls arranged on it to make a beautiful picture. Trays are becoming less fashionable except for special occasions when a host wants to show foreign guests something Japanese or in a restaurant specializing in Japanese culture. Even when the trays are used they will be put on top of short-legged tables.

At formal dinners there is considerable etiquette, with all the dishes served on trays. First comes the soup tray containing soup, raw fish etc., with which is served *sake*. When this is finished the first, second and third trays of the meal proper are brought. The meal consists of one soup and three dishes or two soups and five dishes, or three soups and seven dishes. Then there is the complicated order of how the trays are placed, how to take off the lid of the soup bowls—this one must do carefully for the steam of the soup often causes the lids to stick and careless handling means spilling. Wrong holding of the soup bowl, which must be held in two hands, causes extreme pain for it is a breach of etiquette. Next is the question of how to eat, tasting in a certain order, not eating the rice at one fell swoop and never leaving any in the bowl—another breach—and always praising the soup. Incidentally, if you waste rice your loved one will grow a wart on his face, which seems a little unfair.

All portions are very small, probably because there are so many dishes. Except for such dishes as *sukiyaki* or other chafing dishes, each portion is served individually.

In no other country in the world are there so many festivals so closely connected with food. Every festival brings its own food. 'Doll's Day' features shellfish; 'Boy's Day' carp; the New Year rice and more rice. 'Flower Viewing' days mean food in lacquered boxes for picnics, each layer containing a different dish and arranged as neatly as a layered box of chocolates.

For the interested tourist there is much to discover even in the restaurants of Japan. These range from street stalls and hole-in-the-corner eating houses to those of baronial size. One can walk through the streets of Tokyo and turn into a quiet garden complete with willow tree and stream, enclosed by a bamboo fence, to discover at the end a tempura restaurant spotlessly clean, a blue and white curtain (*yukata* cotton) hanging in the doorway. On a perfect day one lunches or dines in an open-air garden restaurant to try a Ghengis Khan barbecue or try the fairly formalized *sukiyaki* restaurant.

There are small restaurants which serve nothing but several species of sardines or *yakitoris*, offering all kinds of birds on small spits.

Then there are the *sashimi* houses (*see* page 189), or those which serve only *sushi* (*see* page 193), and the *mitzutaki* restaurants which are rather like the *sukiyaki* ones inasmuch as the food is cooked on a chafing dish in front of guests.

Many country inns are renowned for their cooking, always strictly Japanese for the Japanese. When travelling one need never be hungry. The Japanese trains are famous for their cooking, the stations even more so. It all began in the days when trains had no dining cars and enterprising vendors started preparing dishes of noodles, *sushi* and other Japanese specialities to hand out quickly to hungry passengers. One main station cooked noodles in a manner better than anywhere else in Japan and people travelled by train just to try these noodles. The idea grew and now the guard's voice on the intercom announces that the train will stop exactly five minutes at the next station, that we are nearing it and get out quickly to buy noodles, *sushi* or what you will. Tea is brought in a small plastic pot with a built-in cup, and young girls run along the platform calling out their wares.

Most Japanese housewives still prefer to shop daily. All fruit and vegetables for Japanese taste must be fresh, slightly immature even.

Japanese cooking is far more preparation than actual cooking. A cook will spend hours preparing, cutting and chopping, using his razor-sharp knives. Where we would use metal spoons, chopsticks in varying sizes are used and with tremendous expertise. Otherwise many of the Japanese utensils resemble our own.

If dining with Japanese do not pick up your chopsticks until the oldest member of the party has done so. If helping yourself to something from a communal dish, reverse the chopsticks, put the food in your bowl and then pick it up with the right ends of the chopsticks. At the end of a meal the chopsticks are put back into the small envelope out of which they came. And when not using them place them on the chopstick rests. Chopsticks are used with the right hand and if holding a bowl of food, do this with the left hand.

Sake and beer cups are exchanged between host and guests, but the cup is rinsed afterwards as a sign of respect to the guest. Not to exchange is considered rather bad manners to say the least. If you want more *sake* put out your cup, never fill it yourself. If you do not want any more, simply turn your cup upside down. Napkins are not used, at least not the variety we wrap round our knees. Instead hot towels are given for washing hands and men, not so women, rub it round their faces.

The *chanoyu* or tea ceremony as it is commonly known, is peculiar to Japan. Originally it was a monastic custom introduced by Japanese Buddhists who went to China for spiritual studies. In the land of its origin this ceremony has long been forgotten, but it survives in Japan even with today's mighty industrialization. It is considered as an aesthetic pastime, a cult in which the beverage is idealized. It is remarked that devotees of *chanoyu* 'appreciate and worship nature through the medium of the indescribably delicate and refreshing aroma of powdered tea'.

The original tea ceremony dates back earlier than the thirteenth century when an austere Zen priest, Eisai, brought back with him from China a simple form of flower arrangement as an adjunct to the tea ceremony. Some three centuries later appeared Rikyu, a man of considerable influence and well versed in Zen, and it is he who is credited with having founded the present tea ceremony. As practised by Rikyu, there was no pretentious display, only a few persons participated in the ceremony and in a small room where they could take sanctuary and communicate with one another in the manner of close friends. The *samurai* took off his sword and the peasant became equal with the nobleman or such was the intention.

To add to the impression of community with nature, the tea house was set in a garden giving the impression that it was far from the city and its crowds. Subdued colours were there to soothe the senses, and the tea utensils, never left out on display, were taken from their wrappings. The simple ceremony, it was insisted, was in perfect harmony with the Japanese devotion to serenity and simplicity. As such the spirit of tea is symbolized by four written Chinese characters:

1. Harmony between man and the universe
2. Humility and mutual respect among human beings
3. Spotless cleanliness

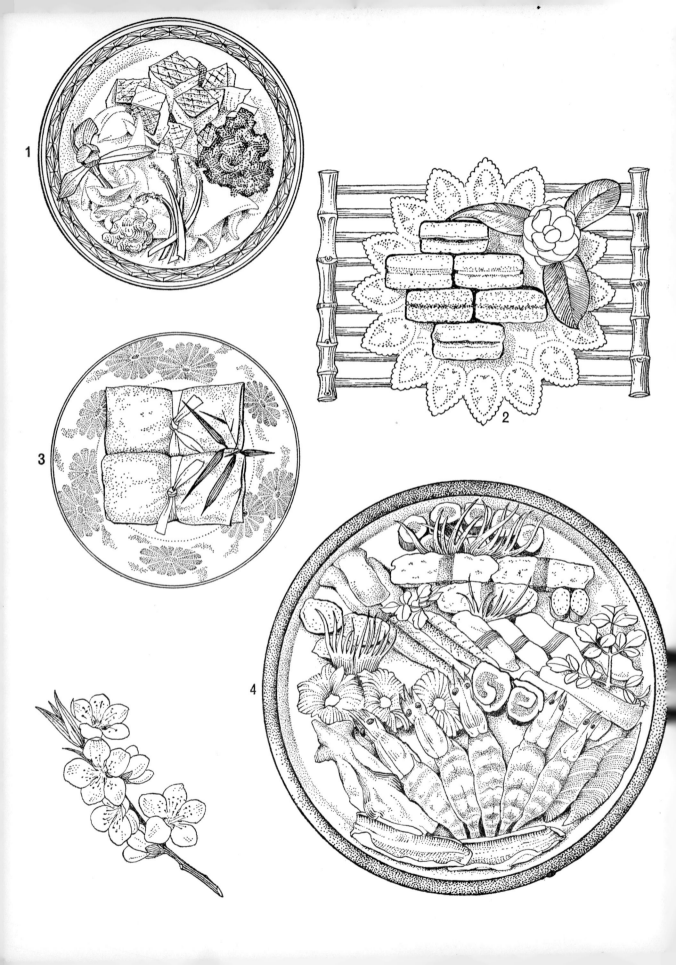

4. Tranquility of environment in order to bring clarity of mind and spiritual understanding.

The tea ceremony, which usually starts around noon, provides a setting for quiet conversation. However much a foreigner might try to enjoy the ceremony or even enjoy it, it can seldom be fully appreciated by him. Even so, he cannot fail to be impressed by the sincere enjoyment evidenced by the Japanese participants. It is a function which still carries with it a trace of its early religious element. While the modern Japanese girl may wear her kimono but rarely, and then only on special occasions, most of them still take an interest in the tea ceremony, attending special classes for its instruction, as we might cooking classes.

TEA (*Cha*)

Apart from the ceremony connected with the drinking of tea, this beverage is important to the Japanese people. They serve it at any time of the day and there are several varieties. Before the 1939 war the most popular tea was green tea but now it seems that black tea is gaining adherents, especially in urban areas.

Looking through my Japanese books of reference none refer to the impulsive Buddhist saint who tore off his eyelids, tossed them away and, where they dropped, there grew a tea plant (*see* page 180). On the contrary, more prosaically, it is recorded that as far as is known the earliest reference to tea drinking was in the eighth century. It was brought to Japan from China and used rather more as a medicine than as a beverage. Tea plants were cultivated in the twelfth century, not far from Kyoto, the ancient capital of Japan, and today tea forms one of the important products of the country.

Japanese green tea is mild and fragrant. It is divided in *gyokuro, sencha* and *bancha*. Then there is a *matcha* or powdered tea, made from old but good plants. This is used in the tea ceremony. All these teas are from the same type of plant, their differences are in the manner in which they are processed.

Gyokuro is the finest of the green teas and for this the finest buds are required. Also it is laid down that it should be brewed in hot water of exactly the right temperature, that is between 60° and 70° F. *Sencha*, the common green tea and usually drunk by tea lovers, is brewed at a temperature of 75–85° F., and for its production the best leaves of the plant are needed. Old-fashioned etiquette demands that either of these teas only may be offered to guests, and one must not overlook that the pot and the cups must be heated to the same temperature as the water.

Finally there is *bancha* for which left-over or inferior leaves are used. It is more nearly a black tea and the 'people's drink'. This needs to be brewed in water at 85–100° F. Thus, the cheaper the tea, the hotter the water. Old tea, say the Japanese, must also be brewed longer than the fresh tea.

According to Japanese taste, one pound of good quality green tea will produce up to 250 cups of tea. Earthenware pots are preferred and these are scalded first. Often the Japanese, when using high-grade tea, will let the water boil first and then let it become lukewarm before pouring it into the pot. Before drinking tea the Japanese will eat something sweet, like a small cake, claiming that only then can they appreciate the subtle charm of its taste and fragrance.

Much has been written the world over concerning the quality of water required for tea drinking. Of the four varieties of water, rain water, well water, mountain stream water and urbanized water, it has been proved that the mountain stream water is best for Japanese tea. Impurities in water will ruin tea, so will chemicals. Rain water is not good for tea making.

(1) *Sashimi*; (2) *Sushi*; (3) *Seaweed Pancakes*; (4) *Mixed Hors D'Oeuvre*

However, I doubt whether tea lovers anywhere in the world can have done what the Japanese tea connoisseurs used to do, send special messengers in a palanquin from Edo (Tokyo) to Kyoto to fetch the water so desirable for tea making. The journey took days and the operation, therefore, was expensive. But, it was said, what is time and money when it is well known that without good water there can be no good tea.

FISH (*Sakana*)

It is said the Japanese are the greatest fish eaters in the world. And that they have more varieties to choose from than any other people. Being surrounded by water and possessing many rivers and lakes, fish is available in any part of the country and, because of both warm and cold currents running along the islands, the variety is enormous.

I went to the great fish market in Tokyo. This is a must for those interested in fish and food. It is a truly mammoth market. I do not know if it is the largest in the world but it must be one of the largest.

Never in my travels have I seen such variety in fish, ranging from a small white fish which, piled on a platter, looked like so much long grain rice (this is mixed with a sauce and served in Japanese eating houses with drinks) to monster swordfish with splendid pink flesh which cuts so neatly into steaks and tastes so good. And the equally monstrous tuna fish which requires two men to push it on a barrow on its last journey before being cut up like so much rich veal or beef. Red is the colour of the market, bright as the artist's palette. The red of the mullet and the snapper, the brilliant red of the octopus, some as exquisite in colouring as in shape.

I noted almost with awe the neatness of it all, the lack of a fishy smell, the immense cleanliness, the swiftness with which the fish was handled and prepared. I watched, spellbound, eels being made ready for the buyer. A spike was thrust through their unsuspecting heads as they were plucked from tubs. Then the head smartly cut off with one stroke of a sharp knife, the same knife cleanly whistled down the length of the eel and in a second it was in two thin slivers. The strips of eel are then deftly handed to a second man who threads them expertly on to bamboo skewers, hands them to a third fellow who packs them neatly into boxes.

All through the market there is this insistence on neatness. Much of the fish is prepared not only for the fishmonger but also for the housewife.

Let me name just a few of the fish which we might recognize in the West. Sea bream, bonito, tuna, swordfish, salmon and cod, sardines and flounder, mackerel and all members of the herring family, shellfish, in all shapes and sizes. *Fugu*, called globefish, blowfish and balloon fish, which only licensed specialists should prepare since, badly treated, it can be deadly poison. Many is the drunken Japanese fisherman who has died a nasty death from carelessly dealing with the *fugu*. There is a Japanese saying which goes something like this—'I would like to eat the globefish but I would not like to loose my life!' The skins of this curious creature are sold to make globefish lamp shades sold as souvenirs. Then there is the abalone so much appreciated in Japan that only the finest is sold. Edible seaweed surely counts as fish and is certainly to be found in the Tokyo market, so are sea urchins from which a delicious but expensive sauce is prepared. Oysters, clams, mussels . . . but why go on, you name them, the Tokyo fish market has them.

SLICED RAW FISH (*Sashimi*)

This is a truly Japanese speciality. It is a dish which often causes people to pull a wry face when it is mentioned.

I took myself alone to a small *sashimi* bar, sat at the round counter and ordered *sake*, and eyed the spotless counter and the glass case in which the raw fish was beautifully arrayed. I started conservatively with a prawn, which was not absolutely raw for it was dropped into boiling water for a second or so. This does not cook it but makes it look less offensive, for raw shelled prawn is not a lovely looking thing; this was followed by thinly sliced bream first dipped into a dish of *shoyu* and then swiftly into another containing horse-radish sauce.

Although *sashimi* is a truly Japanese dish there are legends that it was brought to Japan by early settlers from the South Seas. Whether this is true or not, it is still the custom among Japanese fishermen to consume small live fish straight from the sea.

Almost any kind of fish can be made into *sashimi* but it must be fresh. The most popular are sea bream, carp and tuna, but some shellfish, abalone and even varieties of shark are also considered good by some connoisseurs, so is fresh sardine.

To make good *sashimi* the fish is cleaned and sliced as thinly as possible. It is in the cutting that skill is shown, as *sashimi* sliced by inexperienced hands loses much of its flavour.

Sashimi is cut into various shapes and it is according to the shape and size of the fish that a particular dish gets its name. Different fish are cut into different shapes and styles.

Another important point with *sashimi* is its arrangement. It must be both artistic and beautiful and the various slices of fish must stimulate the appetite. Side by side with *sashimi* is *tsuma* which adds colour to the dishes and is also meant to be eaten. *Tsuma* is mostly leaves but also thinly sliced carrot qualifies, so do edible chrysanthemum flowers, sliced cucumbers, radishes etc., and its function is to freshen the taste between each slice of *sashimi*. '*Sashimi* without *tsuma* is rather vulgar,' I was informed.

It is usual to drink *sake* with *sashimi*. Some people like to have a bowl of cooked rice with their *sashimi*, others take it neat. Another custom is to put thin slices of *sashimi* over the bowl of rice and then pour boiling hot Japanese tea over it all. However, this is considered a very special dish by Japanese gourmets.

The curious thing about *sashimi* is that it lacks both the fishy smell and taste which would be its undoing. It is often so artistically arranged on a plate, which is shaped like a fish and painted with a fish seemingly swimming lazily in a cool pool, that it recaptures nature.

Now for preparing the fish, and I am not pretending this is simple. The fish must be scaled, head, fins, tail and entrails removed. In other words it must be absolutely cleansed. It is washed carefully, soaked in water and the flesh is divided laterally along the backbone, all the bones are scrupulously removed and the upper and lower slices divided again. The skin is taken off and the fish is ready for slicing. There are four main ways in which to slice fish for *sashimi*, but I shall only give one, the most usual method. This is to slice the fish thinly and let the slices overlap, 'like roof tiles'. The slices are cut at a 30-degree angle with a very sharp knife and each slice is cut $1\frac{1}{2}$ inches long and $\frac{1}{4}$ inch wide.

All these slices, for home consumption, are placed with an eye to beauty on a lovely plate and garnished. The garnish can be finely shredded radishes, cabbage, cucumber, lettuce, grated fresh ginger and thinly sliced or grated carrot, not all of these at the same time but taken from this selection. Add for dipping a sauce made from 1 cupful ($1\frac{1}{4}$) *shoyu* sauce mixed with 1 teaspoonful ($1\frac{1}{4}$) of either dry hot mustard or grated fresh ginger. It is also usual to have a bowl of grated horse-radish handy for dipping.

MEAT

Meat in Japan is available in all forms. Beef is the favourite and this has become famous. Of Kobe beef it is said that the cattle are fed on beer, massaged to distribute their flesh evenly and generally cosseted. By the time these spoilt creatures are ready for the slaughterhouse they are contented and fat. Beef cattle are much bred in Japan and not only Kobe produces excellent beef.

Pork and chicken are also splendid and, because all three kinds of meat are expensive, the Japanese housewife has learned to cook it in small portions, making meat an adjunct to vegetables and a little is made to go a long way. There are chops which an obliging butcher will not only trim but will also cook, and the usual sub-divisions of meat, bacon, liver, kidneys and offal generally. Mutton or lamb is not popular.

Poultry and game are easy to find, duck, goose, turkey, capons, rabbit, deer, wild boar, quails, pheasants and partridges.

NOODLES

It is not known when the Japanese first began to eat noodles. There are several varieties. The three most popular are *soba*, a thin noodle made from buckwheat flour, *udon*, which looks like macaroni, and *somen*, which is thin; the last two are made from wheat flour.

Of these three, *soba* is the earliest known. It is said to be of Chinese origin and, as the cultivation of buckwheat increased, so did the consumption of *soba*.

Then there is *harusame* or noodles from soy bean flour, *shirataki* (devil's foot noodles) made from a tuberous root with a gelatinous texture, and a green noodle which is a mixture of buckwheat and green tea.

Pride of place is *soba*. It is eaten both hot and cold (so for that matter is *somen*, but *udon* almost never). It is mixed with a number of varying ingredients to produce some of Japan's most famous dishes. It is much used in soups and one of the most familiar sounds of Tokyo is the shrill whistle of the *o-soba* man as he peddles through the darkening evening with his warming soup to sell to late workers. Or there is the familiar sight in Tokyo of the noodle vendor balancing his boxes of noodles as he cycles blithely through the crowded streets of the city.

And finally, noodles come in several colours, and there are even instant noodles.

VEGETABLES

A wide choice, those we know such as leeks, spring (green) onions, peas, corn, onions, turnips and squash—the latter not so well known to the British as the Americans. Spinach and radishes both figure greatly in Japanese cooking, so does parsley and broccoli, cauliflower and green peppers. There is rhubarb, asparagus, celery, beetroots, mushrooms, tomatoes and lettuce.

Distinctive Japanese vegetables include burdock and *daikon*, which is a long white radish. There are bean sprouts and bamboo shoots and Japanese-style parsley, edible chrysanthemum leaves, varieties of mushrooms unknown in the West, the gingko nut and horse-radish, a most important ingredient in Japanese sauces.

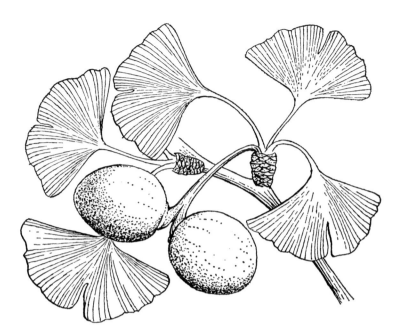

Gingko Nut

Because it is the custom in Japan to cook vegetables lightly they are also harvested at the height of their season, even sometimes when slightly immature, but always when at their best—full of flavour and tender.

FRUIT

All those we know in Europe, besides persimmons, oranges, lemons, mandarins, loquats, huge melons, strawberries which grow in the south amidst the rocks and appear in February, dates, figs, bananas and pineapples. There are apples, called *ringos*, grapefruit and the many berry fruits, and a cool crisp fruit, the pear-apple. Curiously, cherries are not abundant, for the famous Japanese cherry is a flowering variety.

SHOYU SAUCE (*Shoyu*)

Without *shoyu* there can be no Japanese cooking. It is the Japanese soy giving both the smell and the flavour which characterizes Japanese food. Made from barley, soya bean, and salt, millions of litres of *shoyu* are produced annually. Although it is used in small quantities only.

Shoyu was brought from China by a Buddhist priest in, it is thought, the sixth century A.D. At first the use of it was confined to the noble families, but some six centuries later it was manufactured in the region near Kyoto and became increasingly popular.

There are different kinds of *shoyu* sauce which vary according to the manufacturers and in the method of preparation. Basically it is a salty liquid, its colour varying from inky black to almost colourless. Different recipes call for different varieties, although if only one kind is available it can be used.

RICE (*Kome*)

Rice as the principal food of the Japanese has long been regarded as sacred. From the very beginning of history rice was respected by the Japanese people. Whatever rice may mean to Westerners, they really cannot appreciate what it means to the Japanese.

It is his way of life; it has been said that he eats it, drinks it (in the form of *sake*) and wears it (as rice-straw hats). It is the mainstay of his diet, for no Japanese meal would be complete without rice. It is the potatoes and the bread of the West put together, but even more so, for it is eaten three times a day, every day, summer or winter, hot or cold, plain or garnished.

Throughout Japan rice rituals of ancient history are performed. Rice dishes figure in many ceremonies, for the New Year, or the moon viewing and so on.

Curiously enough, rice was not originally produced in Japan, it was brought over by early settlers from the south. It was eaten unpolished in those far-off times, but in the peaceful days of the fifth Tokugawa Shogun in the seventeenth century, the populace became luxurious in their tastes, demanded polished rice and got it. However, recently there has been a campaign against polished rice, its devotees being threatened with beri-beri. So back has come unpolished and semi-polished rice to the Japanese diet.

Consistent eating of rice has developed among the Japanese a definite sense of rice tasting. To cook rice well, they insist, requires skill. It must not be too hard, or too soft but just right, *al dente*, as the Italians would say.

The rice is washed thoroughly, the water being changed several times, and then is left soaking in water for some hours before being used. It is then put into a heavy pan, a special rice boiling pan with a thick wooden lid, and cooked over wood, coal, gas or electricity. The Japanese consider that the best rice is cooked over wood. According to the size of the pan and the type of stove used, the rice takes from 20 to 60 minutes to cook.

Badly cooked rice is sticky and stodgy. More and more Japanese housewives are using modern electric rice steamers which have taken all the chance out of rice cooking. Such units also are available outside of Japan, and when they become better known, should be as much a part of the Western kitchen as the pressure cooker or the electric mixer has become.

BOILED RICE (*Gohan*)

The following is a specific, basic recipe. But it must be remembered that there are many different grades of rice, different types, and each type has its own function.

4–6 servings:

2 cups (2½) long grain rice   **3 cups (3¾) water**

One or more hours before using the rice, wash it thoroughly and drain. Put it into a heavy pan, add the water and stir this well into the rice. Cover with an ordinary tight-fitting lid and bring to a quick boil, reduce the heat to slow and cook for 3 minutes. The pan must be covered. Increase the heat again and cook the rice for 15–20 minutes, it should boil during this time. When all the liquid has been absorbed, it is ready. Turn the heat to high for exactly 1 minute, then take the pan from the heat. Still covered, let it rest for 10 minutes, thus allowing it to steam. By this time the rice should have risen to a dry mound, with all the grains swollen and separated. Do not stir.

VINEGARED RICE (*Sushi-Meshi*)

Vinegared rice is rice of the finest quality cooked especially for *sushi*. *Sushi* is sliced fish or vegetable and other small bits beautifully arranged on rice, in other words, each a sort of small rice open sandwich. They are served as snacks and there are *sushi* bars throughout the country, or one can buy boxes of exquisitely arranged *sushi* to take home. *Sushi* always forms part of a picnic luncheon and Japanese airlines serve them.

Originally *sushi* meant pickled fish and was made by placing fish between layers of rice. After a while the rice fermented and became sour then the fish, according to Japanese taste, was fine but the rice was thrown away. This method of preparing *sushi* is still followed in some parts of the country. In time, however, people came to realize that they could prepare *sushi* and retain the rice by adding vinegar to it thus producing vinegared rice.

In this new form *sushi* became increasingly popular, with two distinct schools of *sushi* makers developing. One in Edo (now Tokyo) and the other in Naniwa (now Osaka). People from the latter town preferred the *oshi-sushi* or packed *sushi*, in which the *sushi* is packed into a square box with the vinegared rice; a weight is then applied and after a while it sets into a mass. Later it is taken out of the box and cut into shapes, squares, oblongs etc. The other method is the palm-packed *sushi*, in which the rice is taken up in the left hand and with the first two fingers of the right hand it is moulded swiftly into shapes. Over this is placed the raw fish and other delicacies. The origin of this, it is claimed, comes from the *kabuki* or Japanese theatre. It was customary for *kabuki* audiences to remain in the theatre the entire evening. During the intervals they would consume these little rice balls, fashioned for their convenience, which took only a couple of bites. Their colloquial name when translated means 'between the curtains'.

Sushi bars are usually built to resemble an old-fashioned house. They are small with a counter or bar at which the *sushi* fancier sits and chooses his *sushi* from the remarkable array displayed on the glass-topped counter. Usually there will be prawns, cuttlefish, bream, scarlet tuna fish which look like thin strips of meat, and a paler and oilier relative, the *toro*; there is abalone and scallops. Then there are several gourd-like vegetables and a sort of omelette.

Behind all this stands the *sushi* maker, an expert at his job. It is a pleasure to watch him as he skilfully takes the vinegared rice from the tub beside him, flips it between his palms and, in a matter of seconds, has his little shapes formed. The customer indicates what he would like to eat and this is deftly placed on the small mound of sticky rice, garnished with a leaf, and served two at a time on a coloured lacquer plate. The *sushi* is eaten with a sauce, usually *shoyu*, and paper-thin slices of fresh ginger. With it is served tiny hot cups of green tea. Cold beer also goes well with *sushi*.

The success of the *sushi* depends largely on the rice and it is important this is cooked properly. The Japanese recommend a starchy white polished rice.

5 cups (6¼) rice
6¼ cups (7¾) water
1 tablespoon (1¼) salt

1 tablespoon (1¼) sugar
4 tablespoons (5) vinegar

Three hours before cooking, thoroughly wash the rice and let it drain completely. Bring the water to the boil, add the rice, and bring it again to the boil. Stir lightly, lower the heat as soon as the rice begins to bubble and let the rice continue cooking for between 10 and 15 minutes. This way of cooking gives the rice its correct firm consistency. Combine the last three ingredients and pour these over the rice. Turn the rice into a shallow bowl and fan it for rapid cooling. It is ready for use.

The usual and simplest shape for the non-expert is to make small ovals which can be shaped in the hands by moistening the palms slightly. The ovals should be 2 inches long and 1 inch wide, and the expert gets all equal and right the first time. On top of each piece a sprinkle of Japanese horse-radish (the Western equivalent can be used in moderation) and on top of this whatever covering chosen, each piece precisely the same length, but not the width, as the rice ovals. Many Westerners outside Japan would perhaps not appreciate the raw fish of the Japanese, but one can cover the rice with strips of smoked salmon, cooked prawns or shrimps, smoked oysters, anchovies, tinned lobster or crab, even sardines and paper-thin slices of cucumber. If these are all deftly and artistically arranged one will have a splendid array of unusual hors-d'œuvre, or appetizers with drinks, to offer guests.

COLD RICE, EGGS AND VEGETABLES (*Chirashizuchi*)

4 servings:

½ lb. (1¼ cups) long grain rice
2 teaspoons (2½) vinegar
salt to taste
1 teaspoon (1¼) sugar
a little fresh ginger, finely chopped

2 teaspoons (2½) shoyu sauce
2 eggs
1 cup (1¼) shelled peas, just cooked
½ cup (⅔) carrots, sliced, cooked but only just

Cook the rice as in the previous recipe until it is very soft but still with some of the liquid remaining in the rice. Take it from the pan and put into a bowl. While still hot stir in half of the vinegar, salt and the sugar. Put the rice aside in a cool place but not in a refrigerator. Soak the ginger in the remaining vinegar, the *shoyu* sauce and sugar for 1 hour.

Scramble the eggs. Arrange the rice on a plate, smooth it out and garnish it with the scrambled eggs, peas, carrots and the ginger-flavoured sauce. The garnishings for this dish may differ but only those vegetables which combine with 'beauty' should be used.

Actually we might call this a rice salad and it can be served with any green salad.

BEAN PASTE (*Miso*)

There is no Western counterpart to *miso*, which is a paste made with *shoyu* or soy bean, wheat or rice and salt. These ingredients are put into a wooden tub, crushed and allowed to ferment to form a thick paste.

There are different kinds of *miso* as well as different forms of manufacture. It is one of the most important items of diet among the Japanese people. To the majority, a breakfast is not complete without it.

As a breakfast dish, *miso* is mixed with a variety of other ingredients and made into a soup. In the main these are vegetables or seaweed, but fish also is used. This soup is called *misoshiru* and, although considered principally as a breakfast dish, it is used at other meals. By some of the farming communities it is eaten three times a day. A large kettle of *misoshiru* is made in the morning and heated up later.

This, like so many Japanese culinary specialities, is one of Chinese origin, brought by Buddhist priests who did not eat meat and, therefore, welcomed the *miso*, which is considered highly nutritious. Old-fashioned nursing mothers take a dish of *miso* with carp, called *koi-kuku*, for it is believed to increase the quantity of their milk. And for the sickly *koi-kuku* is especially recommended.

Apart from appearing in soup form, *miso* is prepared with meat as a kind of thick stew with plenty of vegetables and often small dumplings. Finally it is believed that *miso* is especially beneficial to heavy smokers, since it has the power of removing the effects of nicotine.

Miso, if correctly prepared, will keep for years, suffering no deterioration. It comes in waxed paper cartons in several sizes ranging from 1–5 lbs.

A typical *miso* soup or stock, is made by squashing the paste, adding water, straining it into a pan and then boiling it with vegetables of choice and season. As well as vegetables, small pieces of bean curd are sometimes added, also fish or meat.

SOUPS

STOCK (*Dashi*)

Dashi, the Japanese stock, is a light, clear fish stock quite indispensable to Japanese cooking and has a subtle and delicate flavour. It is made from flaked *katsuobushi* (dried bonito flakes) and *konbu*, which is dried seaweed. *Dashi* has been said to be the cornerstone of Japanese cooking, as well as being the basis of Japanese soups. It is the cooking liquid of many other dishes. It is pale amber in colour, like a perfect chicken bouillon, and has not the remotest trace of fish or seaweed taste. Most Europeans mistake it for a superb chicken consommé. In fact, the only possible substitute for *dashi* would be this—but it is only a substitute, it does not and cannot give the same flavour.

There are a number of *dashi* stocks, used for various dishes. One for general use in soups and the other for vegetables etc.

In Japan *dashi* comes in packages of various sizes and qualities, including an instant one, which makes life very easy. In the West the ingredients for making *dashi* as well as the packaged one will be found in stores dealing with Japanese foods.

5 servings:

5 cups (6¼) water	**½ cup dried bonito flakes**
1–2 square in. dried seaweed	**a good pinch of monosodium glutamate**

Put the water into a saucepan with the seaweed and bring this to the boil. Add the fish flakes. Turn off the heat, add the monosodium glutamate and leave for 10 minutes. Strain for use. Keep the flakes and the seaweed for making a second brew of *dashi*. *Dashi* will keep indefinitely in an airtight bottle. Instructions for dealing with prepared *dashi* come with the package.

CHICKEN AND NOODLE SOUP (*Sumashi Jiru*)

6 servings:

4 oz. (½ cup) Japanese style noodles or the finest obtainable cut into 1-inch lengths
8 dried mushrooms, soaked for 30 minutes in water
½ lb. chicken meat

6 cups (7½) dashi (see page 195) or chicken stock
2 teaspoons (2½) shoyu sauce
salt
6 strips lemon peel

Cook the noodles for a few minutes in boiling water or until tender. Drain. Slice the mushrooms thinly (discarding the stems) and boil separately. Drain. Slice the chicken meat into thin strips. Heat a cupful of water, add the chicken pieces and cook these a few minutes or until tender. Add the *dashi*, stir, the noodles, *shoyu* and a little salt. Finally add the mushrooms and bring the lot to the boil. Divide the chicken, noodles and mushrooms into small bowls, add the soup and garnish each bowl with a strip of lemon.

STEAMED EGG WITH VEGETABLES SOUP (*Chawan-Mushi*)

Chawan-Mushi, which is cooked in small containers called *chawan-mushi jawans*, curiously is called a soup but it appears to Westerners to be a custard and exceedingly good. It appears in several guises throughout the Far East and, although the Japanese are able to compete with it with chopsticks, take refuge in the fact that it is also correct to eat it with a spoon. Apart from being an important item of Japanese cooking, this is a dish which can be used in a Western meal as a starter.

There are recipes using only vegetables, others only white chicken meat, fish, shellfish—especially prawns, crayfish and lobster. Or use fish and vegetables, chicken and vegetables—the rules are elastic. Obviously with different vegetables, fish or chicken, the flavour of the *chawan-mushi* changes, and vegetables are strictly those in season. So bear in mind that the following recipe can be changed according to taste and availability.

According to the Japanese, *chawan-mushi* must be made in a special container with a cover, i.e. the *chawan-mushi jawan*, and one is gravely informed: 'It is not made in the homes of the poor.' However, not having these special containers, I use lidded ramekins.

Usually served with rice or *sake*.

6–8 servings:

1 lb. white chicken meat or half chicken and half prawns
2–3 mushrooms, preferably dried and soaked, but fresh will do
½ cup (⅔) tinned bamboo shoots
4 cups (5) dashi or chicken stock, roughly 4 times the quantity of the eggs
8 eggs

½ cup (⅔) frozen peas
2 tablespoons (2½) shoyu sauce
a good pinch monosodium glutamate
1 tablespoon (1¼) sugar
2 tablespoons (2½) sake or substitute (see page 244)
1 lemon

Cut the chicken, mushrooms and bamboo shoots all into slivers and as near in size as possible. Mix this with the *dashi* and cook for 10 minutes, no longer. Strain off the stock and let this cool. Beat the eggs well but not until they are frothy. Stir the eggs into the warm stock and pour through a muslin cloth. Mix the remaining ingredients together (including the chicken etc.) and divide into 6 or 8 small bowls with lids. Pour the egg mixture into the bowls and place them in a steamer or in a deep frying pan in which is placed 2 inches of boiling water. Cover each container with its lid but leave each slightly ajar; steam for 20 minutes (or until the custard is set) over a moderate heat. Serve in the same bowls, uncover and place a thin sliver of lemon on top of each bowl.

In place of chicken or fish, fine noodles may be used. This then becomes *odamaki-mushi*.

Often the *chawan-mushi* is garnished with strips of string bean and carrot.

CLEAR EGG SOUP (*Kakitamajiru Suimono*)

6 servings:

2–3 eggs
5 cups (6¼) dashi or chicken stock
2 teaspoons (2½) shoyu sauce
salt

2 teaspoons (2½) cornflour (cornstarch) mixed with water to a thin paste
1 piece crushed seaweed, spring (green) onion or lemon juice to taste

Put the *dashi* into a pan, add the *shoyu*, salt and cornflour paste and bring to the boil. Beat the eggs and spread slowly on the surface of the boiling soup. The egg should float in threads. Garnish with any one of the remaining ingredients.

Another version of this pleasant soup is to stir the beaten eggs into the liquid after it has boiled and been taken from the heat and also sprinkle grated fresh ginger and parsley over the top.

VEGETABLE SOUP (*Misoshiru*)

8–10 servings:

8 cups (10) dashi or clear chicken stock
2 eggs
¼ teaspoon (⅓) each salt and sugar
1 tablespoon (1¼) shoyu sauce
a good pinch monosodium glutamate

1 cup radish, grated
4 oz. (scant cup) string beans, finely sliced
1 tablespoon (1¼) miso paste (see page 194)
3 tablespoons (3¾) spring (green) onions, finely shredded

Beat the eggs with the salt and sugar and make two thin omelettes. Roll each like a pancake and cut into thin strips.

Add *shoyu* sauce to the stock and bring this to the boil. Add the beans and cook these until just soft—overcooking will ruin them. Add the *miso* to thicken the soup, stirring all the while, then add the grated radish and monosodium glutamate. Serve the soup hot with the spring onions and omelette shreds as a garnish.

Other vegetables may be used, such as turnips instead of radishes, peas instead of beans, mild onions or leeks when spring onions are not available. If *miso* is not available, thicken the soup with the same quantity of cornflour (cornstarch) mixed to a thin paste with water. The kind of radish usually used in this recipe is *daikon*.

MINCED LOBSTER SOUP (*Ebi Shiru*)

4–5 servings:

½ lb. lobster meat, cooked or tinned

1 cup (1¼) strained miso stock (see page 194)

4 cups (5) dashi (see page 195) or chicken stock

½ square bean curd (tofu), cut into small cubes

grated fresh or ground ginger

Put the *miso* and the *dashi* into a pan and bring to the boil. Add the lobster meat and the bean curd. Reduce the heat and simmer until the soup is reheated. Serve in bowls, each topped with grated or ground ginger. If *miso* is not available you will still get a good soup without it.

FRIED FOODS (*Tempura*)

Japanese cooking has two main ways of frying foods, one *tempura* or cooking by deep frying, batter-dipped foods; and *karaage* or frying in a small quantity of oil after being lightly coated with cornflour (cornstarch).

There are many stories, which almost amount to legends, concerning the origin of *tempura*, one of the most famous and popular methods of Japanese cooking. Some believe it to be a dish of Portuguese origin which has become naturalized and nationalized.

After the argument as to its origin, is another as to whether it first appeared in Edo (Tokyo) or in Nagasaki. But whichever town can boast its origin, one is assured that the people of Edo loved *tempura* above all things and that it was in Edo that it has been refined to its present perfection.

Tempura usually implies batter-dipped and fried fish and vegetables, and most experts use sesame oil in its preparation. However, there is a school of *tempura* making which prefers to use a mixture of olive oil and sesame. But whatever oil is used, the best quality is essential. Another difference of opinion concerns adding salt to the batter. Some cooks hold it makes the fried foods crisper, others the opposite.

Another important detail is the preparation of the batter. It is a lumpy batter, not smooth as the batters of the West. The making of *tempura* batter is supposed to be very difficult, but my charming mentor (who explained that most Japanese families go out to have a *tempura* meal as housewives in Japan are as busy as those in the West) did show me exactly how to make it.

Various kinds of fish are used for *tempura*, shellfish, especially prawns and large shrimps, cuttlefish and sliced vegetables. But whatever fish or vegetables used they must be of the finest quality and absolutely fresh, for *tempura* is considered the best way in which to sample the choicest fresh fish and vegetables. Among these ingredients, prawn or *eki* is the most popular.

First let us consider the batter. *Tempura* when translated means 'wearing a crust of batter, as a woman wears silk gauze, stimulating the desire of the beholder by the glimpses of the beauty beneath'.

Tempura batter is then gossamer light and lacy. It is also somewhat lumpy and its secret is in not overmixing. There are several ways of preparing the batter, but I prefer to give the one I know, which is also the usual method.

8 servings:

2 egg yolks
2 cups (2½) chilled water
2 cups (2½) flour
1 teaspoon (1¼) cornflour (cornstarch)
Sauce:
2 cups (2½) dashi (see **page 195**) or **stock**
2 tablespoons (2½) shoyu sauce

½ teaspoon (⅔) monosodium glutamate or
  **fresh lemon mixed with salt and finely
  chopped chillies**
salt and pepper mixed
**1 teaspoon (1¼) each white radish and fresh
  ginger, grated**
2 tablespoons (2½) sake or **sherry** (optional)

Break the yolks in a big bowl, add the chilled water and beat the mixture very well. Add 1 ice cube to keep it chilled if working under hot conditions. Add the flour and cornflour and 'cut' the mixture with a fork, do not beat. It is a good idea to mix about two-thirds of the flour into the egg mixture first, then add the remainder when this is mixed in.

Mix all the sauce ingredients together and put into several small bowls.

Ingredients for frying:
fresh prawns
oil

flat fish, such as plaice or sole
sweet peppers

The secret of the *tempura* lies in the temperature of the oil. Fill a deep frying pan or saucepan and heat to between 350° and 370° F. Without a thermometer, try out a few drops of the batter. If these sink half-way to the bottom of the pan and scatter rapidly, the temperature is right.

Wash and clean the prawns leaving the tails attached. Clip them diagonally to prevent the oil from spurting when fried; make three slight cuts along the inside and put a tooth pick through the back. This done to ensure the prawns remain straight and do not curl up when fried. Clean, skin and cut the fish into fillets, then cut again into inch-wide pieces. Cut the peppers lengthwise into ¾-inch strips, discarding seeds and cores. Other vegetables, such as carrots, turnips, aubergine (eggplant) etc. are all peeled and cut into thin slices or strips. String beans also are used in *tempura*, broken into halves and trimmed.

Bring the oil to the boil. Dip the pieces, one by one, into the batter and then into the oil and fry to a golden brown. The order is first the fish and then the vegetables, the pan must never be over-loaded, i.e. the pieces of fish or vegetables being fried must have room to play about. A trick of the good *tempura* cook is to drop a tiny morsel of the batter on top of the already almost fried ingredient and this forms a lacy pattern. The prawns are done when they rise to the top of the pan and it is at this point that the extra batter is added. Left-over batter is also fried. Should the batter become thick as you are working, add a little water and again sprinkle in a little flour.

Everything should be cut for easy picking up with chopsticks; dip the pieces as they come piping hot from the pan into any of the small bowls of sauce which are scattered around, and eat at once.

In my opinion, *tempura* is everything that one hears and reads about. In fact, it is not difficult to prepare oneself, although a little practice is required to get the correct batter proportions, and the deftness required to serve the *tempura* pieces as they come at once from the pan. They are drained in just a few moments.

It is another one of those dishes which are best cooked at the table, for it cannot wait; cold *tempura* is not *tempura* at all.

TEMPURA ON RICE (*Tendon*)

Tendon is a big bowl of rice on which hot *tempura* (*see* page 198) is served and eaten with a sauce. It has a special place in the Japanese cuisine and it is preferred by many Japanese to the simple *tempura*. Instead of using one large bowl, you can spoon the rice (which is prepared in the usual manner) into small individual bowls. Fish and vegetables are cooked as for *tempura* and these items are added to the rice and the whole is topped with sauce. *Tendon* must be eaten absolutely hot and it is at its finest with fresh lobster or large fresh prawns.

6 servings:

3 cups (3¾) cups cooked rice
Sauce:
1 cup (1¼) dashi or chicken stock
1 tablespoon (1¼) sugar
2 tablespoons (2½) shoyu sauce

2 tablespoons (2½) sake
grated daikon (see **page 190**) or horse-radish to taste
grated fresh ginger to taste

Bring the first four sauce ingredients just to the boil, add *daikon* and ginger and pour it into the rice and top with *tempura*.

CHAFING DISH COOKING

CHAFING DISH COOKING (1) (*Sukiyaki*)

The first thing to remember is that all the cooking of *sukiyaki* is done in front of the diner. This does not mean any objectionable smell of cooking; on the contrary, it is recognized that the aroma of *sukiyaki* is one of its attractions. It excites the salivary glands and makes the mouth water.

Sukiyaki probably is one of the most widely known Japanese dishes, one which pleases not only the Japanese but also the foreigner. Whether or not it is a dish of Japanese origin, is another matter. Being only some hundred years old, it is therefore considered a modern addition to the Japanese cuisine.

Over the name *sukiyaki*, pronounced *skiyaki*, there is some controversy. The most accepted version is that it was formerly a method of cooking on the blades of a plough and was, therefore, called *sukiyaki*, or plough roasting. In any case, *suki* means to slice, and *yaki* to fry; so this story could well be true, for *sukiyaki* is certainly thinly sliced meat, usually beef but also mutton, pork and chicken, cooked in a thick iron pan.

To create 'atmosphere' for the dish, the guests sit on the floor on a *zubaton*, or floor cushion, in the accustomed Japanese style, legs tucked out of sight. (This posture gives most foreigners acute cramp.) The floor is covered with *tatami*—bamboo matting—soft and fragrant, and the table is low.

In the centre of the table is placed the traditional charcoal brazier. On this rests the Japanese *nabe* or thick frying pan. It is from this word that the *sukiyaki* is sometimes called *gyunabe*—*gyu* means beef and *nabe* pan. On the plates surrounding the *nabe* are the various ingredients required for the meal. Most important, naturally, is the beef, cut into the thinnest possible slices. Next in importance come the leeks, diagonally cut and perfectly white, for the Japanese attribute much to the artistic merit of the dish. White onions are also often mixed into the leeks. Then there is *tofu* or bean curd, bamboo shoots and, finally, a dish of *konnyaku*, a gelatine-like vegetable which looks like silvery spaghetti.

There is a bottle of *sake* which is drunk warm; usually some bowls of Japanese pickles, a little soup stock, a small bowl of sugar and *shoyu* sauce. There is also rice, which is either eaten along with the main course or separately, after the meat and other ingredients have been exhausted.

With *sukiyaki* no other food is served, except a small lacquer bowl of soup and another bowl of rice. *Sake* is taken throughout the meal and tea is offered at the end. It is one of the virtues of the dish that it develops a good thirst owing to the saltiness of the *shoyu* used so liberally.

Apart from variations in meat, vegetables can be changed according to season, mushrooms, celery, spinach and a vegetable popular in Japan called *shingiki*, which is a member of the chrysanthemum family.

One can serve a *sukiyaki*-type meal at home although it can never be quite correct as everything, including the room in which it is served, has a *sukiyaki* tradition. But the meal can at least be a talking point. I will list the essentials to get the meal as near authentic as possible.

1. A round table, preferably low but one across which two people can clasp hands without stretching.
2. A chafing dish or what the Japanese call a *hibachi* or a modern table cooker.
3. A shallow, thick metal pan large enough to contain all the ingredients.
4. A large platter for meat and another for the vegetables.
5. Bowls for the *shoyu* sauce, *dashi*, sugar and the *sake*.
6. Large spoons for stirring if not using chopsticks.
7. Four small bowls, one for each person.
8. Four sets of chopsticks and 4 chopstick rests.
9. Four saucers and 4 napkins.

The *sukiyaki* is made in batches and the quantity of liquids indicated in the recipe is for the first batch. More of all will be required if cooking continues.

4 servings:

1 lb. lean beef, thinly sliced

½ lb. Japanese vermicelli (shirataki); this is very fine

4-6 dried mushrooms, soaked for 30 minutes sliced

10 or 12 small leeks, sliced

6 onions, thinly, sliced

1 cup (1¼) Chinese or white cabbage, shredded

1 lb. fresh spinach, leaves only, cut into 1-in. lengths

1 tin bamboo shoots, drained and sliced

1 block bean curd (tofu) (see page 236), cut into 1-in. lengths

2 tablespoons (2½) sake (this is for cooking)

¾ cup (1) shoyu sauce

1 cup (1¼) dashi or chicken stock

7 tablespoons (8¾) sugar

suet or fat

4 raw eggs, i.e. 1 per person

Prepare *shirataki* ahead by soaking in cold water for 1 hour. Drain and cut into lengths. Arrange the meat, vegetables and bean curd neatly on a large platter. Fill bowls with *sake*, *shoyu*, *dashi* and sugar. Heat the pan greasing the surface with a large piece of suet or fat until it is literally coated with fat. Remove the suet. Add *shoyu*, stir, add sugar to check the tartness—this dish should be a mixture of sweet and sour. Add a dash or so of *sake* then some of the *dashi*.

Now at this juncture either add the meat first or the vegetables, it matters little. Cooks in Japan argue this point and are equally divided. So, let us use the vegetables first—not all of them at once, that is, leeks, onions, cabbage and then the vermicelli, bean curd and finally the remaining vegetables and *dashi*. While these are browning and giving out their appetizing aroma, add the meat, resting it carefully on top of the vegetables. Let this cook for 15 minutes or so.

In the meantime the guests, who are watching this procedure, can begin to consider eating. Each guest breaks an egg in his little bowl and lightly beats it with his chopsticks. First the guests, as soon as all the vegetables are cooked, help themselves to some of the simmering ingredients which they dip into the egg just before eating. Most Japanese feel that the thin coating of egg cools the *sukiyaki* and gives additional flavour. Finally, when all is eaten, start on the rice which is served in large quantities.

It may be necessary to add more liquid or sugar to adjust taste. In a Japanese home it is the man of the house who usually gives the final touches to *sukiyaki* flavours. The Japanese have some delightful *sukiyaki* cookers, colourful as well as small and neat in appearance that are roughly the size of a large cake tin.

CHAFING DISH COOKING (2) (*Jingisukan Yaki*)

Actually all that is needed for this simple dish is a small electric hot-plate and an elegant, fairly deep but large frying pan or an electric frying pan. It is another of those dishes which the guests cook for themselves. It is probably better as a luncheon dish but it can be served at an informal dinner. Some preparation is required beforehand, as indeed with most cooking, but it is very worth while. Only really tender meat or chicken is suitable, otherwise the whole meal becomes a flop.

4–6 servings:

1 chicken or 2 lb. lean and tender pork or chicken and pork together	lemon rind, grated
	parsley, finely chopped
½ lb. green and red sweet peppers	chilli powder
1 lb. onions	butter or oil for cooking
shoyu sauce and lemon juice	

Slice the meat into very thin, almost paper-thin slices. Slice the peppers and onions—discarding the seeds of the peppers. Arrange the sliced meat, onions and peppers in dishes around the table. In the centre should be the hot-plate and the pan. In front of each person a small bowl into which is poured a mixture of *shoyu* sauce, lemon juice, finely chopped parsley, chilli powder and grated lemon rind—all of this is to taste. Heat the hot-plate, put the cooking vessel on top and when this is hot add enough butter to start the cooking—more may be needed as the cooking continues. The host or hostess starts the cooking. Using chopsticks, drop pieces of meat, onion and pepper into the hot fat. They cook quickly and as soon as they are cooked they are picked up, either by the host who deposits them on to someone's plate or more usually by the people sitting around the table, all using, of course, chopsticks. (There are what are called chopforks in America.) Having secured a piece of hot food, dip it into the bowl of *shoyu* sauce before eating.

Continue cooking until all the ingredients are used up.

When *jingisukan yaki* is served it is the only dish. So it is usual to serve a bowl of rice with it; this can be kept hot on a table heater and it is eaten last.

This is an adaptation of Ghengis Khan cooking which is basically garden cooking, and very pleasant

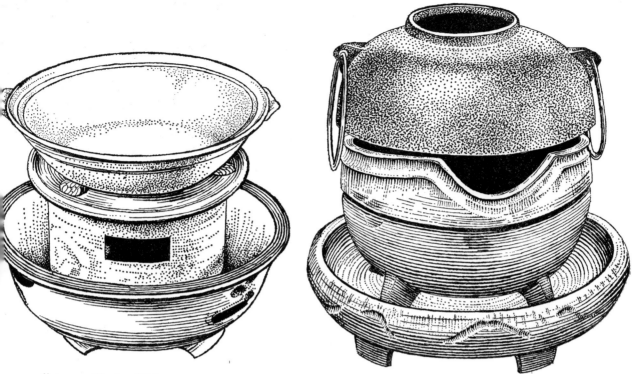

Japanese Chafing Dishes; Sukiyaki; Hibachi

it can be when the weather is right and the surroundings beautiful. This is not difficult to find in Tokyo. The traditional table for *jingisukan yaki* is small and square and in the middle is a large square hot plate or flat grill on which the food for grilling is cooked. Named after Ghengis Khan, the fifteenth-century Mongolian Emperor, this is the Japanese barbecue. It is of recent origin but extremly popular in Japan, especially in Tokyo.

CHICKEN CHAFING DISH (3) (*Mizutaki*)

Mizutaki is a Japanese country-style dish. Traditionally it is cooked in a steamboat (see *ta pin lo* page 112) style of container, but it can be cooked in a chafing dish or even in an electric frying pan instead. Although the following recipe stipulates chicken, it can also be made with fish or beef. For each person there should be a small individual bowl of sauce.

4 servings:

1–2 young chickens, cut into as many thin strips as possible

¼ lb. bean curd, cut into 1-in. cubes (see page 236)

1 tin bamboo shoots, sliced thinly lengthwise

6–8 dried mushrooms, soaked and sliced

1 medium-sized Chinese cabbage or crisp white cabbage, thinly sliced

12 scallions or 6 spring (green) onions, thinly sliced, lengthwise

4 cups (6) dashi (see page 195) or strained chicken stock

Sauce:

horse-radish or red and white radish, grated

shoyu sauce, lemon juice, red pepper

Arrange the chicken pieces, bean curd, bamboo shoots, mushrooms, cabbage and scallions on a large platter. Heat the *dashi* until boiling in cooking vessel on the table. Add the chicken and cook for 15 minutes. Let each person select from the remaining ingredients and drop them into the hot *dashi* along with the chicken. When everything is cooked, the guests should lift the pieces out with their chopsticks (beginning with the chicken) and dip each piece into the sauce before eating.

Mix the horse-radish or red or white radish with enough *shoyu* sauce, lemon juice and a pinch of red pepper to make the sauce.

A variety of the *mizutaki* cooking is the *shabu-shabu* which is paper-thin slices of beef dropped for a few seconds only in boiling water and then eaten with a specially prepared sauce.

GRILLED FOODS

GRILLED FOODS (1) (*Yakimono*)

The Japanese prefer to do their grilling over a charcoal fire on a grid, or spitted on a skewer. However, those of us without charcoal can still follow Japanese recipes to a degree, although obviously electric or gas grilled foods will not taste quite the same. Charcoal fumes invest a flavour of their own.

Most Japanese grilled foods are marinated in a sauce for at least 1 hour, sometimes longer.

Sauce:

1 cup (1¼) shoyu sauce

2 tablepoons (2½) sake (see **page 244**)

½ cup (⅔) sugar

1 teaspoon (1¼) fresh ginger, grated

1 clove garlic, finely chopped

½ teaspoon (⅔) monosodium glutamate

Mix all these ingredients together. Cut whatever ingredients chosen for grilling into bite-size pieces and marinate in the sauce for 1 hour. Grill by whatever means preferred.

Lamb chops, spareribs, shrimps or fish of most kinds may be dealt with in the above fashion.

One recipe I have adds water to the sauce, brings this to the boil and pours it boiling hot over the meat before grilling. This is excellent when meat is not as tender as it ought to be.

GRILLED FOODS (2) (*Yakitori*)

Basically the term *yakitori* applies to all grilling of chicken, white meat, heart, kidneys, gizzard, liver, neck and skin. But it is often applied loosely to other foods which are grilled.

A *yakitori* restaurant ranges from the gourmet spots to the hole-in-the-wall variety. The grills consist of little more than two or three well-encrusted iron bars with a charcoal fire below. The cook grills to order; his food is marinated, or salt encrusted and skewered on sticks. The customer points and in a couple of seconds the food is ready. Food marinated in *shoyu* sauce and sugar is called *momoyaki*; if salted it is *shioyaki*.

Yakitori eating is popular and there are *yakitori* restaurants throughout Japan. Although one loosely calls this food *yakitori*, in actual fact this should only apply to chicken. There is also *kotoriyaki*, which is grilled small birds—and some of these are very small indeed. All parts of the bird are used, head, wings, and feet. If very small, then the bird is grilled whole.

Then there are gingko nuts (*see* page 240), quails' eggs, neatly cut sweet peppers, odd bits of intestines, *tofu* etc., all of which are dipped in a small bowl of *shoyu* sauce before eating.

But anything which can be grilled can be treated in the *yakitori* manner. Provided one has small bamboo sticks or equally small metal skewers, this form of grilling can be achieved in one's own house. Put three or four pieces of liver or fish or bits of chicken meat or whatever you are proposing to grill, on the skewer, baste with *shoyu*, to which is added a little sugar and *mirin* (*see* page 241). Grill quickly over a good heat. The skewers should be lifted three or four times from the fire, the contents basted and then returned to the heat. Overcooking will make the grills dry and spoil the flavour.

Apart from dipping or marinating the *yakitori* in *shoyu* and sugar sauce, some cooks prefer to sprinkle the food with salt, pepper or ground ginger. It is usual to serve grated *daikon* (the Japanese white radish) with *yakitori*, but red radishes may be substituted and are expecially good if mixed with a little grated horse-radish.

If grilling vegetables, these should be parboiled first then marinated in a mixture of *shoyu* and sugar with *mirin* for an hour or so. Vegetables such as aubergine (eggplant), cucumber and turnip are particularly good grilled as *yakitori*.

MISCELLANEOUS DISHES

BOILED SHRIMPS AND BAMBOO SHOOTS (*Umani*)

4 servings:

12 large shrimps or small prawns
2 tablespoons (2½) water
2 tablespoons (2½) shoyu sauce

½ lb. bamboo shoots, thinly sliced
2 tablespoons (2½) mirin (see page 241) or
   substitute

Wash and drain the shrimps, remove the shells if necessary. Bring the water to the boil and add the *shoyu*. Add the shrimps and as soon as they are cooked, a matter of a few minutes only, take them from the pan using a slotted spoon. Put aside but keep hot. Add the bamboo shoots and *mirin* and cook for a few minutes. Return the shrimps to the pan, mix with the bamboo shoots, cook for 1 minute only and serve hot.

SCRAMBLED EGGS WITH PRAWNS AND CABBAGE (*Iri-Tamago*)

3 servings:

6 eggs
½ lb. peeled prawns or shrimps
¾ lb. crisp white cabbage
4 dried mushrooms
3 tablespoons (3¾) chicken stock

2 teaspoons (2½) sugar
1 teaspoon (1¼) salt
2 teaspoons (2½) shoyu sauce
2 teaspoons (2½) mirin (see page 241)
1 tablespoon (1¼) cooking oil

Soak the mushrooms in water for 30 minutes and cut into strips. Trim the cabbage and cut it into 1-inch pieces. Lightly beat the eggs and mix with the stock, sugar, salt, *shoyu* and *mirin*. Heat the oil and quickly sauté the prawns and mushrooms. (If using pre-cooked prawns, hardly cook these at all, cook the mushrooms and cabbage first and then add the prawns.) Add the cabbage, cook this for a few minutes, stirring it until it begins to brown and soften, it does not take long, then add the beaten eggs and lower the heat. As the eggs begin to set lightly scramble in the usual manner. Serve at once.

Ham and peas may be used instead of cabbage and shrimps.

CHICKEN WITH RICE (*Kamameshi*)

12 servings:

1 chicken breast, diced

4 cups (5) rice

1 large piece lotus root (see **page 241**) or mushrooms

vinegar

1 carrot, diced

1 tablespoon (1¼) shoyu sauce

3 cups (3¾) dashi or chicken stock

½ cup (⅔) green peas

sake or substitute

Shred and soak the lotus root, if using, in vinegar-flavoured water. Drain. Marinate the chicken meat, carrot and lotus root in *shoyu* sauce for 15 minutes.

Put the rice into a pot, add the ingredients in the *shoyu* sauce, the *dashi* and peas and bring all this to the boil, lower the heat and cook until the rice is dry and tender. Just before it is ready, add a good tablespoonful of *sake* and serve at once.

Instead of chicken meat, prawns or shrimps may be used. Although lotus root is not in the least like mushrooms, the latter do make a good substitute.

CHICKEN WITH VEGETABLES AND EGGS (*Nimono*)

4 servings:

1 lb. white chicken meat

6 large dried mushrooms

handful snow peas (see **page 246**)

¼ teaspoon (⅔) salt

vegetable oil

1½ tablespoons (2) dashi or chicken stock

2½ tablespoons (3) each sugar and shoyu

2 tablespoons (2½) mirin (see **page 241**)

1 onion, sliced

3 eggs

Slice the chicken into thin strips. Soak the mushrooms for 20 minutes in tepid water, slice thinly and discard the stalks. Wash the snow peas and cook them until tender in salted water. Heat a little oil in a shallow saucepan and add the stock, *shoyu*, sugar, *mirin* and salt. Add the onion and mushrooms. When half tender, add the slivers of chicken, keeping them well on the top of the vegetables. Cover the pan and gently cook until the chicken is tender; drain, add the snow peas and continue cooking.

Beat the eggs until frothy and, while still frothy, pour over the top of the chicken and vegetables while they are still cooking. As soon as the egg sets, take the whole carefully from the pan, for you now have the effect of a crusted pie top, and serve this in 4 portions on plates or deep bowls, depending on whether eating in the Western or Japanese manner. Serve with some of the drained-off gravy poured over each portion.

PORK WITH GINGER AND SHOYU SAUCE

This dish can be served in the casserole in which it is cooked. Use spareribs or pork fillet.

4 servings:

2 lb. pork cut into inch-squares
2 tablespoons ($2\frac{1}{2}$) vegetable oil
a large piece ginger, thinly sliced
2 tablespoons ($2\frac{1}{2}$) sake (see page 244) or substitute

2 tablespoons ($2\frac{1}{2}$) shoyu sauce
1 tablespoon ($1\frac{3}{4}$) brown sugar
a good dash of monosodium glutamate
a good handful French beans
lemon peel, grated

Heat the oil over a moderate heat, preferably in a shallow casserole, add the ginger and fry this for a few minutes, then add the pork pieces and cook these until they are browned all over. Lower the heat, just cover with water, add the *sake* and cook covered over a gentle heat until the pork is quite tender. Add the *shoyu* sauce, sugar and monosodium glutamate and continue cooking until all the liquid has been absorbed. In the meantime cook the beans until only just tender. Break or cut these into inch lengths and add as a garnish to the pork. Serve sprinkled with lemon peel.

BEEF COOKED IN FOIL WITH VEGETABLES (*Gingami Yaki*)

6 servings:

2 lb. tender beef, cut into thin $1\frac{1}{2}$-inch strips
6–8 dried Chinese mushrooms
salt, pepper

butter or other fat
2–3 sweet peppers, seeded and quartered
1–2 stalks celery, cut into small pieces
6 10-inch squares aluminuim foil

Soak the mushrooms in water for 30 minutes, then cut into strips. Rub salt and pepper and fat into the meat. Divide all the ingredients into 6 portions. First place a layer of meat in the centre of each piece of foil, then cover with mushrooms, sweet peppers and celery, in this order. Sprinkle lightly with salt. Wrap securely and cook in the oven at a high temperature for 15 to 20 minutes. Serve the foil packages one per person.

These packages usually are served with a sauce. Mix together some lemon and orange juice with *shoyu* sauce, some finely grated radish, a little horse-radish, finely chopped sweet pepper and enough strained stock to make this into a thin sauce. This is served separately.

Other meats can be cooked in the same manner, also fish, prawns or a mixture of vegetables. For those who like their food cooked longer, prolong the cooking time.

CUCUMBER SALAD WITH CRAB (*Sunomono*)

4–6 servings:

3–4 small fat cucumbers or **1 large**	**white vinegar**
1 medium-sized tin crabmeat	**salt**

Thinly peel the cucumbers in ribs, leaving some fine strips of peel for appearances' sake, rub with salt and leave for about 30 minutes. In the meantime mash the crabmeat and mix it with a little vinegar and salt. Wash off the salt, cut each cucumber in half, scoop out the seeds and centre and fill the hollow with crabmeat. Cut the cucumbers into $\frac{1}{2}$-inch slices and serve with any sauce, mayonnaise, a salad dressing, *shoyu* sauce or even a tomato ketchup.

In Japan, boiled lotus stalks are sliced and marinated in vinegar and served with the cucumbers.

CAKES (*O-Kashi*)

I am not going to attempt recipes for the preparation of Japanese cakes, the variety is enormous. It is possible the Japanese claim to have the largest variety of cakes in the world is more than likely true. Apart from their own cakes, the Japanese have introduced European-style cakes into their repertoire, with the same success that they introduced machinery, cameras etc. All this cake making is encouraged by the Japanese food custom which is to serve cakes at any odd time of the day.

Some of the Japanese cakes I found excellent, others dull. It is difficult to compare the Japanese cakes with the pâtisserie of France, the heavy English cakes, or the cookies of America. The foreign influence in cake making, such as it is, is not entirely of recent years, at least depending on what one calls recent in the ancient East. There is a speciality of Nagasaki called *kasutera* which, it is believed, was introduced by the Spanish or Portuguese who came into the port somewhere in the sixteenth century.

Japanese cakes are considered as being of two classes, *higashi* or dried cakes, and the *namagashi* or undried cakes or confectionery. This type of undried cake is made from an ingredient called 'bean jam'. In fact, the most ubiquitous sweetmeat in Japan is *yokan*, which is made from refined bean jam in its gelatine form. It resembles maybe the popular Turkish Delight but is less refined. Served usually on black lacquer plates, *yokan* appeals to the eye as well as the palate.

Cakes also are divided into spring, summer, autumn and winter cakes and have delightful names. In the spring there is 'night-time plums' or 'misty moon'. Summer cakes include 'firefly-grass' and 'water moon'. Autumn offers 'bush-clover rice cake', or rather nicely, 'chestnut drizzling shower'. Winter suggests 'snow of Koshi Province' and, coldly, 'sleet rice cake'.

Most Japanese cakes are made from such ingredients as red beans, rice, agar-agar (isinglass), rice flour, cornflour (cornstarch), and potato starch, including sweet potato. They add eggs, millet, jelly and other lesser materials. Colourings and aromatic flavours are very important. All these ingredients are easy enough to find in Japan at all times.

On the whole, the Japanese cakes look beautiful and they are superbly packed. Some are painted with *shoyu* or garnished with seaweed. Some taste like lumps of coloured sugar, others seem to be stuffed with chestnuts, which indeed they often are. Some of the bean paste coverings look like pastry. There are hard rice biscuits and cakes which look as though they were made from paper. As I have said, the variety is endless.

STUFFED POTATO DUMPLINGS (*Chakin Shibori*)

This recipe can be made either with ordinary floury potatoes or with sweet potatoes, and when the latter are available I would recommend them, their texture is better. The Japanese use both. I prefer a walnut stuffing to chestnut as potato and chestnut together is rather mealy. A stuffing of maraschino cherries and walnuts I found especially good.

12 dumplings:

2 lb. potatoes
1 cup (1¼) sugar

24 walnuts or peeled and cooked chestnuts
or pieces of glacé fruits

Peel and boil the potatoes. Drain thoroughly, mash and rub through a sieve. Return the potato to the pan, add the sugar and cook for 15 minutes over a low heat, stirring well. Take the purée from the pan and cool.

While this is cooking, shell and skin the walnuts. If these are placed in hot water for some time they will peel fairly easily.

Divide the potato purée into equal portions and in the middle of each push whatever stuffing you are using. Now place the pieces, one by one, in a piece of cloth or a small towel, place this in your left hand and with the right hand twist the cloth, thus giving the potato a twisted onion shape. Take the dumpling from the cloth. Repeat this until all 12 dumplings are made.

Some people serve the dumplings plain, others make a thin syrup with cornflour (cornstarch), water and syrup (a thick syrup from some tinned fruit is good). The size of the balls is bite-size and they are served cold.

Whole tinned chestnuts in syrup are available in speciality shops. If using these, the syrup can be used for the sauce.

EGG BROCADE (*Nishiki-Tamago*)

An egg dish which can be served at teatime or after dinner with coffee. It is extremely good and looks like coconut candy. The bottom of it is white and the top a bright yellow. I recommend it for its taste and because it is unusual and interesting.

12 servings:

12 hard-boiled eggs
16 tablespoons (20) fine sugar

pinch fine salt

Separate the white of the eggs from the yolks. Separately rub the yolks and the egg white through a fine sieve. (This is simpler than it might sound, both go through easily.) Mix the egg white with 3 tablespoonfuls (3¾) of sugar and a pinch of salt. Put this mixture into a mould (I use the ice cube container since I do not have a Japanese mould). Press it down smoothly but lightly. This quantity fills about three-quarters of the average-size ice cube container. Now mix thoroughly the remaining sugar into the yolks and spread this smoothly on top of the white. Put the mould in a deep frying pan or baking dish, cover and steam for about 10–15 minutes. By this time it will have set. Take from the pan, let it cool, put into the refrigerator and when quite cold, cut it into sections, roughly three-quarters of an inch thick.

A more complicated version of this dish is Plum Flower Egg, the difference being in the presentation and the arrangement of the egg to look like a flower.

Korea (The Land of the Morning Calm)

While the cooking of the Korean townsfolk has been greatly influenced by China and Japan, the people of the countryside are still faithful to the old-style Korean dishes, fairly simple, plenty of *kimchi* (*see* page 222) and rice, fish of the less expensive kinds and large quantities of homemade soy bean pastes. This does not mean, however, that the Korean townspeople have lost their taste for their own dishes, on the contrary they have retained them but given them foreign overtones.

A Korean meal is one main dish, that is, steamed rice with side dishes. The rice may be served with other grains, with soup, fish or vegetables, and sauces or even beans, of which the Koreans are inordinately fond. In other words, by a main dish the Korean means a whole number of prescribed dishes all as a complement to the rice.

A Korean meal without vegetables is unthinkable and the most popular of them are radishes and Chinese cabbage, not the small red radishes of Europe but the long white Eastern radish. Koreans love hot peppers and some of their dishes are exceedingly hot. Beans are made into pastes similar to the Japanese *miso* (*see* page 194) which is used to flavour soups and other side dishes. Of the meats, beef and pork are first favourites, but chicken and game are also appreciated.

Surrounded, as Korea is, with waters teeming with fish their diet abounds in sea-food dishes, some of which include unusual combinations of fish and chicken.

One of the results of the Korean idea of one 'main dish' with its many side dishes is that entertaining in Korean homes is not as simple as it was. No longer are there numerous servants busy all day in the kitchen. The one little servant who is cook and everything else, cannot produce a dinner party at a moment's notice. A dinner must produce at least eleven dishes, more if possible, and all must be traditional.

One balmy evening I dined in a typical Korean house. We sat on cool matting on the floor by a low oblong table. A servant brought hot towels on which to wipe our hands. Then she came with dish after dish putting them all on the table at the same time, the usual Korean custom. There were several kinds of *kimchi*, abalone, chicken, beef, a dish of rice, sweet and sour sauces, a hot sauce, jelly fish salad, a large dish of finely chopped meat and livers, a stew and several kinds of vegetables. One samples them all, using silver chopsticks; silver because it detects poison so quickly.

Silver cutlery is usually used and particularly long-handled spoons for the soup. When one is finished the chopsticks and spoons are laid on the table on the right side. To leave chopsticks in the rice bowl is a grave offence since it is a symbol that the food has been offered to the dead. Traditional food containers are, with a few exceptions, shaped in the form of a bowl, rather than a dish, and are made of wood, brass or china.

The usual dining table is low and made of wood, some of considerable ancestral value. In former days oak leaves were used as place mats on which were placed wooden plates.

The meals served for special feasts, such as birthdays and weddings have different names. As we might refer to a 'cold table' so the Koreans have a 'noodle table' which simply means that the basic dish will be of noodles instead of rice. Then there is a 'wine table' at which people entertain with wine rather than food. Since Koreans do not believe in drinking without eating, there are a number of substantial side dishes, cooked and raw meats, grilled fish and even *kimchi* to help the wine along.

Then there is the 'long table'. At this rice will be the main dish, then a noodle soup and other dishes such as rice-cakes, raw fish, meat cooked in several ways, fried fish, honey-water with nuts and persimmons, sweetened water with rice, all kinds of fruit, for the Korean fondness for fruit is pronounced, apples, pears, plums, melons and grapes, and all kinds of nuts including chestnuts, especially pine and hazel nuts.

Then there is the 'large table' for such ceremonies as weddings and sixty-first birthday celebrations. At this table all kinds of delicacies are presented which are not eaten but taken away after their exhibition. Finally there is the 'memorial table' to offer homage to one's ancestors.

For many people, if they consider the matter at all, Korean food is *kimchi*. Equally this word for many foreigners is synonymous with a bad smell and over-spiced food. 'Korean houses,' I was told, are made with plenty of window and draught allowance to let the smell of *kimchi* pass right through the house and out the other side.'

There are a hundred different varieties of this controversial Korean pickle—it could be called the sauerkraut of the Orient—which finds its place on every Korean table at all meals. Some *kimchis* are hot, others mild. Some are fermented others hardly at all.

The saying goes: 'When the *kimchi* is prepared for the winter, half the autumn harvest is done.' In the past *kimchi* was the criterion by which to discover how rich a family was. Court *kimchis* were very rich, prepared as they were from all the rarest fruits and vegetables of the autumn.

A lot goes into a good *kimchi*. Cabbages, radishes, cucumbers, onions and garlic, red peppers galore and often pickled shellfish. All this is fermented in earthenware jars filled with salted water. When the weather is warm fermentation takes place rapidly and the *kimchi* is ready in a few days. The winter *kimchi* jar is buried deep in the earth and taken out as required at each mealtime. It is this buried winter *kimchi* which foreigners find hard to take.

Autumn is *kimchi* time, a period of household excitement. *Kimchi* is, of course, the answer to the lack of fresh vegetables during the long lean winter months. It supplies a large amount of vitamin C, plenty of protein, calcium, carbohydrates and vitamin B. Housewives buy vegetables literally by the cartload and the whole family on the female side, plus some protesting younger males, drop everything and get down to the serious business of cleaning, cutting and sorting. All women working in towns join their families in the country for the *kimchi* making, country cousins are recruited as extra hands and there is tremendous haggling over vegetable prices.

The Koreans have several festivals and for these special foods are prepared, huge round cakes are made which must be both perfect in shape and flavour on which are painted characters, meaning 'long-life' or 'lots of male children' or simply 'happiness', summing up the Korean attitude to life.

EGG GARNISH (Omelette) (*Gyuran-Daji*)

Separate the yolks from the whites of 2 eggs. Separately beat both lightly with a fork. Rub a frying pan with oil, pour the yolk into the pan and make a paper-thin omelette. When set, turn and fry on the other side. Repeat this process with the whites. Cut into fine strips and use as a garnish. They are also part of the Korean hors-d'œuvre, piled separately in small dishes.

ROASTED SESAME SEEDS (*Kaey-Garu*)

Put the sesame seeds in a thick frying pan without fat and cook over a low heat, stirring all the while. When just browned or roasted take from the heat and crush, either in a mortar with a pestle or in a grinder or liquidizer.

Use as a garnish and for flavouring.

SOY AND VINEGAR SAUCE (*Cho-Jang*)

Mix an equal quantity of good quality vinegar with soy sauce. Add a third of this quantity in brown sugar, dissolve this and add pine nuts to taste.

This sauce is used as a dip for fish and is served in small individual bowls.

Some Koreans also add a finely chopped onion or crushed sesame seeds.

BEEF SOUP WITH ONIONS (*Yukkae-Jang-Kuk*)

8–10 servings:

1 lb. beef shank
5 pints (12½ cups) water
1 lb. spring (green) onions
¾ tablespoon (1) red pepper or to taste
1½ tablespoons (2) sesame oil

¾ tablespoon (1) garlic, minced
¾ tablespoon (1) sesame seeds, ground
4½ tablespoons (6) soy sauce
monosodium glutamate to taste

Although served hot, as are most Korean soups, this one is prepared during the hottest day of summer, The Day of the Ox. It is reputed to maintain strength and relieve heat.

Cut the meat into two pieces and cook in the water until almost tender. Remove any scum which might rise to the top.

Trim the onions and cut into 2-inch lengths using the green part as well. Mix the pepper with half the oil.

When the meat is almost ready, add the onions and continue cooking over a medium heat until the meat is very tender. Take the meat and the onions from the pan, cool, then tear both into thin strips. Rub the meat with the red pepper and oil, add the remaining oil, garlic, sesame seeds and 2 tablespoonfuls (2½) of the soy sauce. Add the remaining soy sauce and the monosodium glutamate to the pan.

Bring the stock again to the boil, return the meat and onions to the pan and continue cooking for a further 5 to 10 minutes to reheat.

Sometimes a well-beaten egg is mixed into the soup just before serving.

COLD CUCUMBER SOUP (*Naing-Kuk*)

6-8 servings:

1–2 cucumbers
1½ tablespoons (2) soy sauce
1 tablespoon (1¼) mild vinegar
2–3 spring (green) onions, minced, using
   the green as well

1 teaspoon (1¼) sesame seeds, toasted and
   ground
ground chilli pepper

This soup could not be more simple to prepare with no cooking at all. Cucumbers vary so much in size; use 2 Eastern fat but short cucumbers or 1 medium-sized European.

Peel and slice the cucumbers paper-thin. Mix them with the remaining ingredients and leave for 30 minutes, then add 3 or 4 cupfuls (3¾–5) of water—it depends rather on how much cucumber—put into a refrigerator and serve when icy cold.

If the cucumber slices are too large, cut them into halves, it is much easier for eating. A useful soup for a truly hot day.

A little garlic, white wine and equally well some chopped cooked prawns or shrimps may be added to this soup.

SOY BEAN SPROUT SOUP (*Kong-Namul-Kuk*)

5–6 servings:

1 lb. (2 cups) bean sprouts
½ lb. lean meat cut into thin strips
1½ teaspoons (2) sesame seeds, roasted
   and ground
1 tablespoon (1¼) sesame oil
2–3 cloves garlic, minced

pepper
3 pints (7½ cups) water
1–2 spring (green) onions, chopped, using
   the green part
monosodium glutamate
3 tablespoons (3¾) soy sauce

Wash and drain the bean sprouts. Remove the tails. Mix the meat with the sesame seeds, oil, garlic and pepper in a pan and cook over a moderate heat until the meat changes colour. Add the water, bring this to the boil, add the bean sprouts, cover and simmer for 30 minutes. Add the spring onions, cover and continue cooking for a few minutes but do not take off the lid. Just before serving, add monosodium glutamate to taste, the soy sauce and cook for another 5 minutes.

OXTAIL SOUP (*Kori Kuk*)

8–10 servings:

2½ lb. oxtail
5 pints (11¼ cups)
4 tablespoons (5) light soy sauce
2 tablespoons (2½) sesame seed oil
1 tablespoon (1¼) sesame seeds, ground
and roasted

pepper to taste
3–4 spring (green) onions, minced
1 tablespoon (1¼) garlic, minced, or to
taste

Wash the tail, cut into 8–10 pieces, and gently boil in the water over a low heat for at least 2 hours, or until the tail meat is tender. Take off any scum which rises to the surface.

When the liquid has been reduced to about 8 cupfuls, strain off the pieces of tail (which by now should be very tender) and roll them in half the soy sauce and the remaining ingredients, then return the pieces of meat, together with all the accompanying ingredients to the soup, bring to the boil and serve hot.

BEEF BARBECUE or GRILL (*Bul-Gogi*)

The main meat dishes of Korea are of beef, and *bul-gogi* is one of the most popular Korean dishes both with Koreans and foreigners. It is served often at parties, especially at picnics. The Koreans are great picnic enthusiasts, both in public restaurants with gardens or in their own gardens. They do, of course, have the weather for such activities and the most important part of the picnic ceremony is the *bul-gogi*. The following recipe is basic; the meat is always sliced wafer-thin and spiced. Grilling can be done either on a modern grill or barbecue, or on what is called the Genghis Khan grill, that is, a grill which is rounded and shaped something like a helmet.

8–10 servings:

4 lb. wafer-thin sliced fillet beef
1 cup (1¼) soy sauce
3 tablespoons (3¾) soft brown sugar
½ cup (⅔) sesame oil

½ cup (⅔) sesame seeds, roasted and ground
1 teaspoon (1¼) monosodium glutamate
4–6 spring (green) onions, finely chopped
black pepper and salt

Mix all these ingredients well with the hands, cover and refrigerate until required, at least 3 hours; but better still leave overnight. Grill the slices of meat very quickly over charcoal or, failing a satisfactory grill, fry either in a dry thick iron pan or with the minimum of oil. Do not quite brown.

Watching the maid of a friend of mine cooking *bul-gogi*, I checked with her. When preparing *bul-gogi* for Korean guests she adds more sugar, and, for foreigners, less garlic and onion. Instead of sesame oil another kind of oil can be used, but the meat loses something of its special flavour. The marinade is discarded.

The secret of this dish is the marinade which tenderizes as well as flavours the beef, and the quick cooking which seals the juices.

BEEF KIDNEYS AND SWEET PEPPERS (*Kongpat-Jongol*)

3–4 servings:

¾ lb. kidneys

3 sweet peppers

Marinade:

4 tablespoons (5) soy sauce

2 tablespoons (2½) soft brown sugar

3 tablespoons (3¾) spring (green) onion, minced

3 cloves garlic, minced

1 small piece fresh ginger, minced, or ½ teaspoon (⅔) ground

1½ tablespoons (2) sesame seeds, roasted and ground

salt, pepper and monosodium glutamate

2 tablespoons (2½) sesame or vegetable oil

Other kidneys may be used in this recipe. The Koreans do not consider lamb's kidney—pork or calves' kidneys are the next choice.

Mix the marinade ingredients. Clean the kidneys and remove the skin, gristle and fat. Slice thinly. Mix well with the marinade. Leave for 15 or so minutes. Cut off the tops of the sweet peppers, discard the core and seeds and slice them into thin rings.

Heat a thick frying pan, one that does not burn easily. Add the kidneys, plus their marinade, stir well, add the sweet pepper rings and fry, stirring frequently to prevent burning, although the oil in the marinade helps to prevent this.

To this may be added thin rings of onion.

LIVER SAUTÉED IN EGG BATTER (*Kan-Jon*)

Liver is considered in Korea, as elsewhere, an extremely nourishing food, but possessed of an unpleasant odour. The Koreans feel by using garlic salt this odour is overcome.

3–4 servings:

¾ lb. liver

salt, pepper

garlic powder to taste

flour

2 eggs, well beaten

sesame or vegetable oil

soy and vinegar sauce (see **page 213**)

Clean and trim the liver, discarding all skin, and cut into thin slices. Sprinkle with salt, pepper and generously with garlic salt; leave it for a few minutes. Roll in flour and dip in the beaten eggs. Heat a small quantity of oil and fry the slices of liver on both sides.

Serve hot with the sauce. Calves', pork or lambs' liver may be used instead of beef.

GRILLED BEEF (*Kulbi-Kui*)

This is rather similar to the *bul-gogi* but is preferred by many Koreans. Large chunks of meat are cooked instead of wafer-thin slices. There is certainly no etiquette in eating this, nor, for that matter, with any of the Korean barbecue dishes. It is even acceptable to bite off bits from your chunk of meat and return the chunk to the fire for further roasting.

6–8 servings:

about 3–4 lb. steak with the bone
2 tablespoons (2½) sugar
4 tablespoons (5) soy sauce
4 tablespoons (5) spring (green) onion, minced
2 teaspoons (2½) garlic, minced

1½ tablespoons (2) sesame seeds, roasted and ground
1 tablespoon (1¼) ginger, minced
a good dash pepper
sesame oil

Chop the meat into 3-inch squares with the bone, discarding the fat. Make deep cuts into the meat without cutting through to the bone. Mix the pieces with the sugar and then with the remaining ingredients. Leave for 30 minutes. Grill over a medium heat (in Korea it is charcoal) and take the pieces as they come from the heat all beautifully browned. This recipe can be also prepared with tender chops.

BEEF STEW (*Yukkae-Jang-Kuk*)

4–6 servings:

2 lb. stewing beef, cut into strips
6 sweet peppers
1 cup (1¼) shoyu sauce

a few spring (green) onions
1 teaspoon (1¼) sugar
1 teaspoon (1¼) monosodium glutamate

This Korean stew is cooked very dry, in fact, without any water at all.

Cut the peppers into halves and remove their hot seeds. Put all the ingredients into a thick-bottomed pan, cover, bring to a steady boil, lower the heat and cook gently until the meat is tender. If possible use Japanese *shoyu* sauce in this recipe, not the Chinese soy.

BRAISED SHORT RIBS (*Kulbi-Guy*)

4–5 servings:

2 lb. short ribs
brown sugar
sesame oil
½ cup (⅔) soy sauce
3 spring (green) onions, chopped
2–4 cloves garlic, crushed
1 tablespoon (1¼) sesame seeds, crushed and roasted

salt, pepper and monosodium glutamate
2 cups (2½) water
½–1 cup (⅔–1¼) water chestnuts
pine nuts
1–2 eggs

Have the ribs cut into serving pieces, and score deeply on both sides every half inch. Rub the pieces of meat with sugar and oil. Mix the soy sauce, chopped onions, garlic, sesame seeds, salt, pepper and monosodium glutamate. Rub this all into the ribs and leave for at least 30 minutes or longer.

Put the meat into a pan, add the water; there should be just enough to cover. Leave a space in the middle of the pan and put in the chestnuts. Cook over a moderate heat until the meat is tender and all the liquid has evaporated. Arrange on a hot platter, garnish with pine nuts and strips of omelette.

While the meat is cooking beat the eggs and make one thin omelette. Roll and cut into fine strips.

To the above recipe can be added, dried, soaked Chinese mushrooms, and carrots thinly sliced.

POT ROAST (*Sinsullo*)

This is the chafing dish of Korea, a *pièce de resistance* and a dish for special occasions. When it finally appears on the table, it is the sign for everyone to relinquish the many empty dishes, finish the rice and attack the *sinsullo*.

It is similar to the Chinese chafing dish except that the food is only partially cooked on the table, that is, it is pre-cooked before it comes to the table and continues cooking in the charcoal-fed *sinsullo* pot. This pot can be of brass or silver and comes in varying sizes, from family to individual. It has a chimney in the centre over which a lid with a hole to fit the chimney is placed.

Into the *sinsullo* pot goes almost everything which is edible, which means, therefore, that many of the following ingredients can either be omitted or others substituted. The result is a rather succulent kind of stew.

The ingredients given below are for a pot of some 10 inches in diameter, which means that the ingredients should not measure more than 2 inches in length. Unless served in an individual *sinsullo* pot, which happens in Seoul restaurants, it is usual for everyone to take what they want from the communal pot with chopsticks.

4–6 servings:

¼ lb. lean beef
1 tablespoon (1¼) onion, minced
1 tablespoon (1¼) soy sauce
2 tablespoons (2½) garlic
¾ tablespoon (1) sesame oil
1 teaspoon (1¼) sesame seeds, roasted and ground
1 teaspoon (1¼) sugar
1 abalone, tinned or fresh, thinly sliced
¼ lb. liver
salt, pepper
flour
2 eggs, well beaten

¾ tablespoon (1) sesame oil
 or vegetable oil
¼ lb. each pork and beef, minced
¼ lb. white meat (chicken or veal)
¾ lb. tinned or pre-cooked bamboo shoots
6 dried mushrooms, soaked in water for 30 minutes
watercress or spinach
2 shelled walnuts, soaked in water
½ onion, sliced
2 tablespoons (2½) pine nuts
2 pints (5 cups) meat stock
12 gingko nuts (see page 240), sliced

1. Cut the lean beef into narrow strips and marinate in the next 6 ingredients.
2. Cut the abalone and liver into thin strips and sprinkle with salt and pepper, coat with flour, dip into beaten egg and sauté in sesame oil. Put aside.
3. Mix the two minced meats together. Take the strips of sliced beef out of its marinade, put this

aside, and mix the marinade into the minced meats. Shape this into about 12 or so small balls, roll these in flour, dip in beaten egg, then sauté in oil. Put aside.

4. Lightly fry the slices of beef in a little oil.

5. Thinly slice the white meat and the bamboo shoots and cook these in slightly salted, boiling water.

6. Slice the soaked mushrooms diagonally into thin strips and very lightly fry in oil.

7. Pull the watercress leaves from their stems, dip in flour and beaten egg and lightly fry in a little oil. Put aside.

8. Remove the brown skin from the walnuts, keeping the pieces of walnut as large as possible.

To serve:

Put the sliced meats and onion in alternate layers at the bottom of the *sinsullo*, add the remaining ingredients. The tiny meat balls are best placed at the top of the dish, otherwise they might disintegrate. The nuts are all placed on top, for garnish as much as for eating. Fill the centre of the *sinsullo* with burning charcoal, cover the pot with the lid and bring to the table. One can hear the meat sizzling around the sides of the chimney as it cooks.

To this can be added turnips and carrots, cooked whole and then cut into pieces $1\frac{1}{2}$ inches long and $\frac{1}{2}$ inch wide.

Korean watercress is not like the European variety; it is almost more like spinach, a sort of swamp cabbage.

Making a *sinsullo* is time consuming and not something even patient Korean housewives with expertise would attempt daily.

OYSTERS (*Kul-Hwe*)

Open the oysters but leave in their shells. Sprinkle with finely chopped spring (green) onion, pine nuts and fine strips of hot peppers, preferably red. Immediately before eating, lightly sprinkle with vinegar or lemon juice and soy sauce.

Quite a useful dressing also for mussels.

GRILLED FISH (*Jun-Gol*)

2–3 servings:

4–6 small fish
Sauce:
3 tablespoons ($3\frac{3}{4}$) soy sauce
1 tablespoon ($1\frac{1}{4}$) sugar
1 tablespoon ($1\frac{1}{4}$) ground sesame seeds

$\frac{1}{2}$ tablespoon ($\frac{2}{3}$) sesame oil
small quantity ground ginger and garlic
dash of red pepper and monosodium glutamate

Mix the sauce ingredients thoroughly.

The Koreans use young cod fish for this dish, cutting off the head and tail, trimming and cleaning but leaving the fish whole. Rub the fish in the sauce before it is grilled; during cooking time it should be brushed with sauce at least twice.

Grill under or over a moderate heat. The coating of sauce will give the fish a brown crust which is good to eat but also prevents the fish from becoming dry.

GREY MULLET STEW (*Saingsun-Chickai*)

3–4 servings:

1–2 grey mullet
4–6 large dried mushrooms soaked for 30
  minutes
3 cups (3¾) beef stock
1 teaspoon (1¼) red pepper bean paste (see
  below)

1 tablespoon (1¼) light soy sauce
pinch pepper and monosodium glutamate
2 spring (green) onions, cut into thin
  strips

Clean and scale the fish, cut off head and tail and remove the backbone. Cut the fish into pieces. Slice the mushroom caps and discard the stalks. Bring the stock to the boil, add the red pepper bean paste, soy sauce, pepper and monosodium glutamate. Add the fish, mushrooms and spring onions. Cook until the fish is tender.

It is usual in Korea to serve the fish in the dish in which it was cooked which these days is simple as there are many attractive stove-to-table dishes.

The red pepper bean paste, a local speciality, can be omitted and chilli pepper used instead. Grey or striped mullet is a coarse fish found both in European as well as Atlantic and Pacific waters. Using a meat stock with fish is a usual Oriental practice. The beef stock should be flavoured with ginger, sesame seeds toasted and ground, garlic and onion.

STEAMED or CASSEROLE CHICKEN (*Dak-Chim*)

This is a festive dish of chicken cooked on top of the stove. The original instructions were for a small chicken, cut into 10 or even 20 pieces. I never manage this myself and suggest that the chicken is jointed into 4 or 6 pieces.

2–3 servings:

1 medium-sized chicken
2–3 carrots
4 dried mushrooms, soaked
a little pre-cooked or tinned bamboo
  shoots
1–2 eggs, well-beaten
Marinade:
3 tablespoons (3¾) brown sugar
6 tablespoons (7½) soy sauce

6 spring (green) onions, minced or 2 white
  onions medium size
6 cloves garlic, minced
1-in. piece fresh ginger or ½ teaspoon (⅔)
  ground
2 tablespoons (2½) sesame seeds, toasted
  and ground
monosodium glutamate and pepper
1 tablespoon (1¼) sesame or vegetable oil

Mix the marinade ingredients thoroughly. Put the pieces of chicken into a casserole with 6 cupfuls (7½) of water. Cook this over a moderate heat until the chicken is tender and the liquid is reduced to 4 cupfuls (5). Strain and return the liquid to the pan. Strip off the flesh from the chicken, cut this into thin strips and mix it thoroughly into the marinade. Leave until required.

While the chicken is marinading prepare the vegetables. Peel or scrape the carrots and cut them into short thin strips. Slice the mushrooms and the bamboo shoots into thin strips. Bring the stock again to the boil, add the vegetables, cook these until tender, then add the chicken and the marinade and continue cooking until the mixture is again brought to the boil and the chicken and marinade is really hot. Now at this stage some cooks pour in the eggs so that they make a thin film over the top of the chicken and vegetables, which is excellent if serving the casserole in the same dish in which it is cooked, which is the Korean habit. However, other cooks recommend making a very thin omelette, rolling it up and then cutting it into strips and sprinkling these over the top as a garnish.

CHICKEN STEW 'SOUP' (*Dak Kae-Jang*)

4 servings:

1 large chicken, cut into serving pieces	a few spring (green) onions, finely chopped
2 tablespoons (2½) oil, preferably sesame	chilli powder
4 tablespoons (5) light soy sauce	½ head garlic, finely chopped
dash of salt	1 teaspoon (1¼) monosodium glutamate

The Korean recipe in the original calls for 2 tablespoonfuls (2½) of Korean chilli powder, but of a mild quality.

Put the chicken with all the other ingredients into a pot, stir it well so that it is coated with all flavours and leave for 2 hours. Bring to the boil, lower the heat and cook steadily until the chicken is tender.

As with beef stew (*see* page 217), no water is added. The chicken gains all the additional flavours.

BEAN SPROUTS IN SOY SAUCE (*Khang Namul*)

4 servings:

2 lb. (4 cups) bean sprouts (see page 236)	2 spring (green) onions, chopped
oil	a dash of pepper
1 tablespoon (1¼) soy sauce	
1 tablespoon (1¼) sesame seeds, roasted and ground (see page 213)	

Bean sprouts take a very short time to cook.

Cook the bean sprouts in boiling water until tender, drain off the water, add a little oil, stir this into the sprouts, then add the soy sauce, sesame seeds, onion and pepper. Carefully continue cooking, stirring all the time, until all the seasonings are absorbed into the sprouts.

BEETROOT SALAD IN SOY SAUCE (*Keundae Namul*)

4–6 servings:

6 large uncooked beetroots with tops	a little oil
1 tablespoon (1¼) soy sauce	1 tablespoon (1¼) vinegar
1 teaspoon (1¼) sesame seeds, roasted and ground (see page 213)	1 teaspoon (1¼) each sugar and salt

Wash the beetroots and their green tops. Cut off the green and put aside. Cook the beetroots until almost tender. (This is best done in a pressure cooker.) While the beetroots are cooking, finely chop the beetroot tops and add them to the beetroots. Cook until both are tender. Take from the pan and, as soon as the beetroots are cool, cut them into pieces roughly 1 inch long, $\frac{1}{4}$ inch wide and $\frac{1}{4}$ inch thick. Mix these with the beetroot tops, add the remaining ingredients, mix lightly and serve.

If it is not possible to get fresh beetroots with their tops, then use the seasoning as a dressing to make a beetroot salad with an unusual flavour.

RICE AND MUSHROOMS (*Song-I Pahb*)

4–6 servings:

2 cups (2½) rice
1 cup (1¼) fresh mushrooms, thinly sliced
2–3 onions, thinly sliced
a little lean beef, chopped
2 tablespoons (2½) soy sauce
1 tablespoon (1¼) sesame or vegetable oil

1 tablespoon (1¼) sesame seeds, ground and toasted
1 teaspoon (1¼) salt
pepper
3 cups (3¾) water

Wash the rice if necessary. Mix the mushrooms, onions, beef, soy sauce, oil and sesame seeds, salt and pepper. Cook this in a frying pan, stirring well for 2 minutes. Mix all this with the rice and put into a large pot. Add the water and stir. Cover tightly, bring to a quick boil, reduce the heat to as low as possible and cook for 30 minutes, by which time the rice will be dry and fluffy. Do not uncover the rice, *even once*, during this cooking period. When the rice is cooked, turn it out on to a hot platter and serve at once. This dish is a pilau and can be served as a main course.

CABBAGE OR SPRING PICKLE (*Kimchi*)

1 lb. white cabbage
2¼ tablespoons (3) salt
4 spring (green) onions
2–3 cloves garlic, chopped

1 teaspoon (1¼) chilli pepper, chopped
1 small piece fresh ginger, chopped
water

Wash the cabbage and cut into pieces approximately 1 inch square. Sprinkle with two-thirds of the salt. Mix well and leave for 15 minutes. Shred the onions (including the green parts) into 1½-inch lengths.

Wash the cabbage thoroughly to remove the salt. Mix with the remaining ingredients including the rest of the salt and put the mixture into a stone or glass jar. Add enough water to cover and let it stand for several days. To mature in hot weather, 1 day is sufficient; but in cold weather 5 days are needed. *Kimchi* can be kept in a refrigerator for several weeks. This particular *kimchi* is not one of the variety which frightens foreigners. In fact, it is less odorous than sauerkraut.

Where there is no warm sun the jar of *kimchi* could be put into a warm cupboard, such as the linen cupboard. Soy sauce may be added to the above recipes. Celery is prepared in the same manner.

CUCUMBER PICKLE (*Oye-Sobagi*)

6 large or 10 small cucumbers
1¼ tablespoons (1¾) salt
4 spring (green) onions, minced, using green part
1 small piece fresh ginger, minced

2–3 cloves garlic, minced
chilli peppers, finely chopped or chilli powder
2¼ tablespoons (3) sugar
1 teaspoon (1¼) monosodium glutamate

Cut the cucumbers into 4-inch pieces. Make knife slits through the centre from 3 sides without cutting the ends. Rub the cucumber surface with a little salt and leave for 1 hour. Press out the liquid under a weight. Mix the onion, ginger, garlic, peppers, the remaining salt, sugar and monosodium glutamate and push this mixture into the slits of the cucumber. Fit the cucumbers into jars, press down with a weight, and pour slightly salted water over the top until the cucumbers are just covered. Let this ferment. In hot weather it will take 1 to 2 days; in cold, a week.

Serve as a side dish. As sugar is used in this recipe, candied ginger could be substituted for fresh ginger but lessen the quantity of sugar given in the ingredients.

The milder *kimchis*, such as this and cabbage *kimchi*, are very similar to the Slav and Eastern European methods of preparing pickles.

THE WINE TABLE

The wine table, as its name would suggest, is a table or form of entertainment where wine is served—and technically no food. But the Koreans prefer to eat when they drink, so this table will also be well provided with 'small-eats' such as raw or cooked cold sliced meats, grilled meats, *kimchis* of several kinds, and even small bowls of soup.

Most of the Korean drinks are traditional. There are a vast number of herbal teas, the favourite being *ginseng*, a tea prepared basically from the *ginseng* root (*see* page 240), ginger and cinnamon. This particular favourite has been cherished for generations as a tonic. Cinnamon tea is much drunk for its flavour, while the many ginger teas are appreciated for their refreshing effect. There is another popular tea, with a name that for foreigners is impossible—*ssanghwatang*—originally a speciality of the royal family, containing such items as fruits, nuts, chestnuts and dates. Its reputation is that of a splendid and potent tonic.

Honey diluted with iced water is another popular drink, so is *sikhye*, a sweet rice drink, called a wine, although it is not alcoholic. Then there is a sweetened fermented rice drink; yet another called *sujonggwa*, a liquid 'fruit cake' of mashed persimmons in cinnamon-flavoured liquid, to which dates and nuts are added. Probably, however, the most traditional drink is *hwachae*, or the flower drink, which is flavoured with molasses and magnolia and served with small edible flowers floating on the top. This drink is considered as a festival drink of major importance.

The above drinks are offered on special occasions, birthdays etc. The day-to-day drink is *sungnyung*, which is simply warm water poured into a mass of toasted and ground rice to a drink consistency. It is served after a meal, much as the Chinese and Japanese serve their green teas, even though the host might also serve either tea or coffee in the Western manner. The drink has a distinct flavour of scorched rice and is taken in order to defeat the heat.

However, despite the popularity of the non-alcoholic drinks, Koreans drink plenty of their own typically home-made 'wines'. Three such drinks are *takju*, *yakju* and *soju*—all made from grains or potatoes.

Takju, probably the least expensive of these three drinks, is much favoured by the farming community. Yellowish in colour it sours quickly in hot weather and is made from barley, corn or potatoes. *Yakju* is brewed from rice and is somewhat more alcoholic. While *soju*, also made from grains or potatoes, is quite potent and deceptive as it looks not unlike a drink of plain water. It is a sort of vodka. It is also popular as it does not turn sour even in the very hot weather. It is, therefore, much regarded as a summer drink.

Then there are the regional wines with enchanting names. Sweet Pink Dew is one such name; another Bamboo Shoot wine; Chrysanthemum Wine; Hundred Flower Wine—all reminiscent of grandmother's brews, all just as deceptively potent and all give indications of the fragrant flowers and blossoms which go into their preparation.

The Philippines

The cooking of the Philippines has four different culinary cultures at work. Filipino, Spanish, Chinese and American. It makes eating in Manila, the capital, international but requires some 'digging' under layers of food until what might be called the real thing comes through. One asks oneself, indeed, what is the real thing? So many people have come and gone, all making their mark in many ways, not least in the field of cooking and eating. Indonesian adventurers, Chinese traders, Spanish conquerors, American guardians, each of them has had its influence on the cooking as well as the religious and cultural way of life.

Nevertheless, whatever may have been the origin of many of the Philippines dishes, the islands' cooks have added their own distinctive touch. They use plenty of garlic, vinegar and hot pepper. Their first favourite in meat is pork for in almost every dish, pork or ham is hidden somewhere amidst the ingredients. They certainly use more of the insides of animals than do most Westerners, even the French, and produce interesting and delicious dishes with them.

Obviously with so many islands (there are some 7,000), there are many different styles of cooking. Some are identical with Indonesian cooking, and so much so that some cook books lump them all together. Some of the islanders eat more fish than others, some more spices. But all eat rice, it is the staple food which is eaten as Westerners eat bread.

All Filipinos eat *bagoong*, a fermented salty paste of which there are several varieties. They eat it with rice, pork and vegetables and with salads. From the *bagoong* is drained off a clear liquid called *patis* and this is served over salads as a dressing.

Filipino hospitality is legendary and the average Filipino is happily prepared to run into debt for a fiesta. Such fiestas call for lengthy preparation, occasions for working together for days and nights ahead, for killing the fatted calf or pig and setting a lavish table. A real fiesta is usually an occasion for thanksgiving. A popular urban manner of entertaining is the *Merienda* which is served around 5 o'clock. There are special *Merienda* dishes, both sweet and savoury, served with thick sweet chocolate.

There is no doubt that the Filipinos have evolved some interesting food combinations, for example fish with ginger and an onion sauce; pork and grated cheese; a ravioli type of dish with flaked chicken; crabs and shrimps all in a piping hot soup. *Sinigang* is the Filipino version of the bouillabaisse made with a mixture of fish and garden vegetables. They have a *cocido*, which is chicken, pork, beef, Spanish sausage, cabbage and potatoes, chick-peas and bananas all cooked in tomato sauce and oil. The adventurous foreigner can try *kare-kare*, a stew of beef knuckles, tail, tripe and vegetables, thickened with ground peanuts and toasted rice and served with a shrimp-anchovy paste. The even more daring should try *dinugan at puto*, pig's innards and blood cooked with green peppers and served with rice balls. It is really good, like a dish of unusually flavoured, tender liver. There is chopped chicken with almonds, *adobo*, one of the national dishes, and surely no people roast or barbecue the pig as well as the Filipinos, the skin crisp, its tender flesh melting in the mouth.

Many foreigners are frightened off Filipino dishes. This infuriates the average Filipino, which is not surprising. However, there is a curious dish called *balut* at which even the most ardent Filipino food-fan blanches. It is, in fact, the contents of a duck's egg, eaten raw when the young duck is partially formed and one swallows it beak and all.

A visit to a Filipino food market is positively exciting, especially one which combines fruit, fish, vegetables and general stores. Let us go through the fruit. First, coconuts, both the regular kind which is prevalent throughout the tropical world and a rare variety called *makapuna*, which is solid right through, has no liquid at all and its flesh is white, slightly gooey and very sweet. It is used in many Filipino sweet dishes, especially an iced sweet called *buko*. *Makapuna* is bottled and tinned and made into a coconut honey or jam. The outward appearance of the *makapuna* nut is the same as the regular variety.

Then there is a loofah, for eating, not for washing; the purple heart or blossom of the banana makes good eating; the heart of the coconut palm itself usually made into a salad called millionaire's salad, for a coconut palm must be cut down to dig out the large white heart which nestles so compactly at the top. Coconut heart also provides the filling for *lumpia*, one of the national dishes of the islands, rather like Chinese spring rolls.

Filipino fruits are truly magnificent and there is a fine conceit of them. There is the star fruit or *bilinga*, rather like a sweet watery cucumber which, when cut, produces a star-shaped slice; the star-apple, quite unlike the Western apple which does not grow well in the islands; good guavas, the Java apple, which grows in clusters like loquats; persimmons of bright tomato colour and shape; custard apples, pale green and soft with a flesh like egg custard. When they are really ripe they are literally bursting with sweetness.

Bananas are legion, from finger-size to arm-size—those of us who know bananas in the West cannot visualize 100 different varieties. There are green bananas which are nevertheless ripe and sweet and so tender they whip like cream; others which taste like squashed strawberries; another, the *saba*, which is very dull when raw but becomes sweet when cooked and is served with sugar and coconut milk. There are *rambuttans* and *lansomes*, the latter a curious fruit, slightly astringent; tangerines and mandarin oranges, some of the Valencia type; the pomelo and the expensive but favourite mangosteen; the dark Java plum as well as the lime and *calamansi*, both acid fruits. The latter looks like a small gherkin and is peculiar to the islands. Both are used as we use lemon.

Some of the finest papaws grow in the islands as well as pineapples, so sweet they are almost too sweet. Avocados seem always to be available and are of two main varieties, those with a green skin and those with a deep purple skin. From both a fine ice-cream dish is made, as well, by the way as

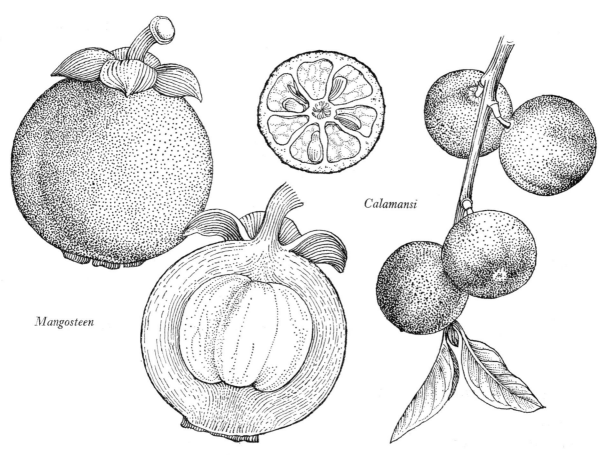

Calamansi

Mangosteen

from the purple yam. This is so good and of such a fine purple colour that most foreigners think they are eating purple grape ice-cream. Then there is *biquai*, a lovely fruit like blackcurrants, which grows in clusters and makes a fine jelly; the forests are full of them. *Roselli*, cherries, all are here.

If the fruit is interesting and good, the vegetables are no less so—yams of all kinds, sweet or Chinese turnips, bamboo shoots, breadfruit which is so good roasted whole in hot embers, sliced and spread with butter. Sweet potato and *taro*, cassava and other starchy roots. There are several kinds of lettuce, white cabbages, Chinese cabbage, swamp cabbage, squash, flowers and fern leaves, all of which find their place in Filipino cooking pots. Long beans and short, winged beans and Chinese, bean sprouts and *mungo* beans. Imagine a dish of beans cooked in a syrup until translucent, looking like fruit gums, and mixed with a custard and topped with purple yam ice-cream. This is a favourite drink concoction. There are all varieties of vegetable squash, long, round, large, small and of all colours.

The islands have plenty of fish, some of them very strange looking indeed, some almost too pretty to eat, some too ugly. There is a type which is as small as bait but which is used in a sauce for rice and which the Filipinos like to eat on a rainy night. There is a tiny shrimp which looks like a mass of oatmeal; only because of its pinpoint black eyes do you realize this is a living mass; it is used mainly to make the local dish called *bagoong*, also used with rice and vegetables and more particularly with a semi-rendered pork fat, added to cooked bitter gourd, a local highlight of cooking.

There are large crabs, an epicurean paste being made from the fat of the female crab. This calls for a lot of crabs. Then there is the coconut crab, shell-less, rather like the hermit crab, and also extremely large prawns.

Of some interest is the smoked fish, which is first cooked and then smoked, unlike our own smoked fish which is smoked while raw. There is the true herring, smoked and shredded and used as a topping for *pancit*, a local dish of noodles with which one is often served some crisply fried and pounded pork crackling.

With all this can one call the Filipinos gourmets? When they give parties the rich come very late and the poor too early. There will be 'small food' and drinks, then finally when dinner is served the guest eats and departs, a custom so often found in the East.

It is noted that even the poor in the Philippines are extremely wasteful with food. Probably because of the tropical conditions, it is a country where the thought of saving for the winter is not inbred in the people. When hungry they can always go out and dig another yam or pick a banana.

In recent years the eating habits of the people have changed. Once they ate only rice; they still do but bread is becoming popular, and they have become great noodle eaters. There was a time when only vinegar and soy sauce was found as a condiment; now there is Worcester Sauce and a variety of ketchups. In flavouring they have a heavy hand, especially with garlic and peppers.

Nature has been kind to the Filipinos for whether he cares much about vitamins or not, they are there. For six months of the year he has tomatoes, for the other six he has his *calamansi*. The poor eat a lot of potatoes, dried fish, shrimps etc. They make a dish called jerky from beef or pork; deer appears often on menus.

FISH SOUP (*Sinigang na Isda*)

6–8 servings:

1 lb. fish (a firm white fish is the best)
2 cups (2½) tomatoes, peeled and chopped
1 cup (1¼) onion, peeled and sliced
4 cups (5) water

2 teaspoons (2½) salt
small bunch young chilli pepper shoots or water cress

Put the tomatoes, onion, water and salt in a saucepan, bring to the boil and continue cooking while you prepare the fish. Clean the fish, remove all the bones and cut it into slices, not too thin or they will disintegrate. Add these pieces to the boiling liquid and continue to cook for about 5 minutes or until the fish is tender. Add the chilli shoots and cook for 1 minute and serve the soup at once.

Other vegetables, cut into small pieces, may also be added to the soup, i.e. aubergine (eggplant), cucumber, gourds and string beans.

BRAISED FISH (*Tinolang Bangus*)

The fish used in this recipe in the Philippines is milk fish or *bangus*, probably the most common fish to be found in the Manila market and is an all-the-year-round fish. It has the same bone structure as the herring.

2–3 servings:
1 whole fish, a young cod will do
2 tablespoons (2½) fat
3–4 cloves garlic, chopped
1 onion, sliced

2–3 potatoes, peeled and sliced
2 cups (2½) rice water, water or strained stock

Clean the fish and cut it into steaks or thick rounds. Heat the fat, add the garlic and let this brown, add the onion, partially cook this, then add the fish. Cover the pieces of fish with the potatoes. Add the liquid and cook over a medium heat until the fish and potatoes are cooked.

Rice water is simply the liquid in which rice has been cooked. It is used a great deal in Oriental cooking.

SOUSED FISH (*Escabeche de Pescado*)

3–4 servings:

3–4 medium-sized fish	1 cup (1¼) vintage vinegar
1 large onion	1 teaspoon (1¼) sugar
1-inch piece ginger	1 cup (1¼) water
5 cloves garlic	salt, pepper to taste
1 tablespoon (1¼) oil	

Finely slice the onion, ginger and garlic. Heat the oil in a large frying pan and sauté these three ingredients. Add the vinegar, sugar and water and stir well. Bring to the boil, add the fish, salt and pepper and cook for 5 minutes. Leave for 24 hours before serving.

There are variations of this recipe. Some cooks add diced green or red sweet peppers to the sauce, which is rather nice; others soy sauce.

Herring and mackerel are good fish for this recipe, and olive oil the best oil as it does not congeal when cold.

BRAISED BEEF (*Estofado*)

6 servings:

3 lb. boneless beef	1 cup (1¼) tomatoes, chopped
¾ tablespoon (1) flour	1 bay leaf
salt, pepper	6 small onions, peeled
cooking oil	2 cups (2½) string beans, broken
2 cloves garlic, pounded	2 small carrots, scraped
2 onions, finely chopped	

Rub the meat with the flour, salt and pepper. Heat the oil, add the beef and fry this until brown. Take from the pan and put aside for the moment. Fry the garlic, the chopped onions and tomatoes, cover and simmer for 5 minutes to make a sauce. Put the beef into a large pan, add the sauce, water to cover and the bay leaf. Bring to a boil, cover and simmer until the meat is tender. Add the remaining vegetables and continue cooking until these are tender. Take out the meat, place on a serving plate, surround with vegetables, add the sauce and serve hot.

STUFFED MEAT (*Morcon*)

A speciality of the Philippines, considered a fiesta dish.

4–6 servings:

1 2 lb. slice of beef
salt, pepper
lemon juice
1 well-beaten egg
3 hard-boiled eggs, sliced
½ cup (⅔) sweet pickles
2 tablespoons (2½) seedless raisins
2 oz. (⅔ cup) each minced ham and lean
    pork

3 tablespoons (3¾) grated cheese
½ cup (⅔) cider vinegar
1 onion, thickly sliced
½ cup (⅔) tomato sauce or purée
soy sauce, pepper
1 bay leaf

The meat must be lightly beaten into a 'sheet' about ¼ inch thick. Spread it out and rub it with salt, pepper, lemon juice and the beaten egg. Cover it with the sliced eggs and spread the pickle, raisins, minced meat and cheese on top. Roll up the meat carefully, as a Swiss or jelly roll, and tie it with a long piece of thread—it must be securely tied. Wrap in muslin and tie again. Put the roll into a large saucepan and cover with water, adding the remaining ingredients. Cook until the meat is tender. Take from the pan, remove the muslin, cut into slices, arrange on a platter, cover with the gravy (reheat in the oven if necessary) and serve hot.

MINCED SAVOURY PORK AND BEEF (*Relleno Suelto*)

4–6 servings:

1¼ lb. minced pork
1¼ lb. minced beef
2 potatoes, peeled
2 tablespoons (2½) fat
1 small onion, chopped

½ lb. tomatoes, peeled and chopped
4 oz. (¾ cup) seedless raisins
½ cup (⅔) cooked chick peas (optional)
2 tablespoons (2½) soy sauce
1 sweet pepper, chopped and seeded

Cut the potatoes into small cubes. Heat the fat and fry these until they begin to brown. Take them out and put aside. Add the onion and let this brown. Add the tomatoes, the meat, raisins and chick peas and stir well. Cook all this for a few minutes, add the soy sauce, potatoes and the pepper and continue until the meat is quite cooked. Serve with rice.

BRAISED PORK AND BEEF (*Carne Mechada*)

4–6 servings:

1½ lb. lean pork
¾ lb. lean beef
5 tomatoes
2 onions
½ cup (⅔) soy sauce

1 cup (1¼) lime or lemon juice
6 peppercorns
1 bay leaf
1 cup (1¼) water
1 crust dry bread

Cut the pork and beef into fair-sized pieces. Peel the tomatoes and onions and cut these into halves. Put the meat into a saucepan, add the soy sauce, lime juice, tomatoes, onions, peppercorns, bay leaf and water. Cover the pan tightly and cook over a slow heat until the meat is tender. Add the bread crust, stir this well into the gravy and serve hot with rice.

The bread is used only as a thickening agent; it can be omitted.

BRAISED PORK LIVER (*Quilowan*)

4–6 servings:

1¼ lb. pork liver	3 tomatoes, peeled
½ lb. lean pork	salt
3 tablespoons (3¾) lard	½ teaspoon (⅔) pepper
5 cloves garlic, pounded	½ cup (⅔) cider vinegar
1 large onion, chopped	½ cup (⅔) water

Cut the liver and pork into small pieces but keep separate. Heat the lard, add the garlic and let this brown, add the onion and tomatoes. Cook until the onion is soft, add the pork, salt and pepper, let the meat brown then add the vinegar and water. When the pork is cooked, add the liver and continue cooking for a few minutes. Serve hot.

MEAT ROLL (*Embutido*)

6–8 servings:

2 lb. pork, minced	3 tablespoons (3¾) sweet pickles, finely chopped
1 cup (1¼) breadcrumbs soaked in ½ cup milk	3 tablespoons (3¾) seedless raisins
2 chorizos de Bilbao (garlic sausage), finely chopped	salt, pepper
2 eggs, beaten	chicken or meat stock

Mix all these ingredients except the stock and shape into a roll. Wrap this up in a white piece of cloth and tie securely at both ends. Put the roll into a saucepan with stock to cover. Bring to a slow boil and simmer between 1½–2 hours. Cool. Put into a refrigerator overnight and slice to serve cold.

Serve with a sauce made by taking some of the broth in which the meat roll was cooked, thicken it with liver pâté or tomato purée.

PORK IN A SOUR SAUCE (*Adobo*)

4–6 servings:

2½–3 lb. pork	salt or soy sauce
1 whole head garlic	2 cups (2½) water
½ cup (⅔) cider vinegar	1 tablespoon (1¼) fat
1 teaspoon (1¼) black pepper, ground	

Cut the pork into pieces about 2 × 1½ inches. Divide the garlic into cloves. Put the pieces of pork into a saucepan, add the vinegar, garlic, pepper, salt and water. Cover the pan and cook slowly until the meat is tender and most of the broth has evaporated. Drain, separate the pieces of garlic from the pork and fry these in the fat until brown. Add the pieces of pork, brown these, then add the remaining broth, simmer for 5 minutes and serve hot.

ROAST SUCKING PIG (*Lechon de Leche*)

There is nothing like the Filipino manner of cooking sucking pig, it is perfect. I shall give their recipe just as it is, attempting no short cuts or substitutes.

Clean well a small pig, up to 12 lb. in weight; drain and stuff it with tamarind leaves. Truss with skewers or tie with string. Put the stuffed pig on to a rack in a dripping pan, brush the entire surface with melted lard, and pour 2 cupfuls (2½) of boiling water over it. Cover the skin with greased paper and roast the pig in a moderate oven for about 4 hours, basting every 15 minutes with liquid from the pan. Or thrust a pole through the pig and roast it turning it slowly over a charcoal fire. Serve with liver sauce.

The crackling is tender but crisp and is usually eaten separately and considered the best part of the dish. Actually most of us will have to omit the tamarind leaves—there is no substitute.

4–6 servings: depending on size of the pig.

Sauce:
4 oz. (½ cup) liver pâté
⅓ cup (½) cider vinegar
1¼ cups (1½) water
⅓ cup (½) dried breadcrumbs
⅓ cup (½) sugar

salt
¾ teaspoon (1) black pepper
2 oz. (4 tablespoons) lard
8 cloves garlic, pounded
6 small spring (green) onions, finely chopped

Mix the pâté, vinegar, water, breadcrumbs, sugar, salt and pepper. Heat the lard and sauté the garlic. When brown take out most of it and put aside leaving only 1 teaspoonful (1¼) of garlic in the lard. Add the onions and fry these until soft. Add the liver pâté mixture and cook over a low heat, stirring constantly until the sauce is thick and hot. Serve the sauce topped with the rest of the garlic.

CHICKEN STEW (*Timola*)

3–4 servings:

1 3-lb. chicken, cut into serving pieces
½ tablespoon (⅔) fat
2 cloves garlic
1 onion, chopped
1-in. piece fresh ginger, pounded

2 cups (2½) green papaws peeled and cut into pieces or vegetable marrow
some spinach leaves
salt

Heat the fat and fry the garlic, onion and ginger, then add the chicken. Mix well. Add enough water to cook the chicken until it is tender. Add the papaw and cook this until it is soft but not mushy. Add salt to taste and finally the spinach—in the Philippines they use sil leaves. Cook a few minutes longer and serve hot.

Green papaw has not a great deal of flavour in itself but it is a tenderizer. In papaw growing countries tough meat is left wrapped in papaw leaves for several hours to make it tender.

FIESTA RAGOUT (*Pochero*)

This dish is served with an aubergine (eggplant) sauce.

5–6 servings:

1 large chicken, cut into small pieces	$\frac{1}{2}$–$\frac{3}{4}$ cup ($\frac{2}{3}$–1) cooked chick peas
$\frac{1}{4}$ lb. each lean beef, pork and ham, cut into small pieces	1 small cabbage, shredded
	2 tablespoons (2$\frac{1}{2}$) sugar
salt, pepper	Sauce:
4–6 under-ripe bananas	4–6 small aubergines (eggplants)
2 potatoes	2 cloves garlic, finely chopped
1 large onion, minced	vinegar, salt and pepper
1 clove garlic	

Put the chicken and meats into a pan, cover with water and cook until tender. Add salt. Peel and cut the bananas into quarters, peel and cut the potatoes into cubes. Add the onion, garlic, chick peas and the potatoes to the pan and cook gently until the potatoes are almost tender. Add the bananas and cabbage and cook for about 10 minutes, or until both are tender. Add pepper and sugar and more salt, if required.

To make the sauce, grill or roast the aubergines over a good heat until the flesh cracks. Cool slightly then peel and mash. Mix this with the garlic and add flavourings to taste. This is an excellent sauce and its flavour comes from the 'burning' of the aubergines.

FILIPINO CARAMEL CUSTARD (*Leche Flan*)

This is the national sweet of the Philippines.

4–6 servings:

Caramel:	8 egg yolks
1 cup (1$\frac{1}{4}$) brown sugar	1 cup (1$\frac{1}{4}$) fine sugar
$\frac{1}{4}$ cup ($\frac{1}{3}$) water	1 strip lemon rind or vanilla
Custard:	
2 cups (2$\frac{1}{2}$) milk	

To prepare the caramel, dissolve the brown sugar in the water and cook over a moderate heat until the sugar caramelizes. With this, line a mould evenly. Serve remainder as sauce.

Scald the milk in a double boiler for 15 minutes. In the meantime beat the yolks with the sugar and flavouring. Gradually add the milk. Pour this into a mould lined with the caramel. Place this in a large pan half-filled with water and bake it in a slow oven until it thickens and sets firmly. Cool and turn out to serve.

PEANUT 'CANDIES' (*Pastillas de Mani*)

About 20 pieces, according to size:

1¼ cups (1½) ground peanuts   ¾ cup (1) milk
½ cup (⅔) sugar

Combine all the ingredients and cook over a slow fire, stirring constantly to prevent burning. Cook until thick. Sprinkle fine sugar over a pastry board, spread the mixture over this with a rolling pin and cut into shapes.

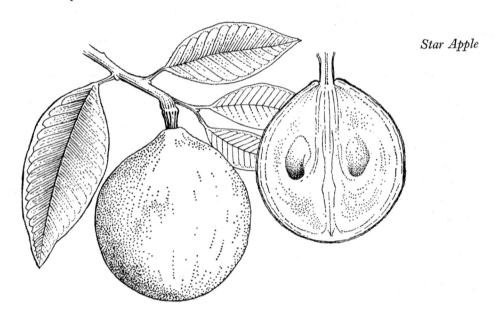

Star Apple

Glossary

ABALONE. This is a gastropod or mollusc belonging to the same class as the snail and sea slug. Its home is an ear-shaped shell, a source of mother-of-pearl. The Chinese purchase it usually in its dried form, soak it for some time and then proceed to deal with it. Tinned abalone is much simpler for it is cured and prepared for cooking. It simply requires thinly slicing and briefly cooking. Too long cooking will toughen it and make it rubbery. Many Chinese prefer to cook with the tinned abalone. It is served with a single vegetable, offered as a form of salad; fried with mushrooms, or is the basis of a favourite Chinese soup. As it comes from the tin, large and somewhat repulsive, the average Westerner might say emphatically no, but correctly dealt with it gains favour.

AGAR-AGAR. A gelatinous substance derived from seaweed and related to laver and carrageen or Irish moss. It is, in fact, a vegetable isinglass prepared principally in Japan but also in other parts of the Far East. Made from the red or *gelidium* seaweed and used much in the preparation of gelatine desserts, it is marketed in several ways, in sticks, in blocks and like 'hair'. Completely tasteless, it is extremely effective and can be used whenever gelatine is called for but usually requires somewhat longer dissolving—but finally produces a dish which will not flop.

ANCHOVY ESSENCE. This condiment is well known in Britain and is simply a thick, bottled, pinkish sauce of concentrated anchovy. Mixed with soy sauce it makes a fair substitute in Oriental dishes for their pungent fish sauces, not always possible to obtain. It is used in Britain for flavouring, spreading on toast and in the preparation of anchovy butter.

ANISEED. The seeds of an umbelliferous annual plant, and member of the parsley family, native to the Mediterranean region but extensively cultivated in Asia. Its flavour is similar to that of licorice and it is considered stimulating and good for stomach disorders. Its colour is a greenish grey and the seeds very similar in shape and flavour to those of the caraway.

ARECA NUT. The nut of the tall areca palm which looks like a slim coconut palm. The nuts hang in clusters below the leaves. Their outer skins are orange and red in colour and about one-and-a-half inches long. The nut looks like a large, fawn nutmeg with white flesh. It is used principally chopped and wrapped in betel leaf and chewed as a digestive. Also used as a dentifrice, first being burnt to a charcoal and then pounded. *See* betel leaf.

ASAFOETIDA. This is a flavouring which, despite all cajoling by Indian friends, I cannot stomach at all. Hobson Jobson says: 'A repulsively smelling gum-resin which forms a favourite Hindu condiment in Western and Southern India as an ingredient in certain cakes eaten with curry.' It was used at one time in Britain for nervous and hysterical ailments 'possibly controlling the erratic nervous phenomena by the psychological influence of its disgusting smell'. (*Everyman's Encyclopaedia.*)

BAMBOO SHOOTS. The bamboo tree is used for food and furniture. It is the young shoots just appearing above the ground which are used in cooking and only in luncheon dishes. Such shoots are sold fresh in the Far Eastern markets and there are two varieties, the winter and the spring shoots. Winter shoots are considered tastier than the spring shoots and are also more expensive. When unavailable fresh they can usually be found in tins, salted or unsalted—unless a recipe specifies salted, it is usual to use unsalted. They are a soft cream colour, rather crunchy and usually cut into shapes to match accompanying ingredients. Tinned bamboo shoots require very little cooking, simply reheating, but the fresh varieties require to be cooked for some time.

BEAN CURD. An ingredient made from curdled soy bean, much used in cooking from Japan to Tibet. It requires a complicated process of preparation, which only experts attempt. But the result of curdling and coagulating the soy bean produces a white substance which looks like a soft but firm white cheese. It is considered highly nourishing and is extremely digestible. It is sold in several forms. 1. Like a watery white custard. 2. Regular bean curd which comes in slabs and the pieces are chopped with the inevitable Chinese cleaver. 3. Dry cakes which can be sliced, shredded and cut into shapes. 4. Cakes, already fried in deep fat. It has its own particular flavour but also blends perfectly with other ingredients. It is good fried in hot fat and served with a mild soy and chilli sauce as an appetizer with drinks.

BEAN PASTE. This is the same thing as the Japanese *miso* (*see* page 194).

BEAN SPROUTS. There are two basic varieties. Those which we usually meet are pea sprouts, not soy bean sprouts. The shoots are the tiny roots issuing from the pea or soy bean, each carrying a little hood. It is usual to remove this hood before cooking, but this is a tedious job and one simply removes as many as one conveniently can when washing them in water. They are very good with or without pods. Pea sprouts are usually white, fine and tender. Soy bean sprouts are crunchy, stronger in flavour than the pea sprouts and of a golden-yellow colour. Both are simple to make at home (*see* page 154) but they can be bought fresh or tinned in the West.

BETEL LEAF or PAN. The leaf of the betel tree which is chewed as an aid to the digestion. For a long time it has been incorrectly called 'betel nut'. The smooth green leaves are smeared with a red paste and rolled into neat bundles, enclosing bits of the areca nut, spices, sometimes tobacco (or even narcotics) and a smear of quicklime. The packages are secured with a clove and for the rich are coated with silver or gold leaf. It produces a blood red saliva which stains the teeth and mouth bright red.

BIRDS' NESTS. *See* page 157.

BLACHAN (*balachan, balachong*). A characteristic condiment of the Burmese and Malaysian cuisines and sometimes called 'the caviar of the Far East'. It is composed usually of prawns, fresh sardines, chillies and other small fish, allowed to ferment in a heap and then mashed heavily with salt. Although at first smell it may not meet with the approval of those unaccustomed to it, there are many Europeans who have learned to like it. Someone wrote it is 'much relished by lovers of decomposed cheese'.

CANDLENUTS. These nuts are the fruit of the candleberry tree, so rich in oil that if lit they will burn like a candle for twenty minutes. Any fatty or oily nuts may be substituted for these in most recipes.

CAPSICUMS or SWEET PEPPERS. Under this name are a multitude of peppers, large and small. There are the large bell peppers, which can be red, yellow or green, all varying in strength from vaguely sweet to some which are extremely pungent; long, hot chilli peppers, both red and green; tiny bird or cherry peppers and many others, too numerous to name. All should be treated with caution, and their seeds removed before using—unless a recipe otherwise specifies.

Most recipes in this book call for chilli peppers which are the fruits of an herbaceous plant belonging to the capsicum family. Usually in the East these are used in their fresh or dried state—they are bought by the pound in the local bazaars. However, in the West this is not always possible, but they are sold ready seeded and chopped in tins.

It is important also to note that chilli peppers vary considerably in strength and flavour. In Goa there is a well-flavoured but mild chilli—so it is not surprising to find there recipes calling for fifty chillies. Kashmir has a pungent, but not especially hot chilli; those in Nepal are fiery. Whenever cutting or removing the seeds of even a mild capsicum wash the hands at once, for should you put your finger in your mouth the sting of the seeds will be painful (*see* page 168).

CARDAMOM SEEDS. These are known among Orientals as 'The Seeds of Paradise' and come from a plant of the ginger family. It grows prolifically on the Malabar coast of India where it is extensively cultivated, as well as in Ceylon and to a certain extent also in Mexico and Central America. Cardamom seeds vary in colour from almost white to a dark reddish brown (known as black cardamoms) but are often bleached to a rich creamy white before being marketed. They have a reputation for stimulation as well as being antiseptic. The texture of the seeds is hard and they are unusually pungent, pleasant and of exotic flavour. Cardamom seeds are used in a large number of Far Eastern dishes, both sweet and savoury and in almost all curries and pilaus. In Kashmir they are used to flavour tea (Arabs also flavour coffee with cardamoms). They can be bought either in powdered form or whole—the latter is better from a flavour point of view. They are also chewed after a meal to flavour the breath.

CAYENNE PEPPER. This is the most pungent of the spices, a very hot biting condiment that is ground from the seeds of several varieties of capsicum. It is a red powdery spice, but its colour is not as bright as that of paprika pepper. It should be used often but sparingly and it can be used as a substitute for the pungent chilli peppers used in so many Oriental dishes.

CHILLI PEPPERS. *See* capsicums.

CLABBER. *See* curd.

COCONUT MILK. Coconut has been described as being like 'a bottle of milk which grows on ice'. But by coconut milk is not meant the thin cool liquid which flows from every coconut when it is opened, but a milk made by squeezing grated fresh or desiccated coconut with either water or fresh cow's milk. To do this with a fresh coconut pierce the three soft 'eyes' at the top of the coconut with an ice pick, or some similar sharp instrument. Pour out the liquid. Revolve the nut in the hand and tap it with a hammer, not too hard, all round the nut until the hard shell cracks and can be pulled off. Take out the meat, or flesh, and slice off the brown skin. Grate the coconut meat—a good sized coconut will yield three cupfuls ($3\frac{3}{4}$) of grated coconut. Coconut milk comes in three qualities, cream or very thick, thick and thin.

Cream or very thick milk. Mix all the grated coconut with $\frac{1}{2}$ a cupful ($\frac{2}{3}$) of warm water. Leave it for twenty minutes, then squeeze it through a piece of fine muslin or even a fine sieve. This liquid will be like a cream, about 1 cupful ($1\frac{1}{4}$) or a little more.

Thick milk. Use the same quantity of grated coconut with 1 cupful ($1\frac{1}{4}$) of liquid—repeat the above process.

Thin milk. Use again the same coconut with 2 or 3 cupfuls ($2\frac{1}{2}$–$3\frac{3}{4}$) of water and repeat the above. One good coconut will yield 2 cupfuls ($2\frac{1}{2}$) of thick milk and 3 cupfuls ($3\frac{3}{4}$) of thin.

Instead of grating the coconut it can be cut into small pieces and put into a liquidizer, adding the same quantity of water—but all of the coconut cannot go in at once. Simply divide the quantities. After letting it whirl for a minute or so, it can be immediately squeezed through muslin.

The above directions also apply when using desiccated coconut, although I use less water. There are several varieties of desiccated coconut, packaged and even tinned coconut on the market—some of the American moist, shredded and hermetically sealed coconut from the southern states makes an excellent substitute for fresh coconut.

If the thick coconut milk is left overnight in the refrigerator a solid cream will form.

CORIANDER SEEDS. These are the seeds of the coriander, a delicate lacy leafed annual. It is far more appreciated in Oriental cooking than in Occidental, although it was introduced into England a long time ago. In certain parts of Britain it has established itself as a wild plant, but there are still people who grow it to provide tender aromatic leaves for salads. It is extensively cultivated throughout the Mediterranean countries, as well as along the coast of northern Africa and to a lesser extent in the United States. In India it grows profusely and it is used where the British and Americans would use parsley. Coriander seeds are tiny and yellowish, extremely aromatic which, when crushed, emit a warm flavour which is a curious combination of sage and lemon peel. They are used in all curries, in pilaus, stews and other savoury dishes. Certain Continental pastries are flavoured with coriander seeds, so are some gins and liqueurs. It is sold both whole and ready ground. It is incidentally the seed which in the old days was sugar coated and sold as comfits or Scotch candy—maybe still is. Sausages, and game, are frequently flavoured generously with this versatile herb—used by the tablespoonful.

CUMIN SEEDS. An extremely aromatic seed with a slightly bitter flavour. The seed of the small annual herb, cumin, which belongs to the parsley family and is sometimes called *comino* in Europe and in Mexico. Native to Egypt, western Asia and the Mediterranean, as well as Asia generally, it resembles in appearance and flavour the caraway seed. It is used both in sweet and sour dishes, invariably in curries and often in pilaus. When cumin is not available, caraway can be substituted.

CURD. *See* page 22.

CURRY LEAVES. These are the leaves of an aromatic bush which have the same taste as *garam masala*, or a curry powder, and are curiously pungent. They are much used in Ceylonese cooking and are usually available at Indian or other stores dealing with Eastern foods (*see* page 66).

DAIKON or Japanese radish. This is the most commonly eaten vegetable in Japan, a long thick white radish, somewhat resembling in flavour the red radish and considered an aid to the digestion, as it contains pepsin. It is much used in making pickles. *Daikons* were first used as 'a fragrant thing' to sweeten the breath and cleanse the mouth, the better to appreciate drink.

DRIED FOODS. These I have mentioned in individual recipes, but a whole volume could be written on the variety of Chinese dried foods. Dried scallops, cod, shark, cuttlefish, octopus and others of this ilk. Dried shrimps, ancient looking oysters, dried to autumn hues, wizened clams, all used as flavourings in soups. Sea-slugs looking as though fossilization had long set in and abalone galore.

But not only fish is dried; eggs, fruits, especially plums, dates, lichees, vegetables, roots—all find a place somewhere on the dried food counters, all looking like old rope, tired rags, tatty rugs, yet all eaten later in an ambrosial sauce. Fantastic is a mild term for what the Chinese and Japanese can do with this fossilized food. The Chinese give them fancy names, exotic and amusing. 'Golden Needles' are dried lilies. 'Ears of Wood' are dried tree fungi. 'Maiden Hair' is black seaweed which is like steel wool. Dried cabbage leaves are served to children 'because they are good for you' and a good Chinese vegetarian cook can include as many of a dozen of these dried vegetables in his dishes. 'One Hundred Unities' are the dried petals of an edible variety of lily.

FENNEL. There are three kinds of fennel. Common fennel, which is the one referred to in this book; sweet fennel often called Florentine fennel or *finocchio*; Italian fennel also called Sicilian fennel. The seeds and soft green lacy leaves of the common fennel both have something of the same flavour as aniseed or licorice. The seeds look somewhat like caraway seeds. Fennel is one of the earliest herbs known.

FENUGREEK. Both the leaves and the seeds of this curiously named leguminous plant are greatly used in Oriental cooking. In India it is served fresh as a salad. It is an annual, brilliant in colour and grown as a crop. In bloom it is a lovely sight. The seeds are sand coloured and come in varying shapes and reputed to be fattening—which might well be one of the reasons for its Asiatic popularity. Their flavour rather resembles that of celery seeds. The leaves of the plant are small, dark green and very bitter, as bitter as spinach. Fenugreek is also used as a fodder plant and is added as a scent in those parts of Europe where the hay is of poor quality. In the United States fenugreek seeds are used to impart a maple flavour to candy, but its chief use is in the flavouring of curries or in flavouring commercial curry powder. In England its country name is Greek Hay Seed or Bird's Food.

FIVE SPICE POWDER. A 'secret' mixture of five essential spices used in many Chinese dishes. It is highly perfumed, a little goes a long way, but its flavour is extremely interesting.

GARAM MASALA. This is a condiment made of cardamoms, cumin and cloves, dry-roasted and powdered, used in curries (*see* page 13).

GINGER. There is romance and tradition in ginger, the root or tuber of a lovely sweet smelling plant looking like a tall creamy iris. It was used medicinally before it became a condiment. Ginger can be chewed as a digestive, Indians use it in all their 'gassy' foods such as pulses and beans and some say that it cures or at least soothes toothache.

Fresh ginger has a hot spicy flavour and resembles a horny or maybe a large coarse potato which has started to grow young potatoes over it. It has a light brown scaly skin, and beneath this is the firm pungent flesh. The older the ginger, the sharper the flavour. There is also a variety of small young ginger, with delicate fibreless tubers which give a subtle flavour to anything to which they are added.

Ginger is indigenous both to India and China but the finest of all grows in Jamaica. It was the first Oriental spice to become known in the West. In the Middle Ages it was second only to pepper in value and the price per pound of ginger was the same as for a sheep. As far as Asian cooking is concerned it is essential, but always fresh. Where fresh ginger is called for in a recipe it can only be substituted by dried ginger, which must be soaked before using. Ground ginger has quite a different flavour and is no substitute at all, except in rare cases which have been noted.

There are recipes which call for ginger juice. This can be made by pounding ginger in a mortar (after peeling it) or putting it into a blender with a little water. When the ginger is thoroughly pulped it should be sqeezed through fine clean muslin. However, ginger juice is seldom called for. (*see* page 168)

GINGKO NUTS. The gingko tree is cultivated in the United States for its handsome foliage, but in Japan the nuts are considered a great autumn delicacy and much used in Japanese cooking. The nuts, which have a gem-green colour, are cooked in a variety of ways, grilled with *yakitori*, roasted and used in soups. They are roughly the size of a small green olive and not unlike it in appearance. (*see* page 191).

GINSENG. A one-foot high plant is native to North China and Korea and is found both wild and cultivated in many parts of North America. The root is from $1\frac{1}{2}$–3 inches long and when fully developed is spindle-shaped and is sometimes forked. It has over the centuries been used as a remedy for almost everything. It is extremely popular in Korea and the Chinese use it as an aphrodisiac. Ginseng has been exported from America since the early part of the eighteenth century.

GRAM FLOUR or BESAN. A flour made from ground chick peas and much used in Indian cooking, especially in the making of Indian breads, or for fritters. It can usually be purchased from Indian stores or one can make a substitute by grinding split peas through a grinder adjusted to the finest grind possible.

JAGGERY or PALM SUGAR. A coarse thick brown sugar made from the various palms. The flavour varies slightly between one type of palm and the other. It is usually made in the form of round cakes. It has its own delicious flavour but the nearest that we have to this flavour in the West is maple sugar or molasses or even black treacle. It can be scraped and used in many of the usual forms of sugar or it is sometimes soaked and cooked to a thick syrup. At one time *jaggery* was such an important ingredient in certain parts of India that it was used as a form of currency.

LEMON GRASS. Used considerably in Burma, Ceylon, Indonesia and certain other countries in the Far East, notably Malaysia. Aromatic, with an odour of lemon or citronelle, it is extensively cultivated in all the countries mentioned and is the same grass from which an oil used in perfumery is taken, marketed as Oil of Verbena. Lemon or lime does not make a substitute. Lemon verbena would, so would lemon balm. Its function is often to take away a fishy odour (*see* page 122).

LIMES. These are the fruit of a small citrus tree, each fruit roughly the size of an egg. Their colour when ripe can be bright yellow, pale yellow or even a deep green. Unlike lemons, whose flavour they greatly resemble, they are nearly round in shape. The average lime contains about one-third more citric acid than the average lemon. In most parts of Asia they are much preferred to the lemon especially for drinks as well as a flavouring. Where limes are expensive lemons may be used as a substitute. Limes are perishable and should be kept in a cool place (*see* page 168).

LOTUS ROOT. From Japan to India, a much used vegetable. It looks rather like a decayed root or tube of no particular interest and one wonders who first thought of connecting it with eating. It is extremely good, crisp and versatile. Its Chinese tone name is the same as for 'many sons'. The underwater root of the water-lily plant, it is cut diagonally. Running through its entire length is a circle of five holes, which the Chinese cooks often stuff with glutinous rice and serve as a sweet. Thinly sliced, the root can be served raw, boiled or fried.

LOTUS SEEDS. Like small hazelnuts, these have a delicate fresh flavour. They can be eaten raw or soaked and cooked with sugar and made into a stuffing for puddings, dates and duck. Asians chew them as a digestive.

MALDIVE FISH. A speciality of Ceylonese cooking and for which there is no substitute. It is dried fish from the Maldive Islands. It is prepared from several varieties of fish and is considered expensive even in Ceylon. The nearest equivalent is Bombay Duck—but this suggestion horrified my Ceylonese friends. Both look like crumbling bits of old wood.

MELON SEEDS. The chewing gum of the East for which a special melon called a wet-melon is grown.

MIRIN. This is a sweet wine fortified with *sake* used in Japanese cooking and made from glutinous rice. When not available it may be substituted by a mild vinegar or dry sherry.

MONOSODIUM GLUTAMATE. An important Japanese and Chinese seasoning and used in the cooking of many of the Far Eastern countries. It is also called '*Aji-no-moto*' and '*Vietsin*'. It is referred to throughout this book as monosodium glutamate. It is considered the finest seasoning of Eastern cooking, comparing with the French *sel-de-celeri*. It is not a salt, nor has it any flavour of its own, but it is used to bring out flavour. The Japanese name *Aji-no-moto* means 'essence of taste' and it is often referred to in Eastern recipes as 'taste powder'. It is used sparingly and is usually generally available.

MUSHROOMS—DRIED. These are usually obtainable in Far Eastern stores and are an important item in the Chinese cuisine. Grey-black or brownish in colour, very wizened they come in varied thicknesses and sizes and require soaking for thirty minutes to expand to their full size. Remove the stems for cooking. Before soaking wash them well, then the liquid in which they have been soaked can be used in stock. Continental dried mushrooms can be used as a substitute, but their flavour is somewhat different.

NAM PLA. A pungent fish sauce, very salty, used extensively in Thai cooking. It is often available in Oriental stores but my own substitute is soy sauce flavoured with anchovy essence.

NAM PRIK. The national dish of Thailand (*see* page 90).

NGAPI. This is shrimp paste which forms the basis of all the Burmese curries and flavourings of most Burmese dishes. It is made from prawns spread out on rough bamboo mats and dried in the sun. When they are dry the prawns are mashed and mixed with a vast quantity of salt. The prawns turn into a black-grey paste which foreigners usually find too pungent. It is also used to flavour many meat and vegetable dishes and is kept stored in small earthenware glazed jars. The nearest thing we have to this is anchovy essence.

NGUOC-NAM. A fish paste used in Cambodian, Vietnamese and Laotian cooking (*see* page 133).

NOODLES. In this book, by noodles is always meant the fine Chinese or vermicelli type of noodles. They are sold both fresh and dried in all Chinese shops and many others which sell Oriental foods. The dried noodles come in different varieties. There are also shining or 'cellophaned' noodles, as well as rice noodles. Failing Chinese noodles, Italian vermicelli may be used instead in many recipes.

OYSTER SAUCE. An important ingredient for many Chinese dishes and, as its name suggests, is made from oysters. It has no particular flavour of its own, but blends perfectly with almost any dish, intensifying other flavours.

PALM SUGAR. See *jaggery*.

PANDAN LEAF. The pandan leaf is a long, sword-shaped leaf, dark green with a very fragrant scent. It is used a great deal in Malaysian cooking, in sweet broths, cakes, syrups and coconut rice. The leaves are also finely shredded and mixed with petals of different flowers called *bunga rampi* for use in religious processions at Easter and Corpus Christi or at a Malay wedding.

PAPAW, PAPAYA. A large and delicious fruit which grows on a sub-tropical tree. The shape is usually globular or oval, but it varies considerably in size, a really fine specimen can reach a weight of twenty pounds. It is rapidly coming to the fore as a source of useful products, including a meat tenderizer. In its countries of origin, its large cut-out leaf is used for wrapping up meat to tenderize it. The flesh is orange in colour and at its best is extremely sweet. When cut open the papaw is seen to be completely hollow inside, and the flesh about one inch thick. It is filled with black seeds which are considered good for the digestion and are chewed by the peoples of papaw growing countries. Unripe, the fruit may be cooked as a vegetable or preserved as a sweet pickle, flavoured with ginger.

It is a most useful tree in the tropics, for its roots yield an excellent nerve tonic and when it is cut down after three years, its heart can be carefully removed, grated and served in the same manner as the heart of the coconut.

Papaw grows rapidly and easily but there are definite male and female trees. One might plant a whole grove of papaw and watch for a crop in vain. The male tree has flowers but not fruit. The female tree can yield a dozen or more of this luscious fruit at one time and there seems to be no end to their productivity. *Papain* is obtained from the half-ripe papaw (*see* page 168).

PARSLEY, CHINESE. This is not the dark crisp stiffly curled parsley of the West but belongs to the coriander group or continental parsley. It has a somewhat willowy stem and is similar also to the Mexican parsley *cilantre* and is lighter both in colour and flavour than the curly parsley.

PEANUT OIL. One of the most important of the many cooking oils in the Far East, especially for the Chinese. It cooks extremely well and has no odour and no flavour, therefore it does not spoil the flavour of any ingredient cooked in it. The best substitute is good quality vegetable oil or where it is obtainable cotton-seed oil. The Chinese always prefer to purify oil before using it. Into 3 cupfuls ($3\frac{3}{4}$) of peanut oil drop 2 slices of fresh ginger and half a leek cut into 2 or 3 pieces. Heat the oil until these ingredients turn brown. Take them from the pan. The oil is ready for use.

POMFRET. A sea fish found along the Indian coasts and highly esteemed. At first glance it is not unlike a smooth silvery plaice with a rounded snout and a small mouth but its flavour is more delicate and could be likened to turbot. There is silver, white and black pomfret. In Pondicherry the French called it *pample* and in most old recipe books it was called *pomplet*—indeed my cook in Bombay still talked of *pomplet*. The name, it has been suggested, may be a corruption of the Portuguese word *pampanos* meaning vine-leaf which it is supposed to resemble (*see* page 106).

POPPYSEEDS. These tiny seeds come from a variety of poppy which is different from the opium poppy—so that any thought of their being narcotic is wrong. The seeds are so tiny that according to the spice trade more than 900,000 go to make up a pound. They are extensively used in Asian cooking, probably because they stimulate the appetite. They have their own especial flavour but curiously no odour. Toasted they have a delightful nutty flavour. The colour of the seeds varies between so-called black or blue, through to white—these latter are grown in India. The white is just as good as the black seed but, since the trade prefers the blue or black, the white is sometimes dyed to conform. Poppyseeds are grown in many parts of Central Europe as well as parts of the United States and Canada. While they appear as a savoury spice in the Far East, in Europe they are used as a base for dumplings and rich pastries and on the crust of bread.

PRAWN. This is a crustacean very much like the shrimp, but larger and more delicate in flavour. Like the shrimp it is in season all the year round but at its best from February to October. The black filament of the prawn should always be removed before eating. For some people this can be positively poisonous. Like shrimps they usually appear on the market ready cooked—so when using them in any of the ways suggested in this book, cook them with caution as they will toughen with over cooking.

Prawns or shrimps are almost everyday items of diet in many of the Far Eastern countries—many of their sauces are a basis of dried and mashed shrimps or prawns and some of the finest curries of the East are those prepared with fresh prawns. Chinese cooking could hardly exist without its prawn dishes.

PRAWNS—DRIED PRAWNS. These are prepared from very small crustaceans—in Britain we would call them shrimps. Usually they are dried in the sun and prepared by village women. Much of the Far Eastern cooking flavours are absolutely dependent on these tiny fish—especially the many important pungent sauces.

PRAWN WAFERS or CRACKERS. Usually these are prepared with tapioca flour which is mixed with shrimps or prawns. They are similar to the Indian *pappadams* (*see* page 24). They are generally sold in those shops dealing with Oriental foods. In Indonesia and Malaysia they are called *krupuk*. They can be fried or grilled and then, like the *pappadams*, they puff up.

ROSE-WATER. An important ingredient in much of Oriental cooking as it was once in English cooking. The best rose-water comes from Bulgaria.

Only the best distilled rose-water may be used in cooking, and it should be kept in a dark cool place as it will otherwise lose its strength and aroma. Buy it in small quantities.

SAFFRON. An important and usually expensive flavouring and colouring ingredient and a *must* in many Oriental pilaus. It is procured from the dried stigmata of the saffron crocus. This species is a beautiful little autumn crocus with slender leaves and pale purple flowers. Native to Southern Europe and parts of Asia, it is a low-growing bulbous plant. Its uses have been known for centuries. The best saffron nowadays comes from Austria and it is highly prized for its flavour and aroma; next comes the French and Spanish saffron—although Kashmiris feel that no saffron is true saffron that does not come from their lovely Valley. It takes over 75,000 hand-picked blossoms to make a pound of saffron— no wonder it is expensive. Each blossom has three saffron stigmata, these in turn, each one of them, must be picked off by hand.

Mexican saffron, while it can be used in place of true saffron, is not saffron at all, but prepared from the stigmatas of a thistle-like plant. Saffron is usually soaked in water, milk or sometimes for sweet dishes in rose-water to release its colour before being used. Although considered an Oriental spice, there was a time when it was much used in British cooking.

SAKE. This is the traditional wine of Japan, but in days gone by no one would consider drinking *sake* alone, so *sake* became to mean drinking parties. *Sake* is served in tiny porcelain cups—not much larger than the average egg-cup—and it is served almost invariably warm. Formerly *sake* was served cold, but *sake* of inferior quality began to be served warm to help its flavour and the habit became so popular that nowadays all *sake* is served warm or even hot. Therefore, the small porcelain cups are the most convenient manner of serving it. Apart from being a popular and national drink, it is offered at shrines of ancestors, and a marriage is celebrated by the drinking of *sake*.

SAMBAL or SAMBOL. *See* page 72.

SAMBEL ULEK. This is simply hot sauce used in Indonesia. It is available in those shops dealing with Oriental foods.

SCALLIONS. Welsh onion or chibol, a bulbless onion with a thick neck like a leek. It is also an onion which starts to bulb but forms instead a strong neck and strong blade.

SEAWEED. This is one of Japan's most popular items of food; it appears in so many recipes, including some delicious biscuits and, of course, *sushi*. In the stores it is draped over counters and overhead rails like streamers. There are some species which are a foot wide and ten feet long. This is used at weddings and is a symbol of longevity. Some species of seaweed are chewed as people chew chewing gum. This is sold in convenient packets for the purpose. It is also used in making soup stocks as well as a general flavouring.

SESAME OIL. Another important Far Eastern oil, one of the purest, much favoured by the Indians. The Chinese who prefer to use peanut oil, however, add a little sesame oil to it simply to give added richness. Unlike peanut oil, sesame has its own distinctive flavour but not as strong as olive oil.

SESAME SEEDS. An aromatic herb very important in Far Eastern cooking and native to the area. It has a delightful warm nutty flavour and when toasted and ground has something of the taste of toasted almonds. Both in India and China sesame is cultivated on an enormous scale. Its colour in seed form varies between so-called white to a grey-black and there is one grade which is a fine orange colour. The seed is the dried fruit of a lovely tropical annual. Apart from being a popular Asian ingredient, it is used considerably in Balkan and Middle Eastern cooking—and has become naturalized in the U.S.A. where they use it in cakes and pastries following the Central Europeans who make sesame rolls and breads as well. It can be purchased whole or ground—but it is far better bought whole, toasted and then ground.

SHALLOT. A member of the lily family, which covers a wide range of flavours, i.e. the onion, garlic, leek, chives etc. The shallot is one of its milder members. It grows in the manner of the onion with one major difference. Instead of being one main bulb the shallot looks rather more like garlic with a series of sections or cloves which come apart easily. It is native in Western Asia. Its name comes from Ascolon in Palestine. It can be used in any of the ways of the onion, especially when a mild flavour is desired.

SHOYU SAUCE. *See* page 191.

SHRIMPS. There are several varieties of shrimps, but the two best known are the brown shrimp and the red shrimp. Of these the brown is the most highly flavoured. It is larger than the pink shrimp which is slimmer in its proportions and also more delicate in its flavour. Shrimps are often cooked in boiling salt water on the fishing boats and they seldom come to the markets in their fresh state. Pre-cooked shrimps, if to be further cooked, must always be treated with caution, otherwise they will become tough. In Britain only the small species of crustacean is called a shrimp, its larger relative is the prawn.

SHRIMP PASTE. A pungent condiment used in Far Eastern cooking, particularly in Indonesia. It is usually available in shops specializing in Oriental foods and is imported in jars both from Indonesia and the Philippines.

SILVER LEAF. A speciality of India used as a digestive and decoratively laid over sweet dishes, pilaus and *pan*. Only the purest and finest type of silver should be used to make it. It is made entirely by hand in the silversmiths' bazaar and several men are required to beat each piece of silver until it is so fine it can hardly be handled—and is literally as thin as a breath. It is sold by the sheet measuring about 3 × 4 inches, placed between sheets of thin paper. It has no flavour but adds a very exotic appearance to the food it adorns. Gold leaf is simply silver leaf which has been coloured.

SNOW PEAS. Small green peas which are used, shell, peas and all. They simply need trimming. Called variously *mange-tout*, French peas and sugar peas. Just to confuse the issue, Americans call them Chinese peas.

SOAPNUT. A most extraordinary small brown nut. It is mentioned but once in this book and this in Thai cooking (*see* page 93). It is extensively used in India, but not usually in cooking, except that its black seeds are used commercially in the preparation of certain sweetmeats to add an opaqueness to the finished product. The brown husk is soaked in water and used for shampooing the hair, washing woollens and also pearls to bring back their lost lustre. In Thailand it is called *kha*.

SOY SAUCE. This is a main ingredient in Chinese cooking, the *shoyu* of Japan. It imparts its own special flavour to any dish in which it is cooked. It is best to get the genuine imported Oriental soy sauce, but when this is not possible remember that non-Oriental varieties are somewhat more salty than the genuine ones. So use less than might be suggested in a recipe. Some cooks recommend Maggi sauce as a possible alternative.

STAR ANISE. A species of aniseed, but the seed of an evergreen tree of the magnolia family grown in Japan and China. The tiny seeds are contained in a star-shaped dark brown pod hence its name. It is curiously different from true aniseed and imparts a most delightful flavour (*see* page 160).

SWEET POTATOES. These are well known to Americans but less so to the British although they were introduced into Britain earlier than the ordinary potato, in fact, they came to Europe 300 years ago. Granger wrote of them in 1794:

> *There let the potatoes mantle o'er the ground*
> *Sweet as the cane sugar is the root they bear.*

It is a native of tropical America and known to the Indians before the time of Columbus. It was the Spanish who took them first to Europe. The flesh is yellow and cooks dry and mealy.

TABASCO SAUCE. This is a condiment well known in the United States of America but less so in Britain. It is simply a very hot sharp seasoning made from capsicums. It can also be used when hot chillies called for in a recipe are not available.

TAMARIND. The fruit or pod of a handsome leguminous tree with delicate feathery foliage which grows to a great height, size and age. The pods are numerous and vary in size and shape even on the same tree. Some are long like beans, while others are sickle shaped. They start life green, then are covered with a thin film which turns them brown. Fresh from the tree the pulp, which has a pleasing sweet-sour flavour, is white and crisp and is said to contain more acid and more sugar than any other fruit. After exposure it becomes a reddish-brown, rather dark. The tree is cultivated throughout India and Burma, as well as other parts of the Far East and the West Indies. It is thought that the acid pulp, which is laxative and cooling, is also good against fevers.

Hobson-Jobson has this to say. 'The origin of the name is curious. It is *Tamar-u'l-Hind*, 'date of India', in Arabic, or perhaps rather in Persian form *tamar-i-Hind*. It is possible that the original name may have been *thamar* (fruit) of India rather than *tamar* (date).'

Tamarind is used not only as a flavouring in curries and other dishes, but also in making chutneys, pickling fish, and there is a highly diluted tamarind syrup used to make a cooling drink also adding bulk and flavour to guava jelly.

Tamarind is available usually in Indian shops, in some chemists and, in the United States, in Mexican shops—they call it *tamarindo*. Failing tamarind, lemon juice or a mild vinegar can be used in roughly the same proportion (*see* page 17).

TURMERIC. The fleshy root stalk of a brilliant tropical plant which belongs to the ginger family. It contains a very heavy bright yellow dye and is one of the principal ingredients in a curry and other Far Eastern dishes. It is native to the Far East generally and also parts of Africa and Australia. Even the colour of the flower of the plant, when grown in hot countries, is a bright yellow, although that grown in China is a dull green. The root of the turmeric is irregularly shaped, the aroma is clean but the flavour is bitterish and faintly resinous. It has been used for centuries because of its colour and its warmth of flavour. It is sold in root form (which is the best way to buy it to obtain its full flavour) or in powdered form. If used in moderation, i.e. simply a pinch, it can be used instead of saffron to give colour—in the Middle Ages turmeric was known as Indian saffron. Too much turmeric will ruin the flavour of any dish.

WAMPI. A citrus fruit found in Thailand. It is about the size of a large marble. When ripe it is yellow and rather like a cross between a grape and a gooseberry. It is used to make jam and also a pleasant drink.

WATER CHESTNUTS. These grow, as their name suggests, in water. In India they grow freely in the plains. They have little resemblance to Western chestnuts. Their flesh is crisp, cool and white, the skin green, which turns black when cooked. They are used extensively in Chinese and Far Eastern cooking and usually obtainable in tins in the West. They are roughly the same size as the regular chestnuts and, apart from using them in Eastern dishes, they are excellent chopped in a salad or lightly fried and served with drinks. There is a Mexican water plant which conveniently combines the flavours of the bamboo and the water chestnut. Called *jicama*, it is readily available in the U.S.A.

YAMS. These are allied to the sweet potato and are of African origin. They have a moist texture and a high sugar content and constitute a staple tropical food. They are the tuber roots of a climbing plant which resembles the hop. Some varieties of yams—and these are many—attain an enormous size. They vary also in colour, with reddish-yellow, greenish-yellow, orange-tinted and mauve flesh. Although the yam resembles the sweet potato, and there is often confusion between the two species, they are from entirely different plants. The flavour is perhaps a cross between the sweet potato and what is often called the Irish potato (*see* page 168).

ACKNOWLEDGMENTS

The publishers and producers of this book would like to thank the Gaylord Restaurant, London, and the Bali Restaurant, Amsterdam, for granting facilities for photography; the Plaza Restaurant, Manila, the Philippines, for permission to reproduce the colour plate of a *Roast Sucking Pig*, which was photographed by Charles W. Miller and Son. The jacket photograph is reproduced by permission of H. v. Irmer, München: the *Nepalese Market* by permission of Paul Popper Ltd, London. The colour plate of the *Rijsttafel* was taken by Lemaire & Wennink, Amsterdam. The remainder of the colour photographs were taken by Kenneth Swain. The drawings are by Ian Garrard.

They would also like to thank Mrs Mariko Maclear for preparing the Japanese dishes, Mrs Eileen Erskine Crum for kindly lending dishes and equipment and Mrs Perez-David for her assistance in obtaining the photograph from Manila.

COMPARATIVE COOKERY TERMS AND MEASURES

BRITISH MEASURES	AMERICAN MEASURES	AMERICAN CUP EQUIVALENTS	APPROXIMATE METRIC MEASURES
1 teaspoon	$1\frac{1}{4}$ teaspoons		6 c.c.
1 tablespoon	$1\frac{1}{4}$ tablespoons		17 c.c.
1 fluid ounce	1 fluid ounce *or* 2 tablespoons		30 c.c.
2 fluid ounces	2 fluid ounces *or* 4 tablespoons	$\frac{1}{4}$ cup	60 c.c.
$2\frac{2}{3}$ fluid ounces	$5\frac{1}{3}$ tablespoons	$\frac{1}{3}$ cup	
4 fluid ounces	8 tablespoons	$\frac{1}{2}$ cup	120 c.c.
$5\frac{1}{3}$ fluid ounces	$10\frac{2}{3}$ tablespoons	$\frac{2}{3}$ cup	
8 fluid ounces	8 fluid ounces *or* $\frac{1}{2}$ U.S. pint	1 cup	240 c.c.
10 fluid ounces *or* $\frac{1}{2}$ Imperial pint	10 fluid ounces	$1\frac{1}{4}$ cups	
16 fluid ounces	1 U.S. pint	2 cups	·480 litre
20 fluid ounces or 1 Imperial pint	$1\frac{1}{4}$ U.S. pints	$2\frac{1}{2}$ cups	·568 litre
$1\frac{3}{5}$ Imperial pints	2 U.S. pints *or* 1 U.S. quart	4 cups	
$1\frac{3}{4}$ Imperial pints			1 litre
2 Imperial pints *or* 1 Imperial quart	$2\frac{1}{2}$ U.S. pints	5 cups	
$6\frac{2}{5}$ Imperial pint	8 U.S. pints *or* 1 U.S. gallon	16 U.S. cups	
8 Imperial pints *or* 1 Imperial gallon	10 U.S. pints	20 cups	4·544 litres

British Standard measuring cup is equivalent to 10 fluid ounces
American Standard measuring cup is equivalent to 8 fluid ounces
In general British and American solid weights are equivalent

British and American weights and the approximate Metric equivalents

1 ounce	30 grammes
16 ounces or 1 lb.	480 grammes
1 lb. $1\frac{1}{2}$ ounces	500 grammes or $\frac{1}{2}$ kilogram
2 lb. 3 ounces	1 kilogram

BRITISH AND AMERICAN EQUIVALENT INGREDIENTS

Caster sugar	Granulated sugar
Icing sugar	Confectioners sugar
Soft brown sugar	Brown sugar
Demerara sugar	Raw sugar
Cornflour	Cornstarch
Wholemeal flour	Graham flour
Single cream	Light cream
Double cream	Heavy cream
Yoghourt	Yogurt
Vegetable fat	Soft shortening
Spring onion	Green onion or scallion
Aubergine	Eggplant or aubergine
Courgette	Zucchini
French bean	Green or string or snap bean
Red or green pepper, or capsicum	Red or green pepper
Sugar or mange-tout peas	Snow peas
Sweet pepper	Pimento
Vegetable marrow	Summer squash
Custard apple	Custard apple, cherimoya or sweetsop
Papaw	Papaya or pawpaw
Patna or long grain rice	Long grain rice
Carolina or short grain rice	Short grain rice
Minced meat	Ground meat
Prawns	Shrimps
Shrimps	Prawns
Scampi or Dublin Bay prawns	Butterfly shrimps or Pacific prawns

Throughout this book British measurements are given first; the American equivalent follows in brackets

Index Recipes by Countries

Index General

THE INTERNATIONAL
WINE AND FOOD SOCIETY

The International Wine and Food Society was founded in 1933 by André L. Simon, C.B.E., as a world-wide non-profit making society.

The first of its various aims has been to bring together and serve all who believe that a right understanding of wine and food is an essential part of personal contentment and health; and that an intelligent approach to the pleasures and problems of the table offers far greater rewards than the mere satisfaction of appetite.

For information about the Society,
apply to the Secretary,
Marble Arch House,
44 Edgware Road,
London, W.2